THE ENTREPRENEUR

An Autobiography of
PRINCE OLABODE ADETOYI
Country CEO, Hi-Nutrients
A Company Member of Neovia Group

# THE ENTREPRENEUR

An Autobiography of
PRINCE OLABODE ADETOYI
Country CEO, Hi-Nutrients
A Company Member of Neovia Group

Safari Books Ltd.
Ibadan

Published by
Safari Books Ltd
Ile Ori Detu
1, Shell Close
Onireke
Ibadan.
Email: info@safaribooks.com.ng
Website: http://safaribooks.com.ng

© 2019, Prince Olabode Adetoyi

First Published 2019

All rights reserved. This book is copyright and so no part of it may be reproduced, stored in a retrieval system, or transmitted, in any form or by any means, electrical, mechanical, electrostatic, magnetic tape, photocopying, recording or otherwise, without the prior written permission of the author.

ISBN: Paperback 978-978-55986-9-8
        Cased   978-978-55986-8-1

Dedication

This autobiography is dedicated to my lovely mother, Princess (Mrs.) Felicia Omoponmile Adetoyi. Mummy, you are the best.

To Bukky, who gives me a life of love.

To Adeola, David, and Daniel, they give joy and meaning to it all.

Table of Contents

Dedication... v
Foreword.. ix
Acknowledgements... xi
Introduction... xv

Chapter One:	2018: Rewards of Hard Work...............	1
Chapter Two:	My Ancestry..	7
Chapter Three:	Prince John Peter Adetoyi...................	23
Chapter Four:	Not Too Young for School....................	35
Chapter Five:	Tamed Champion...................................	41
Chapter Six:	Voice of Destiny (Professor Joseph Bolarinde Obebe)...................................	51
Chapter Seven:	Higher Education...................................	59
Chapter Eight:	The Blessing of Girl-Child Education....	71
Chapter Nine:	On the Streets of Lagos.......................	83
Chapter Ten:	The Beginning of a Budding Career in Agriculture.............................	103
Chapter Eleven:	On the Path of Destiny.........................	117
Chapter Twelve:	Merger and Acquisition........................	143
Chapter Thirteen:	Bukky: My Dependable Intercessor........	181
Chapter Fourteen:	Near Death Experiences......................	197
Chapter Fifteen:	My RCCG Story.....................................	203
Chapter Sixteen:	Poultry Association of Nigeria..............	213
Chapter Seventeen:	My Stint in Politics................................	239
Chapter Eighteen:	International Travel..............................	259
Chapter Nineteen:	Fisheries Society of Nigeria (FISON)....	273
Chapter Twenty:	My Botswana Experience and Lessons for Nigeria in Agricultural Development..	279

Appendix 291
In the Eyes of the People 297
Index 363

Foreword

The Holy Book says "seest thou a man diligent in his business? He shall stand before kings; He shall not stand before mean men" (Proverbs 22:29). This aptly fits the persona of the enigmatic and indefatigable Ezekiel Olabode Adetoyi. This man comes across as one whose zeal is not only infectious but also audacious. My first encounter with him was on one of those trips to the famous International Poultry programme in Atlanta (USA). At every turn, he stood up to be counted and his brilliant and inquisitive mind came across not only to the Nigerian delegates but also to the exhibitors at that programme. He was serious-minded and quick-witted to the extent that, at most of the stands visited, he was the cynosure of eyes and the unwavering energy of the team. This giant of a man showed forth his brilliance and knowledge of the poultry industry during that encounter. Without gainsaying, he became the centre of gravity throughout that expedition.

Bode is irrepressible and highly focused. Every encounter with him is always an inquest of sorts because of his hunger and thirst for learning; he is always probing with a tenacity to push for new ideas and frontiers for Nigeria's poultry industry.

It was another such meeting with Bode that further drew my attention to this vibrant and ebullient young man. It was on one of my official visits to Ghana. Bode spotted me in-flight and swiftly relocated his seat next to mine in order to fill me in on the new vision and venture he had just launched – Hi-Nutrients International Limited. As he ran through his business plan with me, one could not help but catch the passion in his eyes and the fire in his belly. Given his high level of optimism, little wonder that he was able to ride the crest of challenges that came his way ensuring that his company not only became a household brand in Nigeria but internationally as well. That is Bode and his 'can do' spirit.

Looking back today, the birth of Hi-Nutrients has not only fulfilled the dreams and aspirations of Bode the scientist-entrepreneur but has indeed broadened the array of choice and quality profile for stakeholders in Nigeria's poultry industry. It is, therefore, no surprise that Bode is further breaking new grounds as a leading light in the poultry industry with the current partnership journey forged with Neovia. I sincerely wish Bode and his team well as they set to sail on the global poultry arena.

As I conclude this foreword, the words of Robert Bolt in his treatise *A Man for All Seasons* comes to my mind: that is who Bode is.

With Bode attaining the golden age, I believe as we all look back with nostalgia and recall his enormous contributions not only in business but to the church, society (particularly his unyielding commitment to youth empowerment), and his altruistic belief in Nigeria, we can say with all confidence that the best is yet to come. I also hasten to add that Bode, the family man, surely deserves immense commendation for being able to skilfully employ work life balance in making the home front solid, stable and steadfast. As you go through this autobiography, please join me in celebrating this icon at 50 whose life is an all-round testament to good success to the glory of God and the benefit of mankind.

Joe Dada,
November 2018.

Acknowledgements

Whatever I have achieved today, I give God all the eternal glory because they are all products of the favour and grace of God. The only caveat I would add to that is that, unlike some others, I believe that favour only comes to those who expect it; and no one can honestly expect favour with their hands folded in indolent inactivity. You have to be doing something for God to bless you. And I have been busy since my adult life; and God has blessed the work of my hand.

There are several people that God has used to help me. In no particular order, I hereby use this medium to express my gratitude to them and acknowledge their respective roles in my life.

My special appreciation goes to my lovely wife, Mrs. Bukola Adetoyi, for being there for me all the time. The past 17 years would not have been very meaningful without her. In the same vein, I appreciate my daughter, Deola, for being a good influence on her younger siblings. I also appreciate my two sons, David and Daniel, for doing well in school and giving me hope that my labour would not be in vain.

I acknowledge the efforts of my parents, for without them, I would not be here today. I thank them for sacrificing all to educate and take care of me. I appreciate their patience, hard work and prayers. Even though my father is not here today to see me achieve my dream, I appreciate the role he played to make it possible.

Furthermore, all my siblings are wonderful people and they have touched my life in one way or the other. I thank them from the bottom of my heart. I appreciate the Oore of Mobaland, Oba James Adedapo Oladele Popoola, and my fellow royal family members in Otun-Ekiti. I appreciate the entire Otun sons and daughters and all our community leaders. I specially thank the families of Late Hon. Atolagbe, late Mr. Akin Osasona (Akins photo), Pastor D.T. Agboola, Prof. Bolarinde Obebe, they are all models. I appreciate the effort of Pastor D.T. Agboola in his book *The History of Oore and Otun Mobaland*. I appreciate all my extended families of Ibidunmoye, may the good Lord keep us together.

I specially appreciate Neovia Group and its team in France and across the continents because they identified Hi-Nutrients International Limited – the company I founded in 2004 – and considered it worthy of being merged with their multinational establishment. The merger and acquisition of Neovia and Hi-Nutrients is, so far, the foremost in the livestock industry in Nigeria; this merger saw a multinational company acquiring majority shares in a local company with a view to using that local company as a springboard to the African continent as a whole. On a personal level, this merger and acquisition shows that the entrepreneurial spirit in me has been accorded global recognition. It is a thing of joy to think that, in spite of the harsh economic environment for running a successful business in Nigeria, my company has provided a platform for the global announcement of Nigeria's great potential as an investment hub in the African continent.

I will not forget to recognise the impact of all the schools I attended, which all played some specific role in grooming me for excellent achievement: Harvard Business School, Boston, USA; *InsperInstituto de Ensino e pesquisa*, Sao Paulo, Brazil; University of Stellenbosch, Cape Town, South Africa; A & M

University, College Station, Texas; Lagos Business School (Now Pan Atlantic University); Lagos State University; University of Ibadan; University of Ilorin; Oyo State College of Arts and Science (OSCAS) Ile-Ife, Osun State; Comprehensive High School Otun-Ekiti, and St. Peter's Anglican Primary School, Otun-Ekiti. These institutions contributed their respective quota in preparing me for future challenges.

Special thanks to my bosses at various times in my life: Mrs. Funmilayo Olubisi Medunoye of Olubisi Farms; Mr. Olusola Lawson of UB40; Late Alhaji Ola Mohammed of Ola Farms and Trading Company; Dr. U.K. Acholonu of Bio-Organics Limited; Senator Rashidi Adewolu Ladoja, former Governor of Oyo State; Dr. Gbenga Oluyemi, Late Layi Oyatoki, Dr. Peter Bamkole, JID Dada, Abiodun Toki, etc. Your impact in my life cannot be denied and I owe you a lot for adding value to me.

I appreciate my church, the Redeemed Christian Church of God (RCCG), and our General Overseer, Pastor E.A. Adeboye, and all the other pastors in the vineyard of God, for the teaching I have received in the last 23 years of my membership of the church, which have gone a long way in moulding me and having a positive moral and spiritual influence on me.

Thanks to all my Directors at Neovia and also to all the staff and management of Hi-Nutrients International Limited. My political mentors and teachers are also worthy of sincere thanks. These are the people who taught me practical politics and oversaw my baptism into the game that is the only legitimate pathway to power in a civilised society. In no particular order, I thank Otunba Niyi Adebayo (former Governor of Ekiti State); Dr. John Kayode Fayemi, incumbent Governor of Ekiti State; Senator Olubunmi Adetunbi; Engr. Segun Oni (former Governor of Ekiti State); Mr. Biodun Oyebanji (Secretary to the Government of Ekiti State); Senator Babafemi Ojudu, Hon. Opeyemi Bamidele and many others too numerous to mention. My appreciation for you, as senior politicians who have accepted me as your protégé, knows no bounds and I wish you well in your endeavours.

Furthermore, I am grateful to Muyi Ladoja, my former Director and a great farmer. My special thanks also go to all the present and past executives of Poultry Association of Nigeria and our Trustees: Chief Olusegun Obasanjo, GCFR, former president of Nigeria, Chief Folorunsho Ogunnaike, Chief Olatunde Agbato, Late Chief Ladipo Daniel, Chief Olatunde Badmus, Dr. Folarin Afelumo, Mr. Tunde Bello, etc. I also appreciate the executives of Nigeria Institute of Animal Science, Animal Science Association of Nigeria, Fisheries Societies of Nigeria, Catfish Farmers Association of Nigeria, Enterprise Development Centre, among others. Without these bodies, I won't be where I am today.

I remain deeply grateful to the Chairman of Safari Books, Chief Joop Berkhout and his team. Without their effort, this book will not come to reality. I enjoyed working with them. Chief Joop gave me the enthusiasm to put my story together so that the younger generation will learn from my experience.

Finally, hearty thanks to my personal editor, Joe Dauda, who worked with me all through the project. I appreciate his role.

Prince Bode Adetoyi
11th December, 2018

Introduction

Currently, the United States of America is the third most populous country in the world, with a population of well over 300 million people. But the position of the United States is expected to be taken by Nigeria around the year 2050 (just over 30 years away) and Nigeria is expected to hit a population figure of 450 million people. While it may be a good thing in many regards to be ranked the third most populous country in the world, the big and dangerous question is this:

How will these millions of people be fed?

In my view, this expected population explosion will become a terrible nightmare, except it is successfully mirrored by what I would refer to as a food explosion. Whether rich or poor, educated or illiterate, the fact is that, every human being needs some quantity of food to survive and would do virtually anything to get food. This primordial need is not going to change and could lead to unimaginable chaos and even societal disintegration, except something is done to give the vast majority access to food with as little impediments as possible. My autobiography captures my humble attempt to provide answers to this national question through my active participation in the agricultural sector of the Nigerian economy. This journey started as far back as 30 years ago (in 1988), when I became an undergraduate student of Animal Science in the University of Ilorin.

Fortunately for me, I grew up in a farming community (Otun-Ekiti) and life was quite basic. I recall going to the farm countless times with my father. The irony of my life, well captured within the pages of this book, is that, as a young man, I was not interested in farming and was in fact disinclined to farming. Still, this did not stop me from having my own farm, from which I first learnt how to make money: it was my first entrepreneurial venture. So, a careful analysis of my story may cause a keen observer to notice that, perhaps, it was not just that I was not interested in farming: I wanted farming pursued as a business and not just a back-breaking routine with no promise of respite and real wealth.

My background quickly provides evidence that, unlike my namesake (Chief Bode Thomas), I was not born with a silver spoon in my mouth. However, like I have often told people, If you were not born with a silver spoon, you can actually decide to rise up, take up the challenge by working hard and smart, and secure a shiny new silver spoon for yourself, your family, and even generations yet unborn. My story proves that I lived with this concept in mind: while not denying my humble beginnings or trying to escape its unpalatable consequences, I did not allow my situation at birth to stop me from fulfilling my destiny. And my destiny was fulfilled in a rather interesting manner.

I made a drastic detour in life at the point of getting into the university. More than any other single event, it is that detour that is responsible for the height I have attained today. It is that detour that explains the fact that, as at today, apart from being the country CEO of Neovia Group in Nigeria, I am the Vice National President of Poultry Association of Nigeria (South-West), and member of the Technical Committee of experts nominated by the Standards Organisation of Nigeria (SON) saddled with the responsibility of establishing standard for animal feeds, premixes, and concentrates. I am also a member of a Technical Committee of the National Institute of Animal Science charged with the national responsibility of listing of approved ingredients for feed manufacture in Nigeria. Again, I am a foundation member of the Animal Science Association of Nigeria and a registered Animal Scientist of the Nigeria Institute of Animal Science (NIAS).

Many good and very important things in my life happened by accident, but this autobiography you are reading was not one of them. Writing this autobiography was an early objective I set for myself as far back as about 14 years ago. It happened at the same time I conceived the idea of establishing my company – Hi-Nutrients International Limited. This vision began to be fulfilled some months ago when I visited a friend called Patrick Obidoyin who came visiting from the United Kingdom and was hosted by Chief Joop Berkhout, Chairman of Safari Books Limited. Chief Berkhout received me warmly in his house at the Onireke area of Ibadan. After a brief introduction about me and what I was doing as a businessman and what I had achieved in the field of Agripreneur (Agricultural entrepreneurship), he challenged me to put my story down in a book that could serve as a reference point to people who may find themselves in my situation so as to learn how to navigate through life. I took the man rather seriously, and the ultimate product of that advice is what you are now reading.

The Entrepreneur mirrors a life of tenacity, focus, and the firm belief that, where there is life, there is also hope. It chronicles my struggle through school and my determination to do everything legitimate to break the shackles of want and deprivation. It proves that this achievement is possible without breaking laws, cutting corners, having friends in government, or inheriting a fortune from rich parents. A careful reading of this book can train any person to become a wise and purposeful entrepreneur.

This book also captures the essence of employee/employer relationship, navigating through office politics and some of the things that could go wrong; it declares that, like leaders, entrepreneurs are made and not born. The book sheds light on the dynamics of starting a business in Nigeria, growing it in the midst of challenges, navigating through the unfriendly business environment, and running it profitably to the point of attracting local and also international investors.

The Entrepreneur further explores the positive consequences of business alliances within the local and international circle. It teaches some lessons about life in general, the benefits of virtues, the advantage of integrity, transparency, and the things entrepreneurs go through to fund their businesses.

This book also captures the significance of mentorship, family life, the God-factor, and other real aspects of life you may not read about in the news. It elucidates the ingredients needed by every company and business to put things in place and run their establishments from local to global. The successful merger and acquisition of my company with a multinational – Neovia of France – was also captured, as reported by various international magazines in June 2018.

The book also delves into my endeavours in the political scene within the professional circle (through the Poultry Association of Nigerian – PAN; Animal Science Association of Nigeria – ASAN; and Fisheries Society of Nigeria – FISON) and also my attempt to serve my people by seeking a political office, which had to be suspended for reasons that would shortly be obvious to the patient reader.

Furthermore, the book shows how the knowledge and experience gained in international travel can make a positive and remarkable impact in business. Finally, the book did not fail to recognise the critical role of the God-factor in every human endeavour – including the endeavour of entrepreneurship. In an interesting manner, it shows how, God's blessings – like rain on a cultivated soil – waters the dryness of human effort to make phenomenal success possible.

CHAPTER 1

2018: REWARDS OF HARD WORK

Whenever you see a successful business, someone had once made a courageous decision.
Peter Drucker

On Monday, 31st May, 2018, my barely 14-year old company, Hi-Nutrients International Limited, signed a merger and acquisition deal with Neovia of France, which turned the company into Hi-Nutrients by Neovia from that day onwards. This was also announced by Neovia headquarters in various international magazines on Monday 18th of June, 2018. For those who need to know, Neovia is one of the leading players in the agricultural industry, not just in France where it is headquartered, but in Europe as a whole. It is an important player in the European economy and is involved in complete feed production, pet care, aquaculture, premix manufacturing, production of additives, and laboratory analysis, among other activities. Neovia is truly a global company, with presence in 34 countries of the world, and its products are used in over 50 countries. Neovia has close to 10,000 employees, and had just recently reported a turnover of nearly €2b (two billion Euros). Neovia believes in innovative science, feeding mankind and it operates by combining innovation with the sustainable use of natural resources. It is owned by InVivo, which is the leading French Agricultural Cooperative Group, with presence in many countries of the world, and a turnover of 5.5 billion Euros.

On its part, Hi-Nutrients International Limited is the market leader in premix manufacturing in Nigeria, with over 50% market share. Through its own unique brand of patented products (such as Hi-Mix® Layer, Hi-Mix® Broiler Starter and Finisher, Hi-Mix® Growers, Hi-Mix® Breeders, Hi-Mix® Beef and Dairy Cattle, Hi-Mix® Aquafish (Catfish and Tilapia), Hi-Mix® Ruminant Feeds, Hi-Mix® Horse, Hi-Mix® Chicks, Hi-Mix® Turkey Starter, and Hi-Mix® Salt Block), Hi-Nutrients has gained specialty in the production of premixes, vitamins, and minerals for poultry, turkey birds, dairy cattle, beef cattle, horse, other ruminants, and aquaculture. It has achieved and is set to surpass its corporate vision, which is: "to be the number one premix manufacturer, feed ingredients, additives, and veterinary drug supplier in Nigeria and West Africa."

Apart from the fact that Neovia's deal with Hi-Nutrients was the first of its kind in the agricultural sub-sector which I am engaged in, I had actually made up my mind to achieve this exact goal of merger and acquisition deal, fourteen years ago. Although at the time, I had given myself 20 years, not even knowing if I would succeed, but believing I would. And talking about believing, that was something I had done many times in my life. In late 2004, I had nothing but my strong belief in a future that promised to be exciting, but which could also turn me into a laughing stock. I must confess that the fear of things going awry was real, but my faith also seemed to be stronger than my fear. My faith was stronger than the warning of well-meaning friends and even close family members, who all warned me that what I had in mind to do was too risky and even unnecessary. As a matter of fact, my faith was stronger than the chilling forecast I got from my boss, who sternly said that my wife and little child could go hungry as a result of my resignation from a guaranteed monthly income to an attempt to be the Chief Executive Officer of my own company.

Why give up job security for the uncharted waters of entrepreneurship, and that, without any kind of financial backing from anybody?

Why quit a well-paying job for the unknown endeavour of trying to start up a new company?

Why put the livelihood of my young family on the line and bring uncertainty to their daily subsistence?

Why refuse to continue to collect a fat salary at the end of every thirty days?

Why throw away the convenience of a brand new official vehicle, coupled with the paid services of an official driver?

Why withdraw from a company that was at its zenith at the time, and one of the leaders in its niche nationwide?

Why sacrifice the prestige of working for a successful company that was, even then, breaking records and expanding its list of patrons?

Why deliberately turn simple logic on its head by attempting to chase two birds in the bush while letting the one bird in hand go free?

Why?

Why?

Why?

The fact is that I knew why, but, apart from my wife, I did not bother to explain my decision to people who privately thought I was crazy for making such a decision, even though none of them mustered enough courage to tell me so. In some way, these people were right: perhaps I was crazy. And if I truly was, Professor Patrick Utomi, founder and proprietor of the Lagos Business School (today's Pan-Atlantic University), was the main cause of this craziness. Along with Patrick Utomi, there must be Dr. Peter Bamkole, Director of the Enterprise

Development Centre, which is part of the Pan-Atlantic University today. Peter Bamkole was one of my lecturers and he, with a handful of other lecturers at the Lagos Business School, must have been responsible. In fact, anybody that had anything to do with the instructions I received all through the Senior Management Programme of Class 19 (referred to as SMP 19) 2003, must have contributed their quota in making me crazy enough to want to start my own company, and to want it so badly that I was willing to do the unthinkable of quitting one of the best jobs any graduate of animal nutrition could have wished for at the time.

I would not blame Mr. Tony Elumelu because I was already about ten years into this craziness before he met me. Interestingly, Tony Elumelu was eager to shake my hands and smile into my face when we met in 2014 because my craziness had resulted in my company being listed as one of the fifty fastest growing companies in Nigeria. It was the Tony Elumelu Foundation that did the ranking from a list of thousands of Nigerian companies – in conjunction with an international organisation known as AllWorld Network, based in Boston USA: I had nothing to do with the ranking and did not even know about it until my company was officially contacted.

Fortunately for me, my wife, my kids, and almost 100 employees in my company today; in just fourteen years, (even though I had to go through hell and high water), the apparent craziness of 2004 has now been re-evaluated by reluctant supporters, by naysayers, by critics, and even by secret enemies. My audacious act in 2004 is no longer seen as the knee-jerk reaction of an unstable mind. Rather, it is now perceived as foresight, as daring, as bull-headed determination, and as a stroke of entrepreneurial genius. But fourteen years is definitely not fourteen days, or even fourteen weeks; neither is it fourteen months. Like Abraham who knew that he had to move but did not know where he was moving to and did not have a map, I also knew it was time to move on, but, honestly, I had no plan; certainly not in the sense of a roadmap. All I had was some knowledge, some self-confidence, some faith in the ability of God to help me, and a desire for a better life. I also had a history of success to propel me to take this step, which, in retrospect, was a defining moment in my 50-year sojourn in this world. However, to understand my decision in 2004, one has to understand my history. And no matter how amazing or shocking my history may appear, it is a fact – not a fiction.

CHAPTER 2

MY ANCESTRY

> *It's not a question of wanting to be; it's something I was born into and it's my duty. But those stories about me not wanting to be a king are all wrong. It's a very important role and it's one that I don't take lightly.*
>
> **Prince William (of Great Britain),**
> **21st birthday interview with the Press Association.**

I am Prince Olabode Ezekiel Adetoyi. I am not a prince by choice. I am a prince of Otun today based on blood relation with a previous Oore of Mobaland, Otun-Ekiti, and this claim can be verified as a historical fact which could readily be corroborated by the current Oore of Mobaland, Oba James Adedapo Oladele Popoola; some extant documents, and even a book published 17 years ago by an illustrious son of Otun, Pastor D.T. Agboola: *A History of Oore and Otun in Moba-Land,* is the major source of this chapter, as well as most facts concerning the early history of Otun.

According to Otun oral tradition, for one to understand the history of Otun, one must go to the very father of the Yoruba race himself, Oduduwa; because this man was a contemporary of Oduduwa. The progenitor of Otun people was a man known as Omo Olokun. But, from what we came to know, this was not even his real name; rather, it was descriptive, and it was given to him by people who thought he had come out of the sea hence, they believed he was some sort of god. In fact, Omo Olokun means – son of the sea-god. The sea Omo Olokun was believed to come out from was actually a lagoon, and was referred to as Okun Moba, which means "people's sea." The beach where Omo Olokun landed is at an area near Badagry Sea in Lagos known as Ajase. In reality, what is most likely is that Omo Olokun probably used a canoe or some other water vessel to traverse the lagoon such that when he landed on Ajase shore, the locals, who did not know about such vessels, conveniently chose to believe that he had come out of the water like an amphibious animal. And the fact that he emerged dressed in the paraphernalia of royalty made them believe that he was a king.

But Omo Olokun did not land at Ajase alone, his people were with him, and there was soon a battle between him and his people on the one side, and the people of Ajase on the other. The people of Ajase must have felt threatened by the presence of the strangers. Not surprisingly, Omo Olokun and his people were eventually forced out of Ajase area, but they found some respite a short distance away at a place called Epe. There is no evidence that the people of Epe were hostile to Omo Olokun, but, for reasons best known to him, he continued inland with his people until they got to Ile-Ife in today's Osun State, where he personally met Oduduwa. Yoruba history puts Oduduwa's existence around 12th century, therefore, this means that Omo Olokun also lived during that century and made his journey around that time too. At Ile-Ife, Omo Olokun met a kind host in the person of Oduduwa. This would later prove a blessing to Oduduwa because, for reasons not stated, Oduduwa soon became blind. The blindness that afflicted Oduduwa came after his own people and the people of Omo Olokun had already begun to live in peace for some time.

As expected, the people of Ile-Ife tried their very best to restore Oduduwa's sight, but nothing seemed to work, until Omo Olokun stepped into the matter. Omo Olokun was actually an Ifa priest, who soon began divination so as to help his kind friend, Oduduwa. Following the consultation, Ifa directed that, in order to cure Oduduwa's blindness, water had to be fetched from the lagoon through which he arrived Ajase; that is, the Okun Moba itself, which is near Lagos. Oduduwa informed his children about the directive but many of them were not willing to embark on the journey to get the water from Okun Moba. Eventually, one of Oduduwa's children known as Ajibogun, volunteered to go and fetch the water. Perhaps, Ifa had instructed that Omo Olokun could not accompany anybody that went on that trip because, from all indications, he did not make any attempt to go with Ajibogun. So Ajibogun left for Lagos. However, his journey took longer than anticipated to the extent that, the people of Ile-Ife began to believe that he was not coming back. Even Oduduwa himself had lost hope of Ajibogun's return. But Omo Olokun kept assuring Oduduwa and his people that Ajibogun would come back; and by the time he eventually did, most of Oduduwa's children had received their inheritance and had left Ile-Ife to establish their own kingdoms around the various enclaves in Nigeria's south-west.

At the end of the day, the water that Ajibogun brought was used by Omo Olokun to cure Oduduwa of his blindness and restore his sight. In gushing appreciation, Oduduwa called Omo Olokun, "Olu oremi", which means my benefactor, or someone who had assisted me. It is the shortened form of that name, Oore, which is now the official title of the paramount ruler of Otun. What that means is that, Omo Olokun became Oore right from Ile-Ife, and that he was christened as such by none other than Oduduwa himself.

After staying in Ile-Ife for some time, Oore (that is, Omo Olokun) said he too wanted to leave. This was against the wishes of Oduduwa, but Oore assured his host that, anytime he was needed, he would show up. This was how Oore left Ile-Ife, after all Oduduwa's children had left their father. Oore was the last to leave. However, when Oduduwa's children left, each of them sent word back to Ile-Ife whenever they reached where they had chosen to settle. In this way, Oore got to know the different locations of all Oduduwa's children, since he was still at Ile-Ife when their respective messages came to their father. As a backup evidence for the story about Oduduwa's blindness and healing, Ajibogun, who brought the water from the ocean is known as the Owa Obokun, and that is the title of the paramount ruler of Ijesa land in Ilesa, where Ajibogun settled after leaving Ile-Ife. All Ajibogun's descendants who seat on his throne bear that title Owa Obokun, as their official title up till today. Owa Obokun means the king who fetched water from the ocean.

When Oore left Ile-Ife, he settled in various places. He passed through Oke Olodun, Ikirun, and several other places, before finally coming to Ipole. It was indeed a torturous journey. Ipole is about seven miles from the present site of Otun, which the descendants of Oore now call home, and where the incumbent Oore has his palace. But when it was initially inhabited by Omo Olokun and his people, Ipole grew and became a well-established town and would have remained the site of Otun today, if not for something that happened which necessitated the move to the present site.

After staying for a while at Ipole, water scarcity suddenly hit the growing town, and it got so bad that it became an existential threat. In fact, babies were dying simply because there was no water to tend them at birth. Something had to be urgently done; and indeed, something was done. As usual, the first thing was to consult the Ifa oracle. As a matter of fact, previous movements were more or less instructions received from Ifa. So, this case was not odd in any way. After consultation, Ifa oracle instructed the people of Oore to move to the present site of Otun. Ifa also told them that, in the new place, they would get perennial water that would not only be abundant, but that would also flow throughout the year.

Incidentally, the move from Ipole took place during the peak of dry season when water scarcity situation was almost getting out of hand. However, just as Ifa had predicted, abundant water was soon discovered at the new site. The persons who found the sources of water were hunters who had been asked to scout around the area ahead of the actual relocation by members of the thirsty community. These hunters had agreed among themselves to announce the water discovery by shooting their weapon into the air to alert their colleagues. While on water hunt, two hunters who had each discovered water on his own, simultaneously shot into the air. Their names were Abasingin and Abaleti. The source of water Abasingin found was later named Omi Abasingin, while the one Abaleti found was named Omi Eleti. Interestingly, Omi Eleti is the source from which a reigning Oore gets his water, not just for drinking, but also for utility. As a rule, a reigning Oore does not drink water from any other source other than Omi Eleti, neither does he drink water fetched from previous day. The water he uses has to be fetched from the spring daily.

Unfortunately, not very long after Oore left Ile-Ife, Oduduwa died. When he got the sad news, Oore went back to Ile-Ife to perform the burial rites for Oduduwa: he also performed the necessary installation rites for Oduduwa's successor. This act of Oore in the service of Oduduwa became locked into a tradition that is still upheld today that, anytime there is a change of leadership in the house of Oduduwa, the first Oba to be contacted is the Oore of Otun in Mobaland. The reason for this practice is because Oore was the last to leave Ile-Ife after Oduduwa's children, had left. That was why, when Oduduwa died, the people of Ile-Ife sent for him to come and perform the rites. This therefore, became the tradition such that every time there is a passage, they repeat what they did when Oduduwa himself died.

Secondly, because Oore knew the locations of all the sons of Oduduwa, he was the one that contacted them with the news of their father's demise. Today, Oore is given the responsibility of announcing the death of an Ooni stemming from the fact that he was the one who contacted Oduduwa's children to announce the death of their father. And when a new Ooni is to be installed in Ile-Ife, the Oore of Otun must be involved, by virtue of that same history. Nowadays, Oore's physical presence is no longer compulsory, but, at the installation of an Ooni, the spirit of four Obas must be invoked, and one of those Obas is the Oore. So, that is how important Oore is, not only in Ekiti, but also in the whole of Yorubaland.

The last Oore who reigned at Ipole was Oore Owafonran. The first to reign at the current site of Otun was Oore Owafonran's son, known as Abajadiewon. These two men were direct descendants of the very Oore that had healed Oduduwa, whose popular name was Omo Olokun. They belong to the ruling house known as Imoro. After Abajadiewon, the next nine Oores of Otun people were all from the Imoro ruling house, and they all ruled from the current site of Otun. Their official names are as follows:

Oore Owarojo;
Oore Alakuta;
Oore Abegbe Iroko;
Oore Agbonyangoye;
Oore Ajogbo;
Oore Ajiginimorun;
Oore Abawuta;
Oore Abaleyinjuege
Oore Abajimutin.

During the last quarter of the 16th century, after Oore and his people had already spent some decades at the current site in Otun, there was a little rumble in the royal house. This was during the reign of Oore Agbayangoye. Apart from the Oore, there were chiefs that formed part of his leadership council. One of these chiefs is called the Onigemo. It seemed a vacancy came up for this position, and the brother of Oore Agbayangoye, known as Olubalekun, wanted to fill it. But the Oore, showing commendable selflessness and leadership in this instance, refused to allow his brother to become Chief Onigemo. His reason was that it would not be a good idea for him and his brother to lord over Otun people by occupying all the sensitive positions in the hierarchy of power. This apparently did not go down well with Olubalekun, so, he broke away from the Imoro ruling house, being himself a direct descendant of Omo Olokun; after all, Oore Agbayangoye was his brother. But, as Olubalekun was leaving Otun with the intention to settle at Ayetoro (Iyapa), he was prevented from going too far away by his friend, Olelebioke of Imoje. Olelebioke gave Olubalekun a piece of land, on which he settled. Thereafter, Olubalekun named his new location Ileobajeu. After gaining this partial autonomy from Oore Agbayangoye, a second ruling house was thereby formed. But still, the Imoro ruling house continued to produce the Oore of Otun. As already stated after Oore Agbayangoye, the next five Oores (Oore Ajogbo, Oore Ajiginimorun, Oore Abawuta, Oore Abaleyinjuege, and Oore Abajimutin) were all from the Imoro ruling house.

After the successful breakaway of Olubalekun, another direct descendant of Omo Olokun also called Gagagbon, broke away from the original Imoro ruling house and secured his own semi-autonomy. But, like in the case of Olubalekun, Gagagbon was also prevailed upon not to leave Otun by Chief Obadofin, who granted him a piece of land to settle on. Gagagbon named this place Imoya. To this effect, three ruling houses now emerged in Otun (Imoro, Ileobajeu, and Imoya), instead of one. Fortunately, there are no indications that these breakaway efforts resulted in any breach of the peace, neither are there evidences that it was more than just a heated family quarrel.

In spite of the fact that it was Olubalekun that had formed the first breakaway ruling house, namely Ileobajeu (that is the second ruling house after the Imoro ruling house), it was actually Imoya ruling house that produced the first Oore that was not of Imoro ruling house. He ascended the throne after the reign of the 10th Oore from Imoro ruling house had ruled in the current Otun site. That 10th Oore from Imoro was Oore Abajimutin, while the first Oore from Imoya ruling house was known as Oore Adibeoye, and it was only after his very short reign that the first Oore from Ileobajeu ascended the throne. This first Oore from Ileobajeu (who was actually the second non-Imoro Oore to rule Otun) was named Rotimi, and he was one of the sons of Olubalekun. However, in keeping with the tradition of rechristening an Oore, Rotimi's was rename and he reigned as Oore Ajisowo Alade. His coronation was around 1695.

In those precolonial days of 17th century Africa, there were inter-tribal wars as a matter of course, and the new Oore of Otun, Ajisowo, soon found himself embroiled in a skirmish with the neighbouring people of Aaye town. After sixteen years of stalemate, Ajisowo contacted an Ifa priest from Ila-Orangun to help him defeat Aaye town. When the Ifa priest consulted the Ifa oracle, he was told in no uncertain terms that, for Otun to win the war against Aaye, a man from outside Otun had to be crowned Oore. As long as an indigenous Oore was on the throne, the war would persist. As it turned out apparently, Ajisowo was unable to win the war, but, after his death in 1805, the Ifa priest assisted the people of Otun to victory and was crowned Oore, in a very interesting twist to the tale. The name of this Ifa priest who became Oore of Otun after Oore Ajisowo Alade is Adifagbade. As soon as he was crowned, Oore Adifagbade brought his mother and relatives to Otun-Ekiti. However, there was a tradition that prevented Adifagbade from ever seeing his mother face to face again, as long as he was alive. Because of this, he requested for land, and settled his mother there. This area was named Ileyaba (meaning royal mother's quarters) and this became the official name of the fourth ruling house of Otun. At the time, four ruling houses existed, namely: Imoro, Ileobajeu, Imoya, and Ileyaba.

Part of the deal for Adifagbade to ascend the throne was that, after him, three of his children would also rule. The name, Adifagbade, actually means a person who consulted an oracle to become king. It, therefore, seemed Adifagbade, being a diviner, already knew that he would not last long as Oore: no wonder he demanded that three of his offspring rule after him. Interestingly, the man only lasted five years on the throne – from 1805 to 1810.

The people of Otun were very willing to abide by the deal they had agreed to with Oore Adifagbade, the Ifa-priest-turned-Oore who had helped them to defeat Aaye town, but they hesitated to crown any of his three children after his death. The reason for this inaction was that the people of Otun were still concerned about the belligerence of Aaye town. Perhaps through intelligence reports, they believed that they were still preparing for war. These were days when the leader of any community was also a warrior. He would not just sit in the palace to issue orders but actually led his men to war. The people of Otun therefore could not crown any of Adifagbade's children because all three of them were still too young and could not be counted upon to engage in such kind of combat, or even to provide leadership to warriors. They had to find a middle ground: they did not want to endanger their community by having a child as Oore, neither were they willing to become guilty of defrauding a dead man the benefits of the promise they had freely made to him. As a way out of this dilemma, the people of Otun turned again to Ila-Orangun. It goes without saying that, since the threat Aaye town had not been completely neutralised, there was no talk of any person from either Imoro, Ileobajeu, or Imoya to become the Oore, based on the instruction of the Ifa oracle that an indigenous Oore could not defeat Aaye people.

The man that the people of Otun finally got from Ila-Orangun was a hunter and personal friend of late Oore Adifagbade. Obviously, the plan was that this person would rule until such a time when Adifagbade's children had grown up to continue from where their father had stopped. The name of this replacement from Ila-Orangun was Olatubosun, from Isedo compound. He was crowned in 1810 as Oore Obegirimo Olasunkande Awosowoye. Moreover, since the seat of Oore is based on one's bloodline, the male descendants of any man that occupies that seat become princes, and are also automatic potential candidates of Oore. Oore Awosowoye thus became the first Oore from the fifth ruling house of Otun-Ekiti, known as the Ile titun ruling house.

After many years of war between Otun and Aaye, it was now time for peace, and this peace lasted through the reign of my great grandfather, Oore Awosowoye. He became the longest reigning Oore in recent times and ruled for fifty straight years, between 1810 and 1860. He was blessed with many sons and daughters before his death. By the time Awosowoye died, the people of Otun were ready to fulfil the promise they had made to Oore Adifagbade because, by that time, his children had become mature enough to rule the town.

The first of Adifagbade's sons to rule Otun was Okinbaloye, who became Oore in 1860 and reigned until 1886. However, it was during his time that the Kiriji war took place. This war, also known as the Ekiti-Parapo war, was between the people of Ibadan on the one hand, and all the people of all the various kingdoms in the Ekiti area on the other hand. It lasted for sixteen years and did not end until the British, as colonial masters, had to step in. Unfortunately, after the truce was reached, Okinbaloye mysteriously died at the war camp, which was not immediately evacuated by the warriors because of the suspicion that their enemies from Ibadan may still be interested in launching a surprise attack. Oore Okinbaloye's corpse was brought to Otun, and his brother became the next Oore and was named Adifala.

It was during the reign of Adifala that the British mistakenly brought Otun under the general jurisdiction of the Northern Protectorate and specifically under the Ilorin Emirate. This attempt to separate the people of Otun from their brothers in the south-west of Nigeria was resisted by the Oore, who was high-handedly sent on exile to Zaria. We are sure that Oore Adifala was on exile and not in prison in Zaria because, while there, he was paid a yearly allowance of ten British pounds and had servants at his beck and call. The mistake of bringing Otun under the Northern Protectorate was made in 1901 and was not reversed until 1936. But before that time, the Oore of Otun had already been recognised as the head of all the Obas of Ekiti.

While Adifala was in exile in Zaria, his brother was made Oore and was titled Oore Arisile. He was on the throne when Adifala was released from exile in Zaria. But, as Adifala was returning to Otun, with a clear intention of continuing his reign, he heard that his brother had been crowned in his stead. Perhaps to avoid causing civil strife in Otun as a result of conflict between those who will support him and those who will prefer that Arisile continued, Adifala wisely changed his course from Ekan (where he had got the news) and went to

Ila-Orangun, the original town of his late father. He was buried in Ila-Orangun after living the rest of his days there.

Oore Arisile (whose real name was Adegbite) ruled Otun from 1903 until 1919 when he died. His reign marked the fulfilment of the agreement Otun people had entered into with Oore Adifagbade, who had extracted a promise from them to ensure the reign of three of his children. And the three were Okinbaloye, Adifala, and Arisile. It was now time for power to go to other families, and the next Oore was from the Ileobajeu ruling house. This Oore was name, Ariyowaye, and he ruled from 1916 until 1929. Recall that this was a time when Otun was still part of the Northern Protectorate and specifically under the jurisdiction of the Emir of Ilorin. Because of this unpalatable reality, there was no way the influence of the Ilorin Emirate could not be felt in the life and even in the politics of Otun. The Ilorin Emirate, eager to suppress any form of protest by the people of Otun over their separation from their brethren, supported Ariyowaye, who ruled the town with an iron fist and ensured that no grievance was expressed in any way by the people.

After Oore Ariyowaye died in 1929, there was an attempt to crown his son, Dawodu Kolawale, as Oore. But the people of Otun would have none of that. Even the four other ruling houses were stoutly against that idea. Things got so tensed that violence broke out and resulted in the war known as Ogun Opa; that is to say, a war fought with sticks. No houses were burnt and no lives were lost during the Ogun Opa war, but it was such a manifestation of defiance against the Emir of Ilorin that, when tempers cooled down, the people of Otun were allowed to select their own Oore by themselves. But even in this very sensitive matter of selecting an Oore, the Ifa oracle is often consulted, and there is no reason to believe that consultation was omitted in this instance.

The next Oore that was crowned (with the support of the people and the approval of all the ruling houses) was Oyinloye, from the Ile titun ruling house, to which I belong. Oyinloye was crowned Oore Ewedunmoye Olubinyin, and he reigned for the 38 years between 1929 and 1967. He was the second man from my family who ruled Otun as Oore. We are connected because Oore Ewedunmoye is a direct descendant of my great grandfather, Oore Obegirimo Olasunkande Awosowoye.

Oore Ewedunmoye did not find things easy at first. Because he did not enjoy the support of Ilorin and also had to cope with a few disgruntled people from Otun, his palace was burnt down at some point. But the man remained steadfast and focused. One of his major goals was to free Otun people from their bondage to the powers of Ilorin and reunite them with their people in the South-West of Nigeria. Fortunately for this man, he lived to see the fulfilment of his cherished desire: on the 25th of January, 1936, just seven years after he was crowned, the wrong annexation of Otun to the Ilorin Emirate came to an end, and Oore Ewedunmoye and his people were reunited with the people of the South-West.

This terrible error of annexation was initially enacted in 1894 by Captain Bower and Captain Lugard (the same Lugard who became Nigeria's first Governor General) and it was confirmed in the year 1900. Thus, 1936 became a very important year in the history of Otun. It was a day of tears, but the tears were tears of joy. The power of Ilorin over Otun had been broken. The Governor General of Nigeria at that time was Sir Bernard Bourdillon, and, in September of that same year of reunion, Oore Ewedunmoye and other Ekiti Obas went to see him. In fact, Oore Ewedunmoye was able to thank the Governor General in person. In 1947, the preeminent position of the Oore over all the original sixteen Obas of Ekiti was reinforced when the Chief Commissioner of the province presented a Certificate of

Honour to Oore Ewedunmoye. That certificate was issued in the name of King George the 6th of England and presented on the 25th of July.

Like all other men, Ewedunmoye eventually died and his reign came to an end. He was succeeded by Oore Oba Michael Adelowo Adepoju, who was crowned Oore Aroyinkeye in 1968. Oore Aroyinkeye was from the Imoro family and was the first Imoro ruling family member to reign as Oore after the reign of Abajimutin, which ended in the 15th century. Aroyinkeye ruled for 30 years until 1998, and was succeeded by the current Oore, James Adedapo Oladele Popoola, from the Imoya ruling house.

Aroyinkeye had died in 1998, it took almost two years before Oba Oladele was crowned. This delay was due to several factors, one of which was that, at least, three moons duration is required to observe the rites of passage of a deceased Oore. Then, of course, time was also required to consult with the Ifa oracle to determine which family would produce the next Oore.

As the history of Otun has already demonstrated, power does not follow any particular order. Rather, it is decided based on divination by Ifa priests. Oba Oladele has already reigned for 18 years, and at just 62 years of age, the people of Otun, myself included, are hopeful that he will remain healthy and continue with his good works for many more years to come. When he was crowned in 2000, he was titled Oore Odundun Asodedero, which actually means a person who had come to re-organise the communities in the town, inject life in the people, put smile and happiness on their faces, and to ensure that the communities experience progress, development, and peace. Before his ascension, Otun had witnessed a season of periodic unrest that disturbed the peace of the quiet and progressive town.

I, Prince Ezekiel Olabode Adetoyi, am a direct descendant of Oore Obegirimo Olasunkande Awosowoye. As a matter of fact, the man was my great grandfather. It was this Oore Awosowoye Obegirimo that gave birth to my grandfather, Ibidunmoye, his brother, Oladimeji and their other siblings. In his turn, Ibidunmoye gave birth to several children, among whom was John Adetoyi, who later gave birth to me and my siblings.

Long live Oore Odundun Asodedero!
Long live Otun-Ekiti!
Long live Mobaland!
Long live Ekiti State!
Long live Nigeria!

CHAPTER 3

PRINCE JOHN PETER ADETOYI

In the year 2004, three important things happened in my life. The first was as a result of my decision: I chose to set up my own company and had to quit the company I had been working with for more than six years before that time. The second was the birth of my first son, David, who, incidentally, was born just a month after I had already launched my entrepreneurial adventure as the CEO of my new company, Hi-Nutrients International Limited. The third was part of the harsh reality of life and there was little or nothing I could have done to stop it. On the 22nd of September, my beloved father, John Peter Adetoyi, died, and it was just three months before his 87th birthday, which he never celebrated.

In many ways, my late father was my mentor. Although he was born a prince, the reality of life during his teenage days was nothing to write home about. He had to work his muscles on the land and sweat it out many months in a year in order to eat and maintain his dignity. But the man found a way to distinguish himself from his peers quite early. It is no surprise that I seem to have followed in his footsteps.

Not only did John Peter Adetoyi become converted to Christianity and a committed follower of Jesus Christ, he was able to get a job as a cook with a British missionary that was in Otun, who was part of the missionary team of the Seventh-Day Adventist Church. The name of this man was Pastor W.G. Till.

I do not know, and nobody has been able to tell me where and from whom my father was able to learn how to cook so well that a white man would agree to employ him as his personal cook. So, at a very important stage in his life, my father was able to interact with this sort of highly educated, godly, and cultured personality. To say he was more exposed than the average Otun youth in his time would be putting it mildly. As personal cook to the White missionary, my father was not only under godly influence most of the time, but was privileged to receive some grooming on ethics and civility in general, much like Joseph of old in Potiphar's house.

The relationship between my father and his employer got so positively symbiotic that, when the man needed to go to another area to continue his mission work, he took my father along. My father followed Pastor Till to Sapele in Delta State, Ijebu-Ode, Odogbolu, Sagamu, Oyo town, Ibadan, Osogbo, and even to Porto-Novo in the Republic of Benin. His salary as a cook was 2 pounds 5 shillings, which was a huge amount in those days. Of course, I was not yet born at this time, but my father told me about these things himself. Through his extensive travel and work with his white employer, my father became fluent in Pidgin English and was able to expand his circle of influence. In those days, not many people could speak any language other than their mother tongue. Things were quite different and the ability to speak English – even Pidgin English – was nothing less than a status symbol.

My father's friends would often say that, although he was a farmer, he was such a neat man who had the habit of changing into clean clothes after returning from the farm. I am sure this is as a result of the kind of people he was privileged to interact with. This influence must have rubbed off on me also because, in secondary school, even after being appointed Library Prefect, the school noticed that I was probably the neatest student around, and they broke the protocol and made me the Health Prefect, a position I held concurrently with my initial position as the library prefect. These were some of the subtle influences my father had on me. But others were not so subtle and were more direct and based on words he told me in father-son conversations.

Although I have several step brothers today, the fact remains that I am the second of only three sons of my father and my mother. Things were a bit amorphous in those days and my father had many of my elder brothers before consummating matrimony with my mother. An interesting aspect of the marriage is that, even while she was still too young to get married, my mother was betrothed to my father. What happened was that, although my mother was born at Imoko, she lost her parents while she was a little child and was raised by Chief Osasona, who lived at Inisa and was the Obanla (second-in-command) to Oba Oyinloye. But, my mother grew up at Inisa and the connection of her life and upbringing to that street was that her elder sister was married to Chief Osasona. Up till this day, my mother is more associated with Inisa than Imoko, which is the actual place of her birth. In fact, we (her children) have adopted the relatives of her elder sister – persons like D.D. Adeleye, late Awoyinka Osoba Carpenter and co, as our maternal relations.

One day, there was a traditional dance going on as part of an event. Oba Oyinloye was present and he saw my mother, then a young girl, dancing, and he was quite impressed with her. When he asked around, he was told that she was the daughter of his second-in-command, Chief Obanla Osasona. Oba Oyinloye being intrigued by this bit of information, quickly whispered something to Obanla, who explained that, while it was true that the lady in question, Felicia, was a member of his household, she was actually the "last daughter" of his wife, but not his own daughter. Having certified that Obanla had legitimate authority over Felicia, Oba Oyinloye announced, right there and then, that Felicia was going to be the wife of his nephew, referring to my father. So, at that young age, my mother was no longer available to any man and, of course, nobody would like to mess with Chief Obanla's daughter, especially because he was the head hunter and the Chief of Staff of the king. My mother became a protected species from that day onwards and she lived the rest of her youthful days under the watchful eyes of Oba Oyinloye, who waited for her so that his nephew (Adetoyi) could marry her; she was also under the watchful eyes of Chief Obanla, who would not want anything to go wrong with the arrangement. In those days, it was a thing of joy and honour for a man to give his daughter as wife to a member of the royal house. But Chief Osasona's honour was even double: this was not just a matter of giving his adopted daughter (Felicia) to a member of the royal family. In his peculiar case, the Oore himself was the matchmaker, and it was of utmost importance that the Oore was not given any reason to regret his decision.

As for the average father in Otun, the idea of giving their daughter out to the royal family was a dream virtually all of them had, but which not many people saw come true. Apart from the prestige that came from being in-law to royalty, there was an economic angle to the whole matter. The Oore of Otun, by virtue of his position, was a Chief of Chiefs in some way. The various chiefs the Oore presided over were obligated to periodically bring him tributes and gifts. Money raised from taxes in their domain could be part of this also; but it was mostly things like goats, sheep, cattle, game, palm wine, palm oil, foodstuffs, and other goods. Bringing tribute was regarded as a sign of submission to the authority of the Oore and any delay in performing this duty could easily be interpreted as insolence or even treason. In this way, there was a limitless supply of goods in

Oore's palace and anyone who had right to a share in the goods did not need to work. So, the scramble of parents in Otun to give their daughters away in marriage to the royal family could partly be from the desire to share from the wealth of the royal family.

After being shown her future husband, my mother did not just remain idle, waiting to be married off. Rather, having grown with her sister whom we called Mama Igbogun by the name of the street she lived, she began to engage in trade. In those days, they trekked long distances that would be hard for people in this generation to comprehend. My mother's entrepreneurship, which made her to trade in many businesses, did not cease even when she got married. Until a few years ago when I stopped her from further trading and began to pay her monthly allowance, my mother was engaged in trading. She has traded in virtually everything that can be traded, all in an effort to raise money legitimately and meet the needs of her six children.

It is pertinent to note that, before the royally orchestrated marriage between my father and mother would be solemnised, things had already started happening such that, by the time my mother gave birth to her first child, Alice, my father already had a male child. Before giving a list of my siblings from my mother, I would respect the sequence of history and first state the names of my step siblings. My other step siblings in their birth order are as follows:

1. Elder Gabriel Popoola Adetoyi
2. Dayo Adetoyi
3. Kayode Adetoyi
4. Mrs. Yewande (Mama Sade)
5. Mrs. Deborah (Mama Folake)
6. Radeke (Moriadeke); now Mrs. Ayodeji
7. Monisade
8. Olaniyi Adetoyi

9. Olalekan Adetoyi
10. Olanrenwaju Adetoyi; now late
11. Sunday Adetoyi

My mother's children in their order are:

1. Akanke; now Mrs. Alice Odia
2. Deborah (Folake); Mrs. Adeyemi
3. Sarah (now late); Mrs. Abolarin
4. Funmilola (now Mrs. Aluko)
5. Banji Adetoyi
6. Bode Adetoyi
7. Adebola Adetoyi (now late)
8. Dare Adetoyi

I am proud to state that, I have a wonderful relationship with all my siblings, whether directly from my mother or not. In the year before my father died, he displayed some eerie foreknowledge of his impending death by hosting all of us. Then he said that the only favour he was asking was for us to be united. He said he wanted us to be like a bunch of broomsticks. If we were separated, we could easily be broken; but it would be hard to break us if we were a bunch, and that we could sweep away the enemies as a broom. He said that, no matter the disagreement, we must remain one. That is the principle we now live by.

Long before having his first child, my father followed his White missionary employer from one missionary station to another, until it got to a time that the missionary wanted to return to the United Kingdom. The bond between my father and this man had become so strong that he seriously considered my father with him to the UK. Perhaps he was due for a furlough and was not signing off from the missionary activity completely. In any case, since he was not a kidnapper, he returned to Otun to ask permission from Oba Oyinloye, who was my father's uncle.

Unfortunately, after making his intentions known, the request of the missionary was declined. Unknown to the innocent British man, the Oba refused his request because he heartily believed that the plan was to make my father a slave, once he got to Britain. Nobody could blame Oba Oyinloye for taking that position. After all, this was colonised Nigeria, and the relationship of master-servant was the order of the day between a white man and a black man. Besides, slavery was still practiced in some areas at that time, even within Nigeria.

Sadly, the British man left without my father, who now had to return to the hard life of farming. His own father, Ibidumoye, had died at that time, so, he stayed with his elder brother, Olaniran, who was old enough to be his father. In fact, Olaniran's children, until sometime later, truly believed that my father, Adetoyi, was their eldest brother. They had no idea that he was actually their father's brother because they grew up seeing him in their house and relating with their father as his own father. In those days, an elder brother in Otun was addressed with the prefix "Oga." So, to the children of Olaniran, my father was "Oga Adetoyi."

Although my mother was raised a Seventh-day Adventist, she joined the Anglican Church after she got married and has remained an active member up till today. My father was always an Anglican. He was called John Peter Adetoyi because his name at birth was Adetoyi, and his baptism name was Peter. As for the third name, "John," he added that to his name, as a testimony to his Christian faith, for which he was glad. In spite of his early interaction with Pastor Till – a Seventh-Day Adventist – my father was an active member of the Anglican Church until his death. That was why the church handled his burial ceremony and even buried him within the premises of the St. Peter's Anglican Church in Otun-Ekiti.

The history of the Anglican Church in Otun began in 1905, and the missionaries that brought the faith, though of the

Anglican Communion, came under the direct auspices of the Church Missionary Society, popularly known as CMS. It seems that these missionaries did not make an issue out of their Anglican roots and were simply known as CMS missionaries. No wonder, most people in Otun today (especially members of the older generation) would look blank if you asked them about the early days of the CMS in Otun-Ekiti. This would instead refer to the Anglican Church. They would not be able to make the connection; what they know is the CMS. But members of the CMS did not just materialise from nowhere, neither were they nondenominational. They were all members of the Anglican Church in England. Interestingly, even before the Anglican Church came to Otun in 1905 through the CMS, indigenous Christian missionaries had brought the gospel of Christ to the general Ekiti area, beginning from Ado-Ekiti. These missionaries were mostly freed slaves who had regained their freedom mostly from Ibadan and environs, where Christianity had already taken root.

As early as 1787, some British men like Thomas Clarkson and George Fox came together to form The Society for Effecting the Abolition of the Slave Trade. This campaign to abolish the commercial exchange of human beings for money developed alongside international events such as the French revolution, sporadic unrests, and individual acts of resistance from enslaved people in the British colonies. Not many people are aware that the anti-slave trade society had several women as active members. According to historian, Clare Midgley, there was at least one woman in every ten men in that society. This 10% participation of the female folk was made up of well-known abolitionists like Mary Birkett, Hannah More, and Mary Wollstonecraft, apart from a considerable body of working and middle-class British women. Some African slaves, who were brought to Britain and had managed to regain their freedom, were also supported by the movement. One of the most prominent former slave who joined the anti-slave trade movement was Olaudah Equiano. He was kidnapped at the young age of 11. Many people believe that Equiano was of the Igbo ethnic group.

Equiano, who later became known as Gustavus Vassa, was initially sold to a Virginia planter, before being eventually sold to a British naval officer named Captain Pascal. But, as was common in those days, slaves were sold from one man to the other exactly like cars are sold today. Captain Pascal soon sold Equiano to a Quaker merchant. Equiano eventually bought his freedom from the Quaker merchant.

One other notable former slave at that time was Ignatius Sancho, the first African prose writer to have his work published in England. Sancho was brought to England as a slave in 1731 at the age of 2.

After many ups and downs, and support from some British Parliamentarians and even members of the House of Lords, the vision of The Society for Effecting the Abolition of the Slave Trade was achieved. Slave Trade was effectively abolished in the whole of the British Empire in 1833, after an initial abolition in Britain in 1807. After that abolition, it became illegal for British ships to participate in the trade. Moreover, Britain went as far as attacking slave ships belonging to other nations and freeing the slaves. In fact, this was exactly how the popular Yoruba missionary, Bishop Samuel Ajayi Crowther, was released. A notable miracle in Ajayi Crowther's case was that, even though he and his mother had been sold into slavery at the same time and they both had been bought by different slave traders and were to be separated forever, they were both released by the British enforcers of the anti-slavery law and eventually met again on Nigerian soil.

In spite of the abolition of slavery in the British Empire, which Nigeria eventually became a part of in 1860 when formal colonialism began, slavery still thrived in many locations in those days, largely because there was no standing army to enforce the will of the British in every nook and cranny of Nigeria. To find a way around this problem, Christian missionaries came up with a very astute scheme. They would pose as slave buyers, buy slaves before they were shipped off, and then release those slaves, after introducing them to the Christian faith and educating them properly. This highly intelligent and compassionate strategy was the remote cause of the introduction of Christianity to Ekiti because some of those slaves (persons like Famoboni) who were from Ekiti, were able to find their way back and bring their new found faith to their kith and kin. They were able to find their way back to their own land after slavery became a thing of the past all over Nigeria and to return became relatively safe.

To answer the question of how Famoboni and others found their way from Ekiti to Ibadan in the first place, one only needs to recall that, during the Ekiti-Parapo war (already referred to in Chapter Two of this autobiography), the practice was to either capture and kill enemy soldiers, enslave them, or enslave the people of the area conquered, which was initially under the protection of the neutralised soldiers. It was through this means that some people from Ekiti found themselves in Ibadan as slaves. This exciting bit of history was related in person by Venerable Samson Olubunmi Omitade – the venerable currently in charge of the St. Peter's Anglican Church, Otun-Ekiti – with retired Bishop Peter Adebiyi's book, *History of Christianity in Ekitiland*, as his source.

According to Venerable Omitade, even before the CMS missionaries came, the early indigenous missionaries like Baba Famoboni had planted the seed of the gospel of Christ in Ekitiland. In spite of coming to Otun as early as 1905, the CMS missionaries could not make any meaningful impact because, as a result of the wrong annexation of Otun to the Ilorin Emirate, Fulani raiding parties posed a real danger, and this effectively impeded the work of the missionaries. This, therefore, took another 25 years for the CMS to return to Ekiti.

However, in 1922, eight years before the CMS could return, Seventh-day Adventist Church missionaries showed up and began to gain a foothold in the town through their missionary activities. By the time the CMS returned to Otun, they appeared like newcomers, in spite of the fact that they had initially arrived there much earlier.

One point worthy of note is that the first house ever to be roofed with corrugated iron sheets in Otun was erected in 1925 for Pastor W.G. Till and other Seventh-Day Adventist (SDA) Church missionaries; this was the same Pastor Till that my father eventually served as personal cook. Pastor Till worked mainly with a local missionary, I.A. Balogun, to preach the Seventh-Day Adventist message to the people of Otun. They had many converts, including the adopted parents of my mother, who were Seventh-Day Adventists. Today, Otun hosts several old denominations like the Anglican Church, the Seventh-Day Adventist Church, the Catholic Church, the Christ Apostolic Church, and even some new generation churches like the Redeemed Christian Church of God (RCCG); Deeper Life Bible Church, Mountain of Fire and Miracles, and others.

I shall never forget my father whose words I did not understand until now. He would often tell me:

"Bode, do your work at the right time that you are supposed to do it. If you do your work right and well, you do it for yourself."

Today, with the modest success I have achieved by the grace of God, I wish this man was around to share in the fruit. Anyway, he seemed to have known that he would not be around because he rightly told me that, when I would be realising the truth of his words, he would be long gone. How sad that my father was right!

One thing that pains me up till this moment is the missed opportunity of getting some vital information from him. I had started discussing some sensitive issues with him about my background, and we were supposed to continue the discussion at a later time. Unfortunately, that was never to be because he passed on. I will never forget my father and all he did to set me on the right path. I will never forget his devotion and sacrifice. I don't know how he did it, but there is none of his children today that is unable to fend for him or herself. As a prince in Otun, he lived with the honour and dignity of a prince, and died only after unleashing several princes and princesses to carry on the torch after him.

I will always miss my dad, Prince John Peter Adetoyi. My only hope is to see him again on the resurrection morning.

CHAPTER 4

NOT TOO YOUNG FOR SCHOOL

The Nigerian Senate recently passed a bill tagged, Not Too Young to Run. The whole idea behind that bill is to enable Nigerians that are qualified, competent and mature to run for public offices without putting undue restriction on them based on age alone. From the content of the bill, it would continue to be alright for a 35-year-old Nigerian to become a Senator; but a House of Representatives aspirant needs only to have celebrated his/her 25th birthday before aspiring to go to the Federal House, etc. This bill received enough support due to many factors which include the fact that Barack Obama became President of the United States before the age of 50 (he was 47 at the time), and the fact that Australia recently produced one of the youngest leaders of the developed world. In fact, at 31 years of age, Sebastian Kurz is actually the world's youngest leader. Canada's Prime Minister is still less than 45, even after some years in power. Britain's Tony Blair was just 44 when he began to reign over Britain and there have been younger leaders in Europe also, like Emmanuel Macron of France, who was 39 years old when he became President.

In 1973, I was just four years old but was already making my mark as an individual who could not be pushed around. One day, I suddenly decided that I wanted to go to school. What prompted this decision was my childhood friend and next door neighbour, Gbadebo Ajiboye, who was a year older than me. In my young mind, I did not know that Debo was a year older than me and could not understand why he was allowed to put on school uniform, carry a box, and head for school every weekday, while I was told to wait for my time. I did not like the idea one bit, but I endured the insult for some time, until it became unbearable. I had never gone to school by that time, but the anticipation it held in my childish mind was an earthly paradise. I decided that I was done playing with Debo only when he returned from that special place he often went to.

Normally, Debo and I played mostly by making clay mounds with our feet. We would use our feet as a support structure, build the mound by piling clay on our feet, and then try to carefully pull our feet out without causing the mound to collapse. This attempt at imprecise civil engineering was a source of great pleasure to us at that age – especially when our mounds held steady and did not collapse. The only problem I had was that I could only play with Debo after he returned from school. Debo himself did not help matters when he whispered in my ears that, if I followed him to school, we could build mounds there, and I did not have to wait for him to return anymore.

Those who know me today would confess (maybe secretly) that I have a fierce willpower. Many have described me as a go-getter. But some have interpreted this attitude as sheer stubbornness. The problem is that this fierce willpower seemed to have been with me from birth. My mother and older siblings have a handful of stories recounting things I did as a child which were simply hard to believe. In one particular case, I was sitting at the veranda and refused to make way for my sister to enter the house. When she tried to gently nudge me to move aside and wondered why I would not make way for her, I replied her like an adult. I told her that she should not attempt to boss me around. According to those who related the story, I even asked my bemused sister if she did not know that she was talking with Awosowoye. How a young child of my age would know the name of Oore Awosowoye (my great grandfather) and even attempt to claim his privileges was something too mystical for my family to deal with. They basically just ignored me in such situations.

So, as soon as I got the idea that I could play with Debo and build mounds in school, I became upset and began to insist that I wanted to go to school. How I was able to stampede my parents and all my older siblings into acceding to my will is a mystery up till this day. I was told that, three days after my protest started, I was enrolled into the St. Peter's Primary School, Otun, which was under administration of the Anglican Church. The first time I attended St. Peter's, I went in mufti, reason being that my school uniform was still being sown by the tailor, but I was impatient and desperate because I suspected that the issue of my school uniform may be used as a delay tactics. I am quite sure it must have been a war, and must have given them hell to allow me to start attending school even before my uniform was ready.

Ironically, this stubborn boy that appeared set for truancy, rebellion against teachers, fighting with fellow pupils, and general brigandage and poor performance became the best in his class and the best in his school, as far as academic matters were concerned. I don't know how I did it neither can I recollect any kind of serious reading I engaged in while in primary school. I beat the whole class in my first term in Primary One, beat them all again in the second term, and repeated the feat in the third term promotion examinations to Primary Two. I now know that I am blessed with a very strong memory and I think that my strong memory was all I applied at that primary level. As long as I was in class when instructions were given, I seemed able to remember and regurgitate the information during tests and examinations. I mention this because, when I got to secondary school, I realised that the game was different.

It was in secondary school that I actually started to read my books.

In Primary Two, I continued with the merciless trouncing of my classmates and became famous in school. My name was no longer Bode, but "that boy that often took first position." There was a classmate of mine known as Ayangbemile. Like me, she was a native of Otun-Ekiti, but lived on Inisa Street. I soon got to know that she and her father felt that, because her father was an herbalist, taking the first position in class was Ayangbemile's right. It was an open secret that the incisions on Ayangbemile's face during our examinations was often done as part of rituals to ensure her domination of the class. That was how desperately Ayangbemile's father wanted his daughter to take the first position, but, I kept beating the girl. My performance endeared so many of my classmates to me, and I taught them during break time – without having to refer to any notes. My superb memory was enough to put me in that position.

I did not know how it happened, but, for the first time in my school life at the time, Ayangbemile beat me and came first during our promotion examinations to Primary Four. Even though I did not do badly, I lost my first position for the first time. My reaction to this event revealed a part of my nature that was to become more obvious with time. Just for not taking the position I had set out to take, I felt like I had failed that examinations. I went home after receiving my report card and started crying, leaving everybody confused.

"What is wrong with coming second in a class of so many pupils?" they reasoned, but I saw the matter differently. When my father returned home, I tearfully told him that Ayangbemile and her father had used charms to take away my first position. My father may only have been trying to calm me down, but he ended up teaching me a lesson which I have never forgotten.

He urged me to be of good cheer and that, since we were going to church, I should go and personally tell God that I did not want anybody to take my position again, and I did as I was told. Amazingly since then, nobody ever beat me again in the primary school.

When we started Primary Four, I worked hard and in no time returned to my winning ways and dominated the class by taking the first position during first term. I maintained my lead over Ayangbemile and the others until we finished primary school. So, long ago, I had seen the efficacy of prayer when coupled with hard work. Therefore as a Christian and a pastor today, I still correct people who believe that just going to church aimlessly without taking their primary assignments seriously will result in miracles. I sincerely do not believe in that ideology. My school of thought is that, there can be no miracle if one does not work towards it. I stand to be corrected.

I could remember that even at an early age, the traits of working to earn a living had being ingrained in me. While construction works were ongoing on the National Bank in Otun-Ekiti, my mother saw that the workers would need food and she moved to the site to render that services. My siblings and I joined her to give her a support. Funmilola and Banji were preparing the dishes while I was saddled with the responsibility of fetching water. If my parents were expected to pay my tuition and those of my siblings, the least we could do was to also assist them by working in our own little way.

CHAPTER 5

TAMED CHAMPION

According to the book of Judges in the Old Testament of the Bible, Delilah used all her feminine wiles but could not get Samson to tell her the little but powerful secret hidden in the seven locks of his never-before-shaven hair. When she got tired of trying to seduce him into revealing his life's secret, she used the time-tested principle of perseverance.

As a secondary school student at the Comprehensive High School, Otun-Ekiti, I found myself in a drama of destiny that was similar to what happened to Samson over three thousand years ago, even though my situation was a bit different, and only three individuals were involved. In this case, the Delilah was a male and my classmate: his father played the role of the Philistines who had hired Delilah. Although my role in this drama was Samson, fortunately for me, I still have my eyes today and my life is not in any danger.

Because of the way I had dominated academic activities while in primary school, I already had a reputation before getting into Comprehensive High School, Otun-Ekiti. But I was not the only one with a reputation. There were other champions from other primary schools in town and Comprehensive High School suddenly became a platform for a royal rumble. Years past, the World Wrestling Federation based in the United States organised special wrestling matches at certain seasons between successful wrestlers, drawn from different tournaments. They called such matches royal rumbles and it was a high point for wrestling enthusiasts. Comprehensive High School, Otun-Ekiti, was nothing less than an arena for a royal rumble when I arrived in 1981. Several kings were now present in one location, and we immediately went to war so as to determine who will be crowned emperor. There were also pupils from the Seventh-Day Adventist Primary School who had done exactly what I did at St. Peter's Anglican Primary School. There were also pupils from the Catholic Primary School, as well as other schools, who had dominated their class and were undisputed leaders. So when we met at Comprehensive High School, an undeclared contest for supremacy began.

In the first term of Form One, I came first in my class. In the second term, I repeated the same feat. Tension must have begun to rise, but I did not bother to find out. I remained focused and still came first in my class again in the third term. This doubled as promotion examinations to Form Two. If a storm was brewing over my dominance, it blew up after the usual speech and prize-giving day. The speech and prize-giving day was the most important day in the school calendar in those days because it was the high point of a school year. On that day, students, teachers, school administrators, parents, guardians, and well-wishers came together to celebrate the students who had distinguished themselves among their peers.

In the first speech and prize-giving day, I was the most distinguished student in my set, and it was not even a normal case. It was a case of making it look like every other student was playing and that I was the only person who had been serious academically. Like a badly acted movie, parents, guardians and fellow students watched as I was given prizes for one, two, three, four and then five subjects. It did not stop there, I eventually got eight prizes. I actually cleared all the prizes, leaving only one in an inconsequential subject to one of my classmates. It was a total demolition, and there were bound to be reaction.

Although my friend, Babatunde Olofinbiyi, was not one of the kings that had dominated their respective classes he still took what happened during our first speech and prize-giving day personally. This was quite understandable because Tunde's father was at that event. Tunde prayed and wished that, even if it was just in a single subject, he should get something to save his face, but that was not to be. The cause of Tunde's embarrassment must be that boy from St. Peter's whose fame had preceded him.

Tunde's confusion was over the fact that that my father was a farmer – a blood-and-sweat, traditional, muscle-dependent farmer that utilised the same implements used 500 years ago to till the soil and practise crop production. On the other hand, Tunde's father was not only educated but was actually a very brilliant teacher at the Seventh-Day Adventist Church Primary School, where Tunde had obtained his primary education. This man was so cerebral that he was nicknamed, "imaginary professor." Tunde took it as an affront that the son of a subsistence farmer should make him and others (children of schooled parents) look so bad. However, Tunde was a wise young man, and he took his challenge to his father. He believed there should be a way out of his humiliation, which intended to make life in secondary school a living hell and cause the subsequent five years to be his most difficult.

When Tunde's father engaged his dejected son in a heart-to-heart conversation and got to know that my father was a farmer, he decided to be objective instead of sentimental. Tunde was not going to envy the dangerous young man called, Ezekiel Olabode Adetoyi; Tunde was not going to hate him; he was not going to try to poison him so that the threat he presented could be eliminated; he was not going to undermine the boy; he would not even try to compete with him. What Tunde would do was to befriend him. Surely, there was a secret to such academic excellence, and Tunde's father was determined to uncover it. But the process was going to be long and hard – and there could be no mistakes. The results would be rewarding though, but failure would be calamitous. Mr. Olofinbiyi was ready to help his son, albeit his son had to play a key role.

I did not know what Tunde and his father discussed on that fateful day until very recently. In fact, this 37-year-old secret was publicly revealed by Tunde himself inside a church in Ado-Ekiti, Ekiti State. Tunde told this amazing true story during a thanksgiving service to thank God who enabled him to become a qualified surgeon. He remembered the past and was able to recount that if not for my influence in his life, he may have ended up a mediocre and certainly, not the surgeon he came to be.

In expressing gratitude during that church service, he freely confessed the role God had used me to play in his life. He even promised to bring me to the church to confirm his story, and this actually happened just a few months ago. It was from Tunde's own lips that I got to understand how my academic dominance at Comprehensive High School had brought us together. Today, he would describe me as an icon and encourager; his mentor, and leader and even as his helper, and dare anyone to challenge him. In fact, he would go as far as saying I was his teacher, but the process of this special relationship was wonderful and incredible.

After our first speech and prize-giving day was the long vacation that would end with our resumption in Form Two. Tunde's father advised him to use the holiday period to befriend me. But Tunde told his father that I was a proud and snobbish student and that I would not want to relate with him. He wondered aloud what he would do if I rebuffed him, but his wise father insisted that he had to find a way to befriend me, even though he (Tunde's father) did not have an answer to the possible impediment Tunde had pointed out. Tunde was encouraged to act like Delilah in the story of Samson; he was to patiently woo me until he broke any sort of resistance I may have towards him. He was to make a habit of going to my house and sitting with me. The end game of Mr. Olofinbiyi was for me to begin to teach Tunde, and support for this bold strategy came from Tunde's mother too, leaving Tunde with no option but to try. Tunde now had to figure out how to get me to love him to the extent that I could help him improve academically.

I cannot remember the details, but, according to Tunde, when he first started coming to my house, there was no welcome smile on my face towards him, neither did I make any attempt to acknowledge his presence. Tunde claimed that he always met me reading anytime he came to check on me; that instead of encouraging him to stay, I would suggest that he could come the following day and would turn right back to reading my books, virtually ignoring him. This attitude of mine often left Tunde dejected, but he knew he could not report any failure to his father, so he kept coming.

Things did not change much until when we got to Form Two. I kept ignoring Tunde, but he kept coming to my house. Through the period of the long vacation, he had managed to become my acquaintance but could not rightly be described as a close friend.

In Form Two, Tunde noticed that he was a bit more confident in Fine Arts, so he gave his all in a test we had during our first term and performed well. As a matter of fact, he actually did better than other Form Two students. Our Fine Arts teacher, a Ghanaian, came to our class and said that we could consult with the chap in Form Two C that had come first in the Fine Arts test. I was in Form Two B while Tunde was in Form Two C, and the chap the Ghanaian teacher referred to was Tunde.

The weekend of that very week, Tunde showed up in my house as usual and, for the first time, I decided to give him my attention. Apparently, Tunde is a very intelligent person, but perhaps, I did not consider him so initially, at least not before that Fine Arts test. Perhaps I thought he was someone I could not condescend to relate with. Because of my commitment to excellence, I must have felt I had nothing to gain from associating with him. My independent mind-set could not see any reason to be his friend. But here was a new situation to deal with: if Tunde could come first in Fine Arts in the whole set, then maybe he was not such an unintelligent lad after all. In retrospect, I can state that that weekend marked the beginning of a relationship that gave birth to two different champions and has been mutually satisfying for well over three decades now.

Because Tunde had been able to beat me in Fine Arts, I began to open up to him, maybe out of curiosity. After sometime, I began to lend Tunde my notes. At first, I only permitted him to read them in my presence when he came to my house; but as trust and respect for him grew, I began to allow him take my notes home. Tunde also started emulating me in the areas of reading at home and being generally serious with his schooling.

During speech and prize-giving day at the end of Form Two, Tunde won two prizes – one in Fine Arts, and the other in Social Studies. The prize in Social Studies was for being the best in his class. This was a remarkable improvement from Form One. Tunde felt much better than he had ever felt since that terrible day at the end of Form One. I won 10 prizes, but with 2 prizes, Tunde was coming up. To indicate that I had noticed his improvement, it was after our Form Two prize-giving day that I came to Tunde's house for the first time.

There was no doubt anymore: Mr. Olofinbiyi's plan was working even better than initially conceived. I seemed to be rewarding Tunde with friendship in a manner directly proportional to the improvement in his academic performance. Note that what opened me up to Tunde was not just his Delilah–like moves, but also some noticeable improvement in his academic performance.

Also recall that Tunde was not alone in this very astute scheme. When I showed up in his house for the first time, his parents could not hide their joy. It seemed that, in their wildest imagination, all they had hoped for was for Tunde to have access to me: but for me to come and see Tunde at home was something else and too good to be true. Our relationship blossomed from then on. I gradually began to accept Tunde as a friend.

In Form Three, I was moved to Three A and Tunde was moved to Three C. He has since confessed that he liked the idea of the two of us belonging to different classes. His reasoning was simple: he so valued our relationship that the fear of any fracas developing between us made him prefer to give me a wide berth. He felt that, if we were in the same class, something somewhere may cause friction between us and deny him the benefits of our association. So, as far as Tunde was concerned, Three C (or any other class) was fine, as long as Bode Adetoyi was not there. Our relationship had become so strong that sometimes, I went to Tunde's class just to see him, and he also returned the gesture intermittently.

Things kept getting better for Tunde. In fact, once in a while, he would beat me in English Essay assignments. I did not necessarily like the fact that Tunde was now able to beat me once in a while in English Essay, but I was so happy to see his improvement. His amazing progress was exciting. For some reasons I cannot recall, there was no prize-giving day at the end of our Form Three. But it was no longer news that Tunde had joined the group of bright and upcoming students of the school. At the end of Form One, Tunde was 24th out of a total of 130 students; but he was certainly among the first 11, as they say in football parlance.

Just by comparing scores between ourselves, we discovered that Tunde had become the best English student at the end of Form Three. He was also the best in Geography and in Chemistry too. Something remarkable and unprecedented happened at the end of Form Three. We did up to 23 subjects and, I had A-grade in all of them. The surprise was that Tunde Olofinbiyi got A-grade in 17 of the 23 subjects and came second to me, the undisputed "Lord of the Manor." Although Tunde was unable to dethrone me, he was extremely happy to have come next to me. His parents were very happy with both of us, and this deepened our relationship to the extent that Tunde sometimes followed me to my father's farm, and I returned the favour whenever possible.

When the time came to go to Form Four, Tunde was not sure if he wanted to study commercial, arts, or science subjects. But as soon as his father realised that I had decided to study what we then referred to as pure science, Tunde got marching orders to follow me. This was how Tunde joined the science class. Tunde and I were joined by other bright and serious students, thus, we became a group of five friends: Tunde, Ganiyu Raji (now Babayemi Adewale); Bayo Aborishade (Boyo), Ezekiel Jide Asaolu and myself.

Throughout Form Four, Tunde remained unbeatable in both English and Chemistry, but I maintained my position at the top of the pyramid as the best student in the whole set. The joy of this recollection is that, when it was time for West Africa Examination Council (WAEC) examinations, we all did well. So, after beginning with a dismal performance in Form One, Tunde ended up getting one of the best WAEC results in our set simply because he had a very humble and wise father who understood that the spirit of emulation was better than the spirit of envy and jealousy. His fatherly advice changed the destiny of Tunde and did a lot to bolster his self-confidence: but the battle for education did not end with our commendable WAEC result.

Even before passing out my friends and I sat for Joint Admission and Matriculation Board examinations, popularly known as JAMB. I remember that I wrote mine at Ola Oluwa Muslim Grammar School, Ado-Ekiti. We all did well, but not well enough to be admitted to study medicine, which was what I initially wanted to study. Naturally, Tunde also decided that he wanted to study medicine. But, as time would later prove, Tunde had been transformed into his own man. Apart from Tunde and I, all the guys in our group of friends wanted to study medicine too. They were Bayo, Waheed, Wale, and Toyin. At the end of the day, only Tunde and Waheed became doctors. Bayo became a physiotherapist, Wale became a pharmacist, and I became a farmer.

After sitting for JAMB the second time, I decided to go to University of Ilorin to study Agricultural Science. This came as a shock to those who knew me, but it was as a result of the counsel from an elderly man, who I would have more to write about in a later chapter. But unlike me, Tunde stuck to his guns and refused to allow his dream to become a doctor die. I became a student of Agricultural Science at the University of Ilorin in 1988 and was in my 300 level by the time Tunde started his 100 level at Obafemi Awolowo University, Ile Ife – as a nursing student. Tunde wrote his third JAMB examination as an undergraduate at Ife, but still could not be admitted to study medicine in any university of his choice. When he got to 300 level, he wrote yet another JAMB (his fourth) and was able to secure admission into University of Ilorin, joining me when I was already in my 500 level.

Many people tried to discourage Tunde from his razor-focus and dogged determination, but his father stood by him. Mr. Olofinbiyi was not a wealthy man, but what he lacked in material resources was well-compensated for by his love for his son, his wisdom, and by his willingness to do all it took to achieve a worthy goal. The man turned deaf ears to all unsolicited advice from people and allowed Tunde to make the switch and begin his university education afresh, even after already spending several years studying nursing and was at the time close to graduation. The move Tunde made was the defining moment of his life, and he had a smooth ride at University of Ilorin, became a doctor, and eventually a surgeon. When Tunde took a deep breath after this marathon in his academic pursuit and looked back at the last three decades, he knew that the trajectory of his life was determined that season when his father decided that he had to become friends with the brilliant boy, Ezekiel Olabode Adetoyi, that had caused him to be depressed.

Today, Tunde and I are so close that we are like blood brothers, and our relationship of over three decades is a categorical evidence that peer group influence can be both positive and monumentally consequential.

It is amazing to recall that I wanted to study medicine and did not lack the mental ability to write JAMB and score the required marks to secure admission. Many people could not understand why I should give up my desire to study the course of my choice, when I was not known for changing my mind easily. I also did not fully understand my own decision then, but now I do: I did not insist on studying Medicine because God had a different plan for me. The plan that God had for me to make me a happy, healthy, and wealthy man was better than what I had in mind, but the road to that future was not smooth nor was it devoid of serious obstacles.

CHAPTER 6

VOICE OF DESTINY (PROFESSOR JOSEPH BOLARINDE OBEBE)

The first advanced level institution I attended after leaving secondary school was the then Oyo State College of Arts and Science, Ile-Ife, Osun State. For convenience, we referred to the institution using the acronym OSCAS, and I was there in 1987. While at OSCAS, I was admitted into the Ondo State Polytechnic, Owo, (now Rufus Giwa Polytechnic, Owo), to study Food Science and Nutrition, but I chose not to attend. The entrance requirement for my admission into the polytechnic was just my WAEC result; that was the system in those days. Part of the reason for my decision to go to OSCAS was to be equipped to deal a deadly blow to JAMB examinations once and for all. We had been told that, at institutions like OSCAS, what was normally treated on a daily basis was the sort of questions one could expect during a JAMB examination. So, attending such an A 'Level school was to guarantee a very successful JAMB examinations.

The second JAMB examinations I wrote was actually after just one year at OSCAS, and my objective was to study medicine. I filled the JAMB form in the same manner I had filled the first one. I selected University of Ibadan as my first choice, Obafemi Awolowo University (OAU) as my second choice, and University of Ilorin as my third choice and I chose medicine as my preferred course of study in all the three. This shows that I was only interested in going to the university to study one course – medicine – and nothing else. My subjects at OSCAS were Geography, Chemistry, Physics, and Agricultural Science; but, when I wrote that second JAMB, I only got 259 marks. I recalled that I was still in secondary school when I wrote my first JAMB; yet, I got 279 marks, 20 marks more than I managed to get, even after one whole year at OSCAS. With 279 marks in my first JAMB, I had tried to get admitted into the University of Ibadan, but the cut-off mark was a whopping 290. In fact, it had to be reduced from an initial 300 marks. Such was the stiff bar set for medical students.

If, with 279 marks, I could not be admitted to study medicine, what was I supposed to do with 259 marks after one whole year at OSCAS? I knew I was in trouble. When Mr. Ojo, my Chemistry teacher at Comprehensive High School, Otun-Ekiti, heard about my performance in second JAMB examinations, he was very sad. It was so unbelievable and so disheartening. As far as Mr. Ojo was concerned, this was not the Bode Adetoyi he knew; something was wrong somewhere.

On my part, I decided to move fast to salvage my situation. Fortunately for me, I knew about one senior Professor in the University of Lagos, Professor Joseph Bolarinde Obebe, who was the younger brother of Chief Saade Ogunleye, my father's friend from Ogbonisan in Otun. My father's friendship with Chief Saade was an adopted friendship and quite unique. There was a significant age difference between the two of them, with my father being the older. The reason for my father's friendship with Chief Saade was that while he was alive, Chief Saade's elder brother was a friend of my father. But the elder brother at the point of death, pleaded with my father to continue their relationship with his family; that was why Saade who later became a chief, became my father's friend since then.

So, I got in touch with my father, and he described Professor Obebe's house in Maryland, Lagos State, to me. By that time,

I went to stay with Raphael Balogun at Ebute Meta West. Raphael is a distant relative from the family of my paternal grandmother. Armed with the direction I had received from my father, I made it to Professor Obebe's residence and was able to secure an appointment for the next day by 10 a.m. But, not wanting to miss the man, I was at his office as early as 7 a.m. I reasoned that no matter how urgent or busy his day would be, he must at least come to his office before going out for the day's lecture and that I should be around for that.

When the man finally showed up at his office, he welcomed me warmly, and began to talk to me. I realised that he was very familiar with my family as he began to talk about them. This was a bit confusing at first because, before coming to see the man, his reputation from people who claimed to have had dealings with him was that of a person that was reluctant to help. People claimed that he was not accommodating. So I had come to see him only because I was nearly desperate and thought it was better to try and fail than to just believe what people had said about the man.

When Professor Obebe asked me what I wanted him to do for me, I said I wanted him to give me a note to his friends so that I could be admitted to study medicine in the University of Ibadan or the Obafemi Awolowo University, Ile-Ife. My belief was that, as a senior Professor, Obebe must have friends in several universities and so should be able to help me in the matter of securing admission.

Professor Obebe immediately explained an unknown reality to me. He told me that, once a student was rejected by the University of Ibadan (UI), that same student could not be accepted by the Obafemi Awolowo University (OAU); at least not for the same course. The reason was that there was some rivalry between the two universities, with UI having the obvious upper hand. As expected, OAU would not want to reinforce the idea, or appear to reinforce the idea of the superiority of UI by granting admission to a student that had been rejected by UI. That would mean they were taking crumbs from the table of UI, and that was not good for their reputation. I listened quietly and said nothing. But it was later that I got to realise that what Professor Obebe had said was based on facts.

Up till this very moment, the rivalry goes on. But, by the time Professor Obebe was telling me about this, I hardly knew the facts like I do today.

In talking about my third choice – the University of Ilorin – Professor Obebe suddenly changed his posture and looked at me in a manner I could not interpret. Then he plainly said that he could not help me to secure admission into the University of Ilorin to study medicine. Since he offered no explanation, I did not know what else to say to him, but what he had said did not come as a surprise to me. I had already been told that he did not like helping people, and here he was confirming what people had told me. I resigned myself to the worst, but he was not done talking.

Professor Obebe told me that, from my background and what he knew about me, he had an advice for me. Then he started to say some nice things that sounded like he was preparing the ground to tell me something he knew I would not like. He said a lot of nice things about my family. In fact, he was the one that told me that his elder brother, Chief Saade, was only an adopted friend of my father. Then he added that, if my father could humble himself to be friends with Chief Saade Ogunleye, who was younger than his youngest brother, I also had to follow my father's footsteps and humble myself and listen to his advice. I knew that Professor Obebe was planning to drop a bomb, so I began to stiffen in my seat involuntarily. I was too wise not to see that his soft words were a prelude to some hard talk.

Unfortunately, I was right. Before dropping his bomb, Professor Obebe had asked me if I wanted him to be candid with me. Sensing trouble but too curious not to want to hear what he had in mind, I had answered in the affirmative. That was when he plainly told me that there was no need for me to sit for another JAMB examinations. At this, I wondered what he expected me to do. Only after putting me in that listening mood did he say I should go to the University of Ilorin and study Agricultural Science. He even said that I did not need any note from him to get admitted. With my score, the University of Ilorin was going to roll out the red carpet and give me admission promptly because they were interested in bright students going into their agricultural science department, which was one of the strongest in the country.

When he noticed my hesitation, he further urged me to be humble to accept his advice. He said that in case I rejected his advice, he knew I would join those who often accused him of not helping people. He said that the fact was that he often helped people by advising them, to the best of his knowledge, but that the people often would not listen to him, only to later accuse him of not helping them. Being a man of peace, he never tries to force people to accept his advice. This willingness to leave people to do what they pleased was what people interpreted as his aloofness and indifference to their plight.

I told him that I needed some time to think about his advice and then left his office. That day I first met Professor Obebe was like the worst day of my life. As a young man, there was no way I would not have thought about the reaction of my friends to this change of direction that seemed like accepting defeat than anything else.

What would Tunde think of me?
What would Waheed say?
Would Bayo still respect me?

Would Toyin think I had lost my brilliance?

How would people react if I abandoned medicine for Agricultural Science?

I burst into tears when I got home.

But after crying my heart out, I actually did some serious thinking.

"This man has said I should not sit for another JAMB examinations.

So I am not going to wear that white laboratory coat and hang a stethoscope around my neck, as I have envisioned countless times?

This Professor must be wicked and very sadistic. Imagine, he wants me to be a farmer – the very thing my poor father had done for years which has been unable to make him rich.

Is this not exactly what I had been told?

Should I blindly follow this man?

Would I not regret this step in the future?"

But then, I had the presence of mind to remember other things the Professor had said:

"Study a course that would enable you employ people;

Study a course after which you would not need to look for a job;

You can become like Obasanjo;

The wealthiest people in the United States are the farmers; etc."

What he suggested turned my stomach into a war zone. I simply could not endure it. There was something interesting in his advice, that I should go to the University of Ilorin and study Agricultural Science. Obebe told me that, if I heeded his advice and went to Ilorin to study Agriculture, I could graduate and eventually become a farmer – like Nigeria's former Head of State, General Olusegun Obasanjo. That was 1988, and Obasanjo's second coming as civilian president in 1999 was still in the future. In 1988, Obasanjo was well-known in Nigeria as a former Head of State who had retired into active farming. Professor Obebe succeeded in tickling my fantasy by painting a picture in my mind that was very fantastic. I could be like Obasanjo, he said and I would be able to employ much more people than I ever could, even if I succeeded in becoming a doctor or even an engineer. He said that I do not need to look for a job after graduation. He challenged me to emulate Chief Olusegun Obasanjo, the farmer. This was something palatable to my mind, in spite of the bitter pill I was required to swallow in giving up my desire to study medicine.

The counsel from Professor Obebe was too heavy and destabilising for me to respond to at once, even though I still remember that discussion, which I can say was the most important discussion that altered the course of my life.

Suddenly, like a burst of inspiration, a decision was formed in my mind and I knew what I wanted to do. I had peace and a new energy. I was now ready to meet Professor Obebe again. I was not afraid of meeting him anymore.

The following day, I went back to the University of Lagos. Since we did not actually have a fixed appointment, I was there again as early as 7 a.m. so as to increase my chances of seeing him before he became unavailable. There were no mobile phones at that time, and appointments had to be arranged in alternative ways which were often cast in stone, without the flexibility GSM technology now affords.

When Professor Obebe met me at the entrance of his office, he asked me what I wanted. Without missing a bit, I told him that I had thought about his advice and had decided to study Agricultural Science.

If Obebe was pleased with my decision, he did not show it. He simply told me that the matter was very simple. He restated the fact that I did not need any note from him and that he could guarantee that I would be admitted if I went to the University of Ilorin. He actually gave me the name of one of his friends at the university, but quickly added that I did not even need to see the man since I was qualified. All I needed was to go to the department and tell them that I wanted to change my course from medicine to agriculture. The good thing was that the University of Ilorin was already one of my choices, so, my admission would be automatic. I believed Professor Obebe and we parted on that note.

    I did not know it then, but in retrospect, Professor Obebe was in the position of an angel of God that day, and what he said to me were not his words, but the very words of God. Today, I know and can boldly say that his voice that day was the voice of God to me. I was given a divine direction because my destiny was not in becoming a doctor, even though that was what I wanted and wanted so badly that I was actually willing to sit for JAMB examinations a third time.

CHAPTER 7
HIGHER EDUCATION

By the grace of God, I am today a Master of Science Degree holder (PhD grade) from the University of Ibadan. I have also received certification for different courses and trainings both within and outside Nigeria. I have an MBA in Marketing from the Lagos State University. I have attended the Grooming Enterprise Leaders Programme of the Entrepreneurship Development Centre of the Lagos Business School. But before that, I attended the Senior Management Programme of the Lagos Business School. I also attended an Agriculture Business Management Programme (AGB) at the Harvard Business School in Boston, USA, and an executive programme at the *Insper Instituto de Ensino e pesquisa*, Sao Paulo, Brazil. Apart from all of the above, I attended a course at the University of Stellenbosch in Cape Town, South Africa and, two years ago, found time to attend another course at the A & M University, College Station, Texas, in the United States of America, the Redeemed Christian Bible College and School of Disciple, Lagos.

I am a lover of education and I do not love education just for the sake of getting certificates. I actually desire knowledge in the real sense of the word. I want to know, and my search for knowledge has led to some very interesting experiences in my life. I remember in 2008 when I travelled to Santa Rosa in the State of California, USA, just to meet the author of a book. At the time, I needed to know why most companies failed after five years, and, because this man had written a book addressing that issue, I wanted to hear from the horse's mouth what I needed to do so that my company would not fail. You may laugh at my aggressive pursuit of knowledge, but the fact is that, according to available statistics, only 5% of registered companies operate and survive for up to three years after registration. Of the 5% that actually operate and survive for up to three years, 70% pack up at the end of two years, meaning that they fail before their fifth year anniversary. Of the remaining 30% that survive for up to five years, only 10% last up to ten years, at which time they get into a position that ensures their longevity, except for some calamitous events that drastically change the equation.

Mr. Gilbert told me some things the day we met. And who knows if it wasn't some of those things he said to me that have saved my company from failing? As long as I am alive and healthy and have the wherewithal, I shall continue to seek knowledge. Incidentally, the company I run today is knowledge-driven. No matter how a man or woman is, there is no way such a person can be the CEO of the type of company I run without a special knowledge that can only be secured within the walls of a university or a polytechnic. Of course, you may want to be the type of CEO who takes instructions, advice, and ideas from a deputy with the required knowledge; but that is the reality of my particular sector. It is no wonder today that a great percentage of players in the industry I belong to are professors, doctors, and graduates of a number of degrees in varying courses, all having something to do with agriculture.

Even those who did not have any training in agriculture or agriculture-related fields had to attend courses in that line to compensate for their late entry into the sector. For example, the Lagos State branch Chairman of the Poultry Association of Nigeria between 2001 and 2006 was Mr. Olanrewaju Bello, whom we fondly call Lanre Bello. He genuinely influenced the industry even up till today. He made his entry into the industry as far back as 1983, but the interesting thing is that Lanre Bello's first degree was in Political Science. As a matter of fact, he was only preparing for a professional examinations when he fell in love with the poultry business because he found his father's farm a serene place for study. However, he attended several short courses on poultry production before he became an active player. He felt he needed to do this even after securing a Master's degree in Business Administration. That is the reality of the sector I belong to, and for me, the journey of seeking higher education (a journey which has not ended) began at the University of Ilorin.

After my destiny-loaded session with Professor Obebe, I did not waste much time in Lagos. I was the son of a determined, hard-working, poor farmer, whose best had been stretched to the limit even in the endeavour of seeing me through secondary school. There was no need to deceive myself that I could get financial support from my father. My mother on her part was doing her best, but the man in me felt she deserved everything she was getting from her kolanut business, which had blossomed. I often reluctantly accepted anything she was willing to give. Professor Obebe had alluded to my sorry financial situation while advising me to go to the University of Ilorin and study agriculture. He had said that, because my father was poor, it would actually be easier to cope in the University of Ilorin than in the University of Ibadan, or the Obafemi Awolowo University, Ile-Ife. Professor Obebe was right. He was also right about the ease with which I was going to be admitted.

Shortly after arriving Ilorin for the first time in my life, I became an undergraduate of Animal Production in the faculty of Agricultural Science of the university.

The University of Ilorin was established by a Decree of the Federal Military Government of Nigeria thirteen years before my admission, but it did not gain autonomous status until 1977, when its first Vice Chancellor, Professor O.O. Akinkugbe, was appointed. Before 1977, the University of Ilorin was a University College affiliated to the University of Ibadan. It was one of seven institutions of higher learning established as part of the implementation of one of the directives of the Third National Development Plan. This plan was actually conceived and launched by the General Yakubu Gowon regime shortly before that regime was truncated by a coup led by General Joe Garba. It was that coup that gave birth to the Murtala Mohammed/Olusegun Obasanjo regime, which established the university and others within one month of coming to power.

Nigeria's Third Development Plan (with an implementation period from 1975 to 1980) was a robust plan developed by Professor Adebayo Adedeji, with input from many technocrats. This was meant to make Nigeria basically an industrialised nation. Professor Adedeji was the same person who drafted the treaty of the ECOWAS. ECOWAS was established in May 1975 – around the same time the Third National Development Plan was launched – and there was much confidence that Adedeji's plan would provide a roadmap for Nigeria's greatness. Not surprisingly, education was a key component of this plan, which explains the establishment of such a number of higher institutions at once in 1975. It was clear to the thinkers in Nigeria that, without rapid educational development, Nigeria would be unable to achieve the goals of its founding fathers. The University of Ilorin became part of the nation's effort to compete with and even overtake the Asian Tigers, which were attempting to rise at approximately the same period.

I would ever remain grateful that Ilorin did not turn out to be a very strange place for me. I met a few classmates there that were from Ekiti (which was then still part of Ondo State). The most consequential of them was Olanrewaju James Atolani, whom we call Lanre for short. I wasn't meeting Lanre for the first time in Ilorin, neither did we know that we were going to meet at the University of Ilorin; so, in some way, it was a pleasant surprise and a real reunion. The reason I refer to Lanre as the most consequential of my friends at the University of Ilorin would soon become obvious.

Although Lanre had his primary education in Ilorin, we were both students at Comprehensive High School, Otun and he was just a year ahead of me. I remember we used to represent our school in debates and other competitions. Lanre is also a native Otun. In fact, his father, fondly known as Baba Ilorin became famous for hosting people from Otun who travelled to Ilorin. Sometimes, people transiting from Otun to other states in Nigeria would sleep in Baba Ilorin's house in Ilorin, instead of staying in hotels. Such was the kindness and magnanimity of this man that he almost always had visitors in his house. If not relatives, there would be students; if not students, then there would be members of the Otun community who just happened to be in the town. Even Muslim pilgrims on their way to Mecca in Saudi Arabia formed part of the traffic. Apart from serving as host, Lanre's father was an unofficial courier and his house was the clearing house for people who send luggage to and from Ilorin. Students who expected foodstuffs from their parents could tell their parents to send whatever they had for them through Mr. Atolani, who frequented Otun not less than twice every month. It was so convenient for the students and their parents, and the man did not mind the inconvenience he had to go through for the sake of others.

The practice in the University of Ilorin was for students in 100 level to get automatic accommodation; so, that first year went smoothly for me, as far as where to stay was concerned. In 200 level, Lanre and I squatted with one Bunmi Fabiyi (now in the United Kingdom), our friend, who had guaranteed accommodation on campus all through his study in the university because he was a medical student. This preferential treatment for medical students was not unique to the University of Ilorin but quite common in most Nigerian universities. So, through our connection with Bunmi, Lanre and I had a place to squat in 200 level. We continued to squat with Bunmi all through our 300 level. Bunmi is also from Otun-Ekiti, but had his secondary education at a nearby school known as Moba Grammar School, which was the first community-funded school in Otun, while Comprehensive Secondary School was established in the 1970s, Moba Grammar School was established in 1965.

Apart from Lanre and Bunmi, there was also Olaitan Alatise. Alatise and Lanre had both attended Ondo State School of Science, Ikare, for their A' Level. They were at Ikare while I was at OSCAS. On another level, Bunmi, Lanre and I had all been members of a social club in Otun. So the friendship in our group had bonds connected by more than just one strand. Since Bunmi would, as a matter of course, spend more time with his buddies in the department of medicine, it was Lanre, Alatise and I that became quite close because we were in the same department under the faculty of agriculture.

Lanre had a habit of going home on weekends. After sometime, I joined him and began to spend weekends in his house, even though I had a sister in Ilorin. We were that close. When Lanre initially asked his father for permission for me to spend my weekends with the family, he got an interesting response after telling him whose son I was. According to Lanre, as soon as he told his father that I was the son of Adetoyi, his father was excited and said I was welcome to spend weekends in his house. He made it look like it was a privilege to host me. The man did not know that I was going to end up taking the relationship further and deeper than that. Luckily for the man, the threat I posed to him and his family was a harmless one. I got to know Lanre's family so well that I became more or less a part of the family. I knew his sisters, one of whom was quite young and still in secondary school at the time. His youngest sister was probably still a toddler.

The interesting twist to this tale (details of which will be provided in a subsequent chapter) is that the young girl that was still in secondary school is now my very wife. But while in the University of Ilorin, no one knew that, in visiting Lanre's house every weekend and eating their well prepared food for free, I was already being served by my in-laws. None, but God Himself, knew what was in store for me and that family because the fact was that, we all related as siblings with no strings attached. There was not the slightest inkling of romantic interest in my future wife; not even as a momentary thought.

All through my days at the University of Ilorin, I never failed to bear in mind the words of Professor Obebe. He had said that I will become wealthy if I could graduate and establish a farm like Chief Olusegun Obasanjo. This became my mantra and it inspired a tremendous focus in my affairs. I had a target, and there was little to distract me from moving towards it. Like Lanre would say, I was either in class, or in church, or in the hostel – the typical triangular student. The only other place one could find me was deep in the quiet section of the university library, either reading, or doing my assignments.

I remember when I travelled to Otun to prepare for my programme at the University of Ilorin, several people openly made jest of my father and were telling him that his so-called brilliant son that had said he wanted to study medicine now wanted to become a farmer. The fact that farming in the minds of both my father and his jesters, was not the commercial type of farming, but the subsistence type they were used to, meant that my father suffered emotionally under the weight of their mockery. The vision of my coming to join him in the bush with cutlass and hoe instead of wearing the white laboratory coat doctors were known for was too much for him to bear. In spite of his initial excitement about the fact that I was the first of his sons to have ever secured admission into the university, he became downcast. I had to talk to him. I had no option.

I gave my father the same pill Professor Obebe had given to me: I was going to graduate and establish a farm, not like his own, but like Chief Olusegun Obasanjo's. I explained to my father that, where he was thinking of cultivating one hectare, my farm would be so large that I could cultivate 100 hectares: that I would incorporate technology into my farming. I tried my best to explain the miracle of modern agricultural practices to my father. I told him not to be discouraged and promised to make him proud. I cannot remember what exactly it was I said that eventually convinced him, but he eventually brightened up. He was then able to endure the sadistic taunts and jeers of those who saw nothing more than a future of subsistence agriculture for me. My father decided to put faith in me and tried to ignore his traducers. He was my first convert in the gospel that had initially been preached to me by Professor Obebe.

I had wonderful and committed lecturers at the University of Ilorin. One of the most influential of them was Professor Job Olutimehin Atteh, whom I still stay in touch with. Professor Atteh was the one that supervised my undergraduate project in Agriculture, with specialisation in Animal Production. He was a father and a mentor in those days. Fortunately, he still is.

Amazingly, while in the University of Ilorin, I did not completely give up on the idea of becoming a doctor. Somehow, that dream refused to die. It was Professor Atteh that initiated and taught me how relevant to the society the knowledge I was acquiring would be. Under his influence, I began to agree in the deepest recess of my heart that I would actually not make further attempts to study medicine, but would focus completely on agriculture. He succeeded largely in making me accept my course of study and begin to conceive a future around it.

Professor Atteh is an expert in mono-gastric nutrition and has remained an academic staff of the University of Ilorin for the past 33 years. He became a professor at the age of 38, after bagging a first class honours in Animal Science from the University of Ibadan and doing his Master's and PhD programme within a 3-years and ten-month period. He did both postgraduate degrees at the University of Guelph, Ontario, Canada. Notably, he published a paper that was adjudged the best by the Poultry Science Association of the United States, and, in 1984, he won the Poultry Science Research Award. He is a core academician with worldwide recognition, and he has won several poultry research awards.

As far as Professor Atteh is concerned, his coming to the University of Ilorin was part of destiny. He believes that I was part of why he rejected a job he was offered after bagging his PhD, and rather chose to lecture in the University of Ilorin, where he eventually met me as a student in his class. He was the one that taught me *The Principles of Livestock Production*, which gave me the theoretical knowledge of how to make premixes. I would later learn the practical aspect of this skill through employment and the effort of other mentors. I remember that I contacted Professor Atteh for guidance when I went into premix production as an entrepreneur. At that time, most of the premix found in the country were imported. But I was willing to take the risk.

Today, Professor Atteh claims I am one of the reasons he feels fulfilled as a person. And, interestingly, he still teaches the course and has even published a book titled *The Theory and Practice of Livestock Feed Manufacturing*, which has a chapter on how to make premixes. While lecturing, he has a habit of asking his students if they had ever heard about Hi-Nutrients International Limited. After getting their affirmative response, he would proceed to proudly tell them that the owner of that company, Bode Adetoyi, was his student and that he once sat exactly where they were sitting. Professor Atteh holds me as a standard and uses my story to challenge his students. My joy is that I can say something similar about the erudite professor. To me, my life would have been very different if I had not met him.

The Dean of the Faculty of Agriculture in the University of Ilorin at the time was Professor Femi Balogun, who also contributed to what Professor Atteh was doing, while I was under their collective influence. He changed my perspective about agriculture and was able to quench that primordial aversion I had for farming and even converted that aversion to interest; thereby changing my view about farming.

Apart from Professor Atteh and Professor Balogun, I met a distant cousin of mine, Mr. Ibidun Taiwo, who was a student of Agricultural Economics. Mr. Taiwo agreed that I should squat with him, which I did sporadically between my 200 and 300 levels. According to him, he was studying Agricultural Economics but intended to work in the banking sector after graduation. He told me that after studying Animal Production, I could also work in the bank. This point of view was different from that of Professor Obebe's, Professor Atteh's, and Professor Balogun's. Honestly, the idea that I had a fall back option, also helped me to inwardly settle down and focus on being academically successful at Ilorin.

There were some other students I met at the University of Ilorin who happened to be from my constituency. There was Femi Kupolati, who is now a senior engineer with Lafarge Cement Company. There was also Niyi Fasanmi, who now works as a senior engineer with Nigeria Breweries. As obvious, both Femi Kupolati and Niyi Fasanmi studied engineering at Ilorin. Then there was Oni Joseph, who studied Chemistry and now works with Berger Paints as a senior chemist. Johnson Ojo studied biochemistry from Ilorin also and was with Coca Cola for some time before leaving to become a full-time pastor of the ministry he founded.

After bagging our first degree, Lanre, Olaitan Alatise and I, went on to the University of Ibadan, where we successfully completed our Masters of Science programme. Only after that did we really part ways. Lanre is still in Lagos running his business, Alatise now works with the government of Ekiti State and is based in Ado-Ekiti, and I am also in Lagos; a city I came to, a city I saw, and a city I conquered. But I would not have been able to get through the University of Ilorin without the devoted support of my elder sister, Alice.

CHAPTER 8
THE BLESSING OF GIRL-CHILD EDUCATION

In the world today, there is feminism, and then there is female empowerment. While I would have nothing to do with the former, I am a firm supporter of the latter – and for a good reason also. Without the support of my eldest sister, Mrs. Alice Akanke Odia, the story of my life would have read very differently and would probably not have recorded the current crescendo, for which I am thanking God today.

My sister, Alice, is several years older than I am. In fact, in many ways, my siblings and I see her as the second mother of the house. My autobiography will be incomplete without highlighting the role of this great woman, whose productive and beneficial life has provided additional evidence that, indeed, an educated and empowered woman is an asset to the society. Perhaps, it is my belief in this idea that is responsible for the fact that, Deola, my first and only daughter (as at the time of this writing) is, today, a student in a Canadian university. I want Deola to be educated to whatever level she desires because I believe in female empowerment.

Like most of the many children of my father, Alice was born in Otun. After her secondary education at Moba Grammar School, she attended the Government Technical College, Otun, and from there she took off and did not stop, until in 2017 when she retired as an Instrumentation Engineer with Seplat Petroleum Development Company Limited. She was actually seconded to Seplat from Shell Petroleum Development

Company (SPDC) where she had worked for 29 years (from 1981 to 2010) as an instrument maintenance technician. From my analysis, the secret to this great career in the oil industry was made possible only because Alice attended Government Technical College, Otun. If she had not attended that school, there is no way she would have attained that height in life. There is empirical evidence for this assertion because there were some of her colleagues who terminated their education after attending Moba Grammar School. While their condition could be said to be better than those who did not go to school at all, the difference in their respective conditions remains as clear as crystal, when compared to that of Alice.

Before preparations for the setting up of the Government Technical College Otun were concluded, Alice had already filled her application form. This was because, being a member of one of the ruling houses in Otun, she received privileged information from the Oba at the time, who urged her and some others to apply for the technical school, which he had been told was about to be set up by the government.

Alice spent three years at the college. But while in their final year in 1980, she and her colleagues sat for an examination organised by Shell Petroleum Development Company to select those that would be trained and eventually employed by the company. It would appear that the examination by Shell was open to all final year students, but only nine of them passed. Of these nine students, at least four were ladies, one of whom did not join her colleagues to Warri, where they went for their first training after graduating from the Technical College. For some other reason, a male student who had passed also did not go to Warri. As for the lady that skipped the opportunity, the reason given by her father was that Warri was too far and that he would not allow his daughter to go that far away from home.

On his part, my father reminded Alice that he had followed a White missionary all the way to Sagamu to be his personal cook and that, if not for the misgivings of his parents, he would have followed that same man to England. My father encouraged Alice and assured her that there was nothing wrong in her going away to Warri. It was for her progress, and she was not going to regret it. Alice was encouraged to make the move and she attended the one-year training and passed all the necessary examinations. She was soon employed as a staff of SPDC.

I vividly recall that I was still in secondary school when Alice began working with SPDC. I would say that my parents were still the primary sources of my financial support by that time. But when I graduated from secondary school and informed my father of my desire to go to OSCAS for my A' Level, he bluntly told me that he could not afford the cost of that endeavour. Without mincing words, he laid that responsibility on my sister, Alice, who did not mind taking it up. She actually encouraged me to make the move and said that, by the grace of God, she was going to stand by my side. It was at that point in life that Alice became the main benefactor in my life, even though I received occasional support from several others. Alice continued to play this role for the longest time, until I graduated from the university, served my country through the NYSC programme, and even became employed.

Not surprisingly, while I was in the University of Ilorin, I spent my holidays with Alice. I remember a particular holiday when things nearly got out of hand. If not for the divine intervention of God, I would not have lived to tell this tale: I would have been killed and there would not have been any evidence of what had happened to me. I would have become part of the sad statistics of missing persons. I was in my 200 level at the time.

I had spent the holiday in Warri and was on my way back to school. In her usual display of magnanimity, my sister, had given me ₦14,000. ₦12,000 out of that amount was my school fees, and the balance of ₦2,000 was my pocket money. That amount is equivalent to today's ₦250,000. At that time, the transportation network within Nigeria was still developing and it was very difficult to get public transport from Warri all the way to Ilorin. The usual route was to take a vehicle from Warri to Benin, and then from Benin to Ilorin. This was the route I had taken every time I came for holidays in Warri and had to return to Ilorin. After bidding Alice and her family goodbye, I went to the park in Warri to take a vehicle that would convey me to Benin, before the onward trip to Ilorin. The vehicle I ended up boarding had only male occupants, and I had no idea that they were all members of a robbery gang. As we were moving towards Benin, the driver suddenly said that there was going to be a traffic gridlock ahead of us, and to avoid that gridlock, he was going to take a shortcut that passed through an untarred road flanked by cassava farms.

Only when we got unto the lonely road did I understand that I was in trouble. By then, it was too late to cry. Any form of resistance then would have been met with instant and permanent liquidation. After all, they were all men and would have easily killed me. I wisely cooperated with them as they robbed me of my very precious ₦14,000. It seemed they were only interested in the money and not my life because, as soon as they robbed me, they abandoned me in the bush and drove off.

When I recovered from the shock of that very dangerous encounter, I trekked back to the nearest park, which was quite a distance. I had to ask for directions from people I met on the road because the place was strange to me. It was one 'good Samaritan' that finally took me to the motor park. I met the chairman of the park and explained what had happened to me. The man had compassion on me and put me in a vehicle scheduled to go to Warri, offering to pay the driver himself. That was how I returned to Warri without a dime and had to trek for several miles back to Sister Alice's house, located at Ijakpa road, which was on the way to the Nigeria National Petroleum Corporation Refinery in Effurun, Warri. This was around 1990, and GSM technology was still ten years away. Until she returned from work and met me face-to-face, my sister had no inkling of my kiss with death.

When Alice came back from work that day, I narrated the ordeal I had been through and instead of scolding me for any carelessness on my part, my sister was grateful that I was alive. She had heard stories of people being killed for ritual purposes and had a better grasp of the miracle of my deliverance than I did. She was glad to have me back, but ₦14, 000 was a lot of money in those days. It took another week for her and her fiancé at the time (Engineer Odia) to put that money together, which they graciously gave to me. I was very relieved, to say the least.

I believe that Alice's empathy for me could not be divorced from a similar experience she had while still a young girl attending Moba Grammar School. At the time, her school fees was 10 pounds – a princely amount in those days. One day, after collecting her school fees from my father, she was making her way to school when she decided to pass by a shop to buy a loaf of bread. It seems this was where her 10 pounds fell down from her pocket, unknown to her.

When Alice got to school and realised what had happened, she tearfully returned home to report the sad event to my father. This was nothing but a disaster of monumental proportions. Money was so difficult in those days. No matter how much my father wanted to, there was no way he could have given Alice another 10 pounds, and the reason was simply that he did not have such an amount to give. Farmers of those days went through a lot to raise any amount of cash, partly because everybody was a farmer and could only grow enough food to eat.

My father objectively told Alice that, in the circumstance, there was nothing he could do: the only way out was for her to temporarily stay out of school. Anytime he got the money, she could return to school. In order to effect this plan, he thought he needed to inform the school principal. So he followed Alice to school and told the principal what had happened, and his decision to withdraw Alice from school in the interim.

The Principal, for whatever reason, disagreed with my father. He said that Alice was going to remain in school. My father could do his best to try to raise the 10 pounds, but Alice was not going to have her schooling truncated. In fact, Alice recalled recently that, whenever other students were being chased home because they had failed to pay their school fees, the principal would publicly tell her that she should not to go home and warn her that, if he caught her loitering in the town under the guise of being chased from school, he was going to personally deal with her. That was how Alice was specially protected until my father was able to raise another 10 pounds for her school fees. The potentially sour situation passed by without any damage. Nobody knows if other factors may have come together at that material time to terminate Alice's education. After all, these were days when parents felt that sponsoring a girl-child to school was a waste of resources.

When it was time for me to return to Ilorin, several days after the robbery incident, Alice decided that I was not going to pass through Benin anymore. I was put in a vehicle going to Akure; at Akure, I boarded another vehicle to Ilesha. It was from Ilesha that I finally took a vehicle to Ilorin, bringing the sordid experience to an end. I cannot forget this kindness of my sister. If she needed an excuse to stop sponsoring my education, the loss of the ₦14, 000 she had sacrificially given me for school fees and pocket money was a very genuine excuse. Nobody in their right senses would have blamed her if she had said that she could not raise another money for my school fees, but my sister went the extra mile. I can say that the impact of that sacrifice cannot be overemphasized in my success story.

Apart from me, Alice was also a sort of bulwark for virtually every member of my family – both nuclear and extended. The only partial exception to this rule would be my elder brother, Banji, who got a job as a messenger after his secondary school and went on to sponsor himself in the university through his enterprise as a very hard-working farmer. Banji succeeded in getting a BSc in Accounting and rose through the ranks over many years. He is now a Director of Finance in the Ministry of Health of the Ekiti State Government. He is one of the most hard-working men I have ever known in my life. There is not an iota of indolence in DNA. No wonder, he used to scold me mercilessly whenever I was reluctant to participate in farm work. As far as Banji was concerned, I was his lazy younger brother. Today, he readily admits that he is amazed that I eventually became a farmer. He can hardly comprehend the switch and the irony it represents.

My younger brother, Dare, is just a year younger than the first son of Alice, Mayowa, and the joke in the family is that they are twins – born by the same mother, namely Sister Alice. This joke is not far from the truth because, Dare is the youngest in my nuclear family and actually a younger brother to Alice but their age difference is so much that Dare is virtually age mates with her first son. Due to this fact, he grew up with her and both Dare and Mayowa were treated as siblings. It got to the extent of buying them same colour of clothes – as is the tradition with twin babies.

After Ilorin, I went to serve in Calabar and did so well that I won an award – my first award in life. Perhaps as a fallout of this award, I was offered a job with the Cross Rivers State

Cocoa Board, where I had served, having been initially posted there from the Cross Rivers State Ministry of Agriculture. In Cross Rivers State, a lot of cocoa is produced and it was the responsibility of the Cocoa Board to buy cocoa from the farmers and then process it, before selling it to the public. We used to go around the villages in the area to sell this processed cocoa; sometimes, we went even as far as some villages in Cameroon. My boss was Mr. Abang, who was a Director in the ministry and was seconded to the Cocoa Board to serve in the interim. He was from Bendege village in Ikom Local Government Area of Cross Rivers State. I remember that Mr. Abang had two young boys then, between ages 9 and 14. The last time I checked, both of them are now medical doctors practising in the United States and the United Kingdom respectively.

In spite of the very warm relationship between myself and my boss, whose recommendation must have played a part in the decision of the Cocoa Board to retain me after my service year, I decided to ignore the opportunity to work in Calabar. And I had two reasons for rejecting the offer: my first reason was that, not being a native of Cross Rivers State, I felt that it may not be easy for me to rise through the ranks and eventually achieve my goal. My second reason was a bit controversial. At that time, there were rumours (though largely unsubstantiated) that the people of Ugep were cannibals. Ugep was a town near Calabar. When they got to find out about this rumour, Alice and every other member of my family told me in no uncertain terms to decline the job offer, which was going to require my staying in Calabar. Alice was particularly frantic about it: she said I should get back to Warri as fast as the next vehicle could drive, and that was what happened.

When I returned to Warri, Alice did everything she could to get me a job. She even tried to get me some ad hoc work with Shell's community development project, which they did as part of their Corporate Social Responsibility (CSR) to their host communities, but things just did not work out. This was why I returned to Lagos to continue the struggle.

After the initial stress of her early years, Sister Alice has been enjoying the softer side of life on earth, and I am so happy for her. All her children have graduated from the university. She is currently living in a decent neighbourhood in Warri, and two of her daughters had their Master's degree in the United Kingdom, after securing their respective first degrees in Nigerian universities. Sometimes I wonder: if not for the mercy of God in positioning Alice to play her supportive role in my life, I may not have been able to go beyond the secondary school level. I may not have been able to attend OSCAS; I may not have been able to attend the University of Ilorin. Without graduating from the University of Ilorin, how would I have gone for my Master's degree at the University of Ibadan? I may not have secured a job with Bio-Organics; I may not have set up Hi-Nutrients; I may not have built Hi-Nutrients to the level it got to before Neovia decided to acquire it. My life would have been very different. Thankfully, the story is progressing on this wonderful note. The ignition point was, as I earlier stated, the fact that Alice attended the Government Technical College, Otun.

This story provides an opportunity to even see a bigger picture, that is, the things that are likely to happen when a woman is not empowered by quality education. It is a sad tale, but, for the sake of others, it has to be shared, and this would be done without revealing the identity of the person or persons involved. The very lady whose father had prevented from going to Warri for the training that would have eventually made her a staff of Shell Petroleum Development Company eventually went to a teacher training college and later became a teacher. Recall that this lady must have been very brilliant. She was part of the only nine who had passed the Shell examination in the whole school; yet, her father bluntly refused to allow her pursue a lucrative career.

Shortly after this debacle, the same father that had denied this lady the opportunity died. The lady later got married. Unfortunately, her husband died after she had given birth to some children. I wonder how life would have gone for this lady if her husband had not died, but his death revealed what was always under the surface, waiting only for the right opportunity to manifest.

As soon as her husband died, his family members came around and stripped her of his belongings. As if that was not enough, they drove her away from the house she was occupying: and they never supported her or her children. Alice saw this lady recently and saw her standard of living. She is now a petty trader selling call cards. Alice could not but wonder how this lady was fending for her children. She was told that it was through the support of the lady's own family members that she was coping with her many challenges. Anyone reading this should consider how the story could have been vastly different if this same lady had gotten a job with Shell Petroleum Development Company as early as 1981. Through a misguided action by her father, her life story changed, and her father wasn't even alive to behold the calamity his decision had caused.

As a member of the Poultry Association of Nigeria, I am delighted to note the active participation of women, even in this industry. Ogun State is a strong enclave in the poultry business in Nigeria today; yet, the Ogun State branch of the Poultry Association of Nigeria is being led by a lady, Mrs. Blessing Osioma Alawode, who is also the Managing Director of Demir Farm. In my base in Lagos, we are yet to have a female chairman of PAN; but we are close to that. Some years ago, we had a Deputy Chairman in the person of Mrs. Tolu

Fashuwape, and the current Deputy Chairman is also a woman, in the person of Olabisi Ayo-Hamilton, of Bivera Enterprise. All over the world, the story is similar. Women, when given opportunity, do very well and many times, better than men. Indeed, there are serious benefits of girl-child education and girl-child empowerment.

Thumbs up to my big sister, Alice.

CHAPTER 9

ON THE STREETS OF LAGOS

When we graduated from the University of Ilorin, Lanre, Alatise and I dispersed for a while but eventually converged in Lagos after a whole year. Our break in transmission was because we had to attend the compulsory National Youth Service Corps (NYSC) programme. I went to serve in Calabar, Cross Rivers State; Lanre went to Misau in Bauchi State, and Alatise served at Biu in Borno State. Apart from my visit to Lagos to see Professor Obebe, I had actually started visiting Lagos since I was in Form Four in secondary school; so Lagos was not that strange to me. I had to escape from home to make my first visit to Lagos. The endeavour was as exciting as it was risky.

In 1984, I had just finished my Form Four and was on vacation which preceded our resumption to Form Five. I was a bit bored during this period. At that very time, my elder brother, Dayo Adetoyi, who was undergoing tailoring training in Lagos, suddenly visited Otun. I asked my father for permission to visit Lagos with Dayo. I had heard so much about Lagos and could not wait to see it for myself. Perhaps due to my terrible reputation for doing anything and everything to avoid going to farm, my father saw my attempt to travel with my brother as a veritable plot to stay away from farm. He would have none of it. So, he declined my request. I was very interested in the idea of going to Lagos. By now, one would begin to know what happens when I am very interested in achieving something. Fortunately for me, I found an ally in Dayo, who also thought there was nothing wrong in my intention to go to Lagos.

So Dayo and I came up with a daring plan. I pretended to abide by my father's order, while I planned to do the exact opposite. In those days, there was only one transport truck that came from Lagos to Otun. If you wanted to go to Lagos and you missed that truck, you would have to wait until it returned after a few days. Dayo and I agreed that on the day of his departure, I would leave the house earlier and go ahead of him to hide inside the bush along the road where the truck would pass through on its way from Otun to Lagos. The risk of danger did not even cross my mind since things like kidnapping and ritual killing were not common in those days.

Our plan worked out and I was picked up at the agreed location. That was how I first visited Lagos. When I returned from Lagos at the end of my vacation to face the wrath of my father, his plan to punish me for disobeying him was successfully thwarted by my mother, who interceded on my behalf and told him to forgive me. After that trip, I promised myself that I would visit Lagos at every opportunity.

Naturally, I stayed with Dayo the first time I visited Lagos. While I was in the University of Ilorin, most times I also visited Lagos, and I stayed with my relative, Popoola Adeyeye, aka the Popular Tailor. After my service year, and a brief stay at Warri with my elder sister, Mrs. Alice Odia, it was time to look for a job.

I arrived Lagos after my NYSC to hear a sad news: Popoola Adeyeye aka Popular Tailor, was dead. I was so sad to learn of this but, life goes on. My elder brother, Dayo was not that buoyant at the time, and Raphael Balogun, whom I had stayed with when I came to see Professor Obebe at University of Lagos, had travelled abroad. So I stayed briefly with my friend, Jide Asaolu, who was working with Coca Cola then. The interesting thing about this stay was that it was symbolic in a very funny way. Jide had a girlfriend, but it was through my influence that they became friends. If I did not have any sort of influence over this lady, there was no way I would have been able to sway her into Jide's arms. My stay with Jide became a kind of insurance policy for his relationship with the girl.

How could Jide deny me the favour or abandon me subsequently, when the unspoken fact was that, at the nod of my head, his relationship could come crashing. I certainly did not behave in such a crass manner or try to blackmail my friend, but this was actually the underlying dynamics of the tripartite relationship between Jide, his girlfriend and I. Jide's house could not be compared to a suite at the Sheraton Hotel and Towers, but, at least, it provided shelter and prevented me from being included in the statistics of homeless people in Lagos, who normally slept under bridges.

My uncle, Elder Olaniran, was in Lagos at the time, and his wife, whom we called Alhaja, was a director at Ashaka Cement Company. Using her influence over banks that worked with her company, she secured jobs for my two elder brothers, Niyi Adetoyi and Lekan Adetoyi at the Union Bank. When I got wind of this development about my brothers, I contacted them and asked for their help in the area of shelter. Lekan was still single then, and it was decided that I should leave Jide's place and come to stay with Lekan. This was how my situation began to improve. At least, I was now staying with my blood brother, the son of my own father. No matter how kind or obligated Jide was to me, it did not change the fact that I was a squatter; besides, his girlfriend was with him. So, staying with a family member like Lekan was a bit more relaxing. Lekan was staying at Palmgrove at the time, and that was where I was for quite a while. Lanre Atolani had an uncle in Gbagada and an aunt in Surulere; so he also decided to stay with his aunt in Surulere. Olaitan Alatise stayed at Ketu in the Shangisha area with his brother. We kept communicating with one another so as to know what was happening in the labour market.

Eventually, Lekan got married and I kept looking for a job. I even attended a couple of interviews, but nothing came out of them. After sometime, the couple was blessed with a child, whom they named Damola. I was still there looking for a job.

Not too long after, the couple was blessed with another child, whom they named Debo. This time without being told, I was old enough to know that I needed to excuse them and allow the privacy they deserved. I tried harder to secure a job so I could afford to stay on my own, but nothing was forthcoming for some time. I was being fed, housed and even clothed, it did not help my manly feelings. I prayed earnestly for a breakthrough.

One day, as I was returning home from somewhere I had gone to, I was called upon by Pastor Gilbert Aimufua, a Redeemed Christian Church of God (RCCG) pastor that occupied the main duplex in the compound we were staying. Lekan occupied the Boys' Quarters in the compound at the back of the main building, hidden from view.

Pastor Gilbert told me that he had been observing me. It was apparent that I was an applicant; the man also knew that I had graduated from the university and was willing to work if I could get a job. He said that I could get help from some people, but that I had to join the Redeemed Christian Church of God because some of these persons would prefer to employ someone from the church, perhaps in the interest of trust and reliability.

I heeded Pastor Gilbert's advice, and that was how I joined the RCCG sometime in 1995. Before then, I normally followed Lekan to the Apostolic Church at Onipanu, Lagos. The Redeemed Church parish that Pastor Gilbert directed me to was located at Palmgrove junction. It was known as Glorious Parish. In Nigeria at least, the practice is that every Redeemed Church branch has its own unique name. This system of giving names to every branch of the church is not common in other Pentecostal churches as it is with the RCCG.

As instructed, I reported myself to the resident pastor of RCCG, Glorious Parish, Pastor Jayeoba. When he got to know that I had been sent to him by Pastor Gilbert, he spoke highly of Pastor Gilbert and told me that they were friends. Pastor Jayeoba then said that, since I had become a member of the church, it was going to be a matter of first things first: I had to join a group known as Workers-in-Training. I joined the group and it was through that group that I met Kunle, who is now a manager at Obasanjo Farms. I started with the workers programme and attended church programmes regularly. As a worker, I was assigned to wash the toilet and I did this with my usual vigour. I had no idea that it was from this humble engagement that God will raise me up and give me enough to take care of myself, with so much left over to give to many others.

I was busy with my work in the toilet one day when one Mr. Olusola Lawson greeted me. I replied him and then realised that I had never met him before. When he asked who I was, I told him that I was new in the church. I was less busy that day, and so had just asked Kunle for the key to the toilet because I wanted to wash it. We got talking and the man came to realise that I was a graduate. He did not share his thoughts with me, but, the following Sunday, he met Pastor Jayeoba and told him that the young man that had been assigned to the toilet was a graduate. He also told the pastor that he would like to engage me on a part-time basis. He had just secured a contract with a company that manufactured toilet soaps, toothpaste, and other bathroom products. When Pastor Jayeoba later told me about Mr. Lawson's offer, he encouraged me to take it and said that, by doing this part-time work (no matter what it paid), I would be positioned to meet others that would help me secure a salaried job. I heartily and thankfully accepted my pastor's advice and began to work with UB40, which was the name of Mr. Lawson's company. UB40 was an advertising company that was involved in sales promotion. If for nothing, this job with UB40 allowed me to leave the house every week day, and that was a blessing in the circumstance I found myself at the time, I had become weary of staying at home like a small boy, waiting to be fed and sheltered freely, even though my brother, Lekan, did not show any signs of fatigue in hosting me. Still, as a man, I preferred to be on my own.

My work with UB40 started immediately and proceeded smoothly. The condition of the employment was that I would be paid based on service rendered, and I was able to make some money for the first time after my NYSC programme. Pastor Gilbert had given me *carte blanche* to join them for dinner anytime I wanted, and I cashed in on that offer several times. But when I started working, I began to be scarce at the Gilberts' dinner table. It got to a point that Mrs. Gilbert noticed my absence, added two and two together, and told me that I should stop spending my money on food, but rather come to their house to eat anytime I wanted to, so as to save my money for other things. I felt better than I had felt in a long time. But this was just the beginning of my staggered independence.

After the soap-making company, Mr. Lawson got another contract; this time around, it was with Nestle, the international beverage makers. Nestle had a very strong presence in Nigeria and they were about to pioneer the sales of one of their beverages called Milo, in sachets. Nestle used to sell Milo in 450g tin containers, and tin containers with larger weights, but nothing less than 450g. They had never tried to sell in 10g sachets before. So, they felt the time had come, and UB40 was sub-contracted to promote the sale of Milo sachets, with secondary schools as its area of primary focus.

We began this sales promotion in earnest, and Mr. Lawson later promoted me to be the sales supervisor when he noticed my commitment and discovered that all the products given to us were often well-accounted for. The sales promotion included a demonstration where we proved to students that the Milo beverage in the usual tin containers was not different from the one in the new 10g sachets. We did this by pouring Milo from the normal tin and from the sachet into different containers (with the students watching), we then encouraged them to taste the two to see for themselves that it was the same delicious Milo that they were used to seeing in tin containers that was in the new sachets.

As salesmen, we were given six 450g tins of Milo every week to use anyhow we deemed fit. We could drink all of them and end up with a running stomach if we chose to; we could sell them to whomever we wanted to; we could give them to friends and family, or just keep piling them in our shelf to form a Milo pyramid. I think we and other stakeholders connected to Nestle served as an efficient conduit for dumping tin containers of Milo because Nestle wanted to focus on sachets. What better way to deal with the Milo already in tins than to give them away to people within their system? It became a win-win situation.

Part of my work as a sales supervisor for UB40 entailed making arrangements for sales promotions. I would go to motor parks and negotiate price with drivers of buses popularly called *Danfo*, after telling them that we needed to hire their buses for a week or a number of days. I was also responsible for securing permission from principals of schools on our target list. Some of these schools were boarding schools that had to feed their students, and it was easy to convince them to begin to use Milo in sachets for their students. We targeted students because we wanted them to be convinced so that they could in turn convince their parents at home that there was nothing different from the Milo they used to see in tin containers, and the Milo now packaged in sachets. This early exposure to marketing was an experience that would later prove useful in my life. I learnt how to make contact with prospective clients and how to engage in marketing, which precedes sales.

It did not take long for me to realise that I could make money with my weekly six tins of Milo. I then came up with an idea that proved that the juices of entrepreneurship were already flowing within me. I got ice block in a container, got a cup, and began to excite children around my area in Palmgrove about the treat, and they stood to enjoy my cold tea. Many did, and, at a point, children around the area who patronised my cold tea had to form a queue to be served. But I also repackaged and sold my Milo in small quantities, using plastic bag. I became known all over the Palmgrove area. That was how far I went to legitimately and honestly earn a living. I sold my cold tea wherever I could set up my mobile shop and made money in that way. My financial institution at the time was none of the existing Nigerian Banks. I snubbed them all. My financial institution was my elder sister, Sarah Abolarin, who is now late. I miss Sarah a lot. At the time I was hustling, she was living in Ketu with her husband. Sometime later, I opened my first bank account with First Bank. Coincidentally, when I set up my own company, my first corporate account was with First Bank. Even beyond that, my first loan ever as a business man was secured from the bank.

The contract with Nestle also eventually expired, and I temporarily left UB40, but things had changed. I was no longer as despondent as I used to be before starting to work with UB40. I now had some cash with my sister and this feeling reminded me of what I used to do when I was still a young boy in Otun. Although I was very reluctant to go to my father's farm, I recall that I managed to have my own farm. I cultivated yam and other crops in my farm and was able to sell the harvest and raise some cash, which I often gave to my mother to keep for me. Whenever I had a need, I would ask her to give me some amount from my savings to meet that need. In that way, I had my own fork, my own spoon, and was able to buy clothes for myself by informally engaging the services of people who went to shop at Ibadan. I remember the sheer pleasure I used to have just eating with my own cutlery, or wearing a shirt that had been bought from cash raised from my farm.

After the UB40 contract with Nestle came to an end, I still did not just sit at home. I developed the habit of going to the news-stand to check newspapers for job vacancies. I was no longer a stranger to the newspaper vendors, who knew me as a determined and industrious young man, following my endeavours, especially my cold tea business. It was on one of those trips to the news-stands that I saw an advert announcing a vacancy for a farm supervisor. The farm was Olubisi Farms in Ogijo, Ogun State, and the announcer was one Mrs. Medunoye Olubisi. Someone once said that truth is stranger than fiction. For those who doubt that, I would like to pose this question:

How likely was it that my sister, Sarah Abolarin, would actually work as a maid with the family of Chief and Mrs. Olubisi?

In spite of how unlikely this could have been, it was the case. My sister, as I came to discover to my amazement, was already working with the owner of Olubisi Farms. When I applied for the job and Mrs. Medunoye Olubisi realised that I was Sarah's younger brother from the same parents; she became eager to employ me, obviously because of a good working relationship she already had with my sister. I do not believe that Mrs. Medunoye would have considered me for the job if she was on the verge of sacking my sister due to one infraction or the other.

Work with Olubisi Farms started without much ado, but it was not an easy ride. I had to take the popular Lagos buses known as *Molue* from my base at Palmgrove as early as 5a.m. because I was expected at Olubisi Farms 7a.m. every work day. Due to the distance also, I normally got back home around 9p.m., even though I closed from work by 6p.m. The transport system in Lagos is famous (or infamous) for providing opportunities for such protracted trips.

Working with Olubisi Farms was a mixed bag of experiences. This was in 1996, and my salary was eight thousand naira (the equivalent to eighty or one hundred thousand naira today) and I was having poultry farm experience. It was my first salaried employment in life and the pay was not that bad. I was not completely happy about the distance and some other extraneous issues. As farm supervisor in Olubisi Farms, which was a layer farm, I was responsible for the care of the farm in general. Like the average layer farm, Olubisi Farms was fairly large and it contained thousands of chickens that were bio-engineered to lay at least one egg per day as soon as they reached maturity. The chickens would continue to do so for several months non-stop until they began to taper off gradually and eventually stopped to produce eggs. It was my first job at a real farm, and I was eager to see the connection between what I had been taught at the University and the reality of an animal farm. I had to keep referring to my books, even on the farm, because I was eager to learn and have functional knowledge.

How else could I set up my farm – like Chief Olusegun Obasanjo – and become an employer of labour, according to the gospel of Professor Obebe?

There was a particular book I had with me all the time: *Poultry Production in the Warm Wet Climate,* by Professor O. Oluyemi. It was a practical guide for persons in my situation, and it came in handy while I was at Olubisi Farms. I would study this book and others at my disposal in the night and try to apply what I had learnt during the day. I maintained my relationship with a particular vendor at Palmgrove while I continued to work for Mrs. Medunoye. This was my first full-time job, but it was not going to be my last.

I returned from Olubisi Farms a bit earlier one evening and took a walk to see my vendor friend. He was rather excited to see me. Out of love and loyalty to me, he had been checking for job vacancies on my behalf and had found one – at last. He told me that he had seen a job vacancy advert by a livestock farm and had copied the address of the farm. It was located at Ikotun and the rest was left to me, if I was interested. I thanked my friend and did the needful. That was how I left Olubisi Farms. I had only spent nine months there, but I was not the rookie animal production graduate I used to be when I first took the job. My confidence had risen, and was beginning to understand what animal production was, outside the classroom.

The farm my vendor had told me about was Ola Farms and Trading Company, and it was located at Km1, Abaranje Road, Ikotun, Lagos. Ola Farms was owned by Alhaji Mohammed Ola and was being managed at the time by his son, Wasiu. It is sad to report that both Alhaji Ola and his son are late. Alhaji died four years ago and, Wasiu reportedly died just last year. But when I met both men in 1996, they were both full of vigour at the time and were engaged in raising pigs, sheep, and goats, apart from layers for egg production.

It was at Ola Farms that I began to interact with veterinary doctors who came periodically to examine or treat the animals on the farm. I remember Doctor Bayo Olufunwa, who was the consultant to the farm. We became close and I used to ask the doctor a lot of questions and he was patient and competent enough to satisfy my virtually insatiable appetite for knowledge. It was by interacting with Dr. Olufunwa that I began to develop interest in the marketing aspect of animal farming, which, I got to know, involved providing services. My salary at Ola Farms was ten thousand naira, and, for the first time, I had my own accommodation in a farmhouse close to the farm. It was at this time that my stay at Palmgrove came to an end.

I learnt a lot at Ola Farms, thanks to my inquisitiveness and the opportunities to reliable answers from persons like Dr. Olufunwa, as well as my working experience itself. Dr. Olufunwa was one of the early players in what is now the Poultry Association of Nigeria. The association used to be based almost exclusively in Lagos. It was formed in the early 1980s and Dr. Olufunwa was already so active in the association that he became a Secretary General as early as 1984. By 1988, he was already State Chairman, and he remained in that position for four years, until 1992. He is one of those persons we rightly refer to as elders in the association.

Back in 1997 when I met him at Ola Farms, he was much agile than he is today. He was the one from whom I learnt about brooding, growing, laying, feed production, sourcing of raw materials, and animal health. He taught me how to detect diseases in poultry, and when to vaccinate them, among other poultry management practices. But instead of this knowledge to satisfy me, it only made me want to learn more. So, after sometime, I began to fidget because the things I was beginning to learn would not allow me to settle down at Ola Farms.

While I was working at UB40, Olubisi Farms, and then Ola Farms, my friends were also gainfully engaged. Lanre was engaged in packaged water production. This packaged water (better known as pure water today) had just made its debut in the market, and the wife of Lanre's uncle was a business woman with interest in its sales. At his uncle's behest, Lanre had enrolled for a training programme at the Federal Institute of Industrial Research, Oshodi (FIIRO) and had become proficient in packaged water production. He was fully engaged in that and the production of soda drinks, while Alatise, whose brother in Canada had sent some computers to in Nigeria, was managing a computer school.

University of Ibadan ran a one-year Master's Degree programme unlike other universities in Nigeria where most of them required at least eighteen months; while some would not take less than two full years for the programme. My friends and I got information about the programme and decided to enroll. I remember that I had to send money to Lanre to help me obtain the form. I had graduated from the University of Ilorin with Second Class Honours and was admitted for the Master's programme without much stress. Both Lanre and Alatise were also admitted. So, I left Ola Farms.

Naturally, Alhaji Ola was reluctant to let me go; he even tried to dissuade me, but my mind was made up. The decision to leave Ola Farms was highly significant and epochal because it was the first time in my adult life that I would leave the known for the unknown. This was different from my move from Olubisi Farms to Ola Farms because, in that case, I was moving from one job to another. The first job paid eight thousand naira and the second job paid ten thousand naira. But the move from Ola Farms to the University of Ibadan was different because there was no guarantee that I would get a job after I finished my programme, and the University of Ibadan Master's Degree Programme was not an employment opportunity that promised or guaranteed any sort of income. Instead of being paid monthly as I was used to at Ola Farms, I would actually be required to spend money running the programme, apart from paying my tuition; but I did not pause to think about all these. Once my sight was set on going for a Master's degree, nothing else mattered; not the ten thousand naira salary I was getting, not the accommodation I had, and definitely not the subtle pressure from Alhaji Ola. This kind of decision (leaving the known for the unknown and doing so wholeheartedly) later propelled me into becoming one among 50 CEOs of the fastest growing companies in Nigeria. No doubt, the height I have attained today is by the grace of

God and by my faith in that grace, which propels me to take certain risks.

Once again, Lanre, Alatise and I, assembled at the same location. It was a reminiscence of our time at the University of Ilorin, and we all felt at home. We were already used to academic excellence, so, the University of Ibadan posed no spectacular challenge, even though the students we met there were spectacular in their own way. Alatise and I studied Animal Science, while Lanre studied Agricultural Bio-chemistry and Nutrition.

My decision to go for postgraduate degree without a part-time job by the side and without sufficient savings was not a bad decision. I knew that I needed money and that I did not have enough. I knew all these; but, I had only taken a step of faith in going, and God came through for me. I began the programme with the money I had saved; so it was not as if my faith was without some supporting action. I started by spending the money I had saved, hoping for some miracle that would enable me to have the funds I needed to finish the programme, and that miracle came in the following manner.

I went to see Mr. Lawson of UB40 one day. That move was divinely inspired because the man said I had come at the right time. As you read this story, you must put it in context to correctly understand it. This was in 1997, when there were no GSM phones. Only a few rich people in Nigeria had mobile telephone, which was made possible in selected cities through the M-tel platform. Mr. Lawson had no way of knowing where I was and I did not know that he needed me at that material time. Yet, I just felt like going to see him.

Mr. Lawson told me that his contract with the soap manufacturing company had been renewed, but the company had said that, because Lagos was getting saturated, they needed a presence in Ibadan. According to Mr. Lawson, I was going to be UB40's supervisor in Ibadan. The company had an office at Bodija area of Ibadan and I was going to operate from there. I had told Mr. Lawson about my Master's degree programme, but that was not going to be a problem. My job as a supervisor was not going to require my consistent presence and would not interfere with my education. What it really required was not my presence as much as it required a person Mr. Lawson could trust as overseer. All I needed to do was to assign the goods that will be taken out on a work day and then to return in the evening to take the account for that day's activities. For this supervisory job (which was no job at all as far as I was concerned), I was going to be paid five thousand naira every week, equivalent to twenty-thousand naira every month. Recall that my salary at Ola Farms (my last employment before UI) was ten thousand naira. Many writers of motivational books have stated that you have to give up to go up. I am sure I do not need to read any of those books because I have experienced the reality of giving up to go up in my life and have successfully internalised that philosophy to the point of making it a lifestyle. Through the fat allowance from UB40, I was able to meet my needs and hold my head up while studying for a Master's degree programme. Jehovah Jireh reigns!

At the end of one year, we all graduated successfully from the Master's Degree programme at the University of Ibadan with PhD grade.

While still at the University of Ibadan, I had an interesting encounter that eventually secured me a very good job – the most important job I have ever had as an employee. An exhibition was organised by the university and companies came around to promote their products. The exhibition was more like a trade fair than anything else. Different companies had their respective stands, where they displayed their products and interacted with their target clients. Dr. Olufunwa had exposed me to some products and their role in animal production. In fact, he often brought these products to Ola Farms, and they were critical to the production process as a whole. I noticed a company that had a stand promoting these kinds of products and went close to observe their activities. I wanted to establish contact with the suppliers of these products so that, after graduation, I would be able to achieve some things using them as leverage.

The company whose stand I was attracted to was known as Bio-Organics, and the Managing Director was there at the company stand in person. Of course, I did not know who was who at the time. But I politely offered to help them with some of their work and they allowed me. At the end of the two-day exhibition, the MD of Bio-Organics was happy with the helpful role I had played. He tried to express his appreciation by giving me some cash, but I was more interested in having his company as a possible future supplier than in any cash he had to offer me. I gently declined to accept the money offered and the man was, to say the least, shocked. He wondered aloud why I had refused to collect the money, but I explained that I was happy to have rendered the help. I told the man that I loved his products and just wanted to interact with them. This MD already knew that I was a postgraduate student at UI; my action was so refreshing and strange that he asked me when I was going to graduate. We were already about nine months into the programme, with just three months to go, and I told him so. Then he looked me over and said that persons like me were uncommon and hard to find. He there and then promised to give me a job and handed me his business card, with instructions to see him when I was through from UI. As a goodwill gesture, I was given a pen, a jotter, and other souvenirs, all branded with the company's logo, name, and contact details.

This was how I got employment, just by applying the wisdom that God had given me. But the job with Bio-Organics did not come on a platter of gold. As with most good things in life, there were challenges on the way.

I did not wait until after graduating from the University of Ibadan before I went to see the MD of Bio-Organics. I wanted to locate the company so that it would be easy to get there when I eventually finished my studies, and I used the opportunity of a short break to deal with that issue. When I showed up at Bio-Organics' office, located at that time at No 4, Oje Imavan Close, off Oregun Road, by Clay Bus Stop, Lagos, I received a warm welcome from the MD, Dr. Uzoma Kenny Acholonu. He introduced me to some of his staff and told them, in my hearing, that I was the one he had been expecting to come and work at Bio-Organics after my graduation. With the way the staff treated me, it was as clear as day that Dr. Acholonu had already told them I had been pencilled in to work with them. I was introduced as someone that had already been discussed. I was understandably excited by all this, of course. When it was time to say goodbye, Dr. Acholonu gave me some cash.

As soon as I concluded my Master's programme I did not wait a moment to celebrate that achievement. I readily packed my bags and headed to Lagos, to Bio-Organics, where an interview was set up for me. I did not expect a competition, but there was one: and this one was potent. He was the son of Dr. Acholonu's friend. Except I performed very well, there was no way Dr. Acholonu, would jeopardise his relationship with his friend just to give me a job. He could always tell me to wait or tell me one of many executive lies, but it seemed I performed creditably well as Dr. Acholonu got evidence that I had the brains he wanted.

But what would he do with the son of his friend, who did not do well to be employed? It was a dilemma. The man resolved it in an interesting manner: he decided to employ both of us. But I was the only one that lasted the distance. After just one month, the son of Dr. Acholonu's friend quitted Bio-Organics, out of his own volition. I later heard that, before coming for the interview, his father had told him that he was going to be employed and given an official vehicle. After a month without any official vehicle, the young man was disappointed, and he bounced off in anger, leaving me in a more secured position. As a matter of fact, I also wanted an official vehicle, but I was willing to wait.

I had not forgotten how my older cousin, Yomi Oyinloye, came to Otun with his official vehicle many years earlier. I was so shocked that Yomi could have a vehicle at that age. He was so young – and he even had a driver. Moreover, the vehicle was brand new. I remember the vehicle brand was Daewoo, made from South Korea. All this was too much to take in at once. When I recovered from my shock, I asked Yomi how he had managed to acquire the vehicle, and he told me that it was his official vehicle from the company he had secured a job with. I knew that Yomi had attended the university and I reckoned that he had gotten the job because he had gone to school. This caused a determination in me to ensure that I also went to the university and succeeded. I believed that if I did that, I too would one day get my own official car. This dream of an official car in the future helped to keep me focused and to endure the difficulties I faced while climbing the academic ladder. I would eventually get an official car from Bio-Organics, but it was going to be about two years down the line.

My work with Bio-Organics was a very important and even critical grooming experience for me. In all, I spent slightly over six years there. No matter what I become in life, I will never forget my time at Bio-Organics, and the key role played by Dr. Acholonu, from whom I learnt quite a lot, in my life. The man was remarkable in his own way. He was a business man and a true professional in his field. Before setting up Bio-Organics, he had worked with multinational companies and had even worked in the United States for some years. That was long before he came to Nigeria. I enjoyed my years at Bio-Organics and achieved a lot for the company. But I knew, in my mind that I would have to leave one day. The company was into premix production and I was part of the sales team before eventually becoming the sales manager. This was good, but this was not exactly the ultimate destination, according to the gospel of Professor Obebe. I needed to set up my own business. Fortunately for me, I got a push from some things that began to unfold at Bio-Organics. There were disappointing developments. But as a matter of fact, "every disappointment is a blessing."

CHAPTER 10
THE BEGINNING OF A BUDDING CAREER IN AGRICULTURE

In 1994, Little Brown & Co published the autobiography of former South African President, Nelson Mandela. This book, titled *Long Walk to Freedom*, chronicled Mandela's interesting life from his own point of view. The most remarkable aspect of Mandela's life was the nearly 27 years he spent as a prisoner on Robben Island under the apartheid regime of South Africa. Like a fairy tale, apartheid crumbled, Mandela was eventually released in 1990, and he went on to become the first black president of South Africa in 1994; the same year his autobiography was released.

The greatest challenge of Mandela's life was his time at Robben Island. His imprisonment drew the attention of the whole world to the situation in South Africa, which made him to become popular. Without the experience of Robben Island, Mandela would not have been a different individual. Mandela's survival of Robben Island made apartheid to eventually fall; it also made him to forgive his former enemies and bring about peace in South Africa. It was because Mandela came out of Robben Island that he eventually became President. I would not compare my time at Bio-Organics Nigeria Limited with Robben Island (because I was not in jail), but, in terms of its implication in my life, the two are very similar.

Since 2014, my company, Hi-Nutrients International Limited, has been the leader in premix manufacturing for feed in Nigeria. Even before the merger of Hi-Nutrients with Neovia of France, Hi-Nutrients had successfully reversed the clock a full 180 degrees. When Hi-Nutrients made an entrance into the premix subsector of the livestock business, there were older and very formidable companies on ground. In fact, it was on the basis of this fact that some of my friends, who showed commendable concern but nonetheless misinterpreted my determination, advised me not to attempt to do the impossible. It is to the glory of God alone that it can be said, using the very paradigm of these very advisers, that what Hi-Nutrients has achieved was seemingly impossible initially.

This unimaginable turn around and the speedy rate of growth of the company has become a case study for the Enterprise Development Centre (EDC), which is part of the Pan-Atlantic University (formerly Lagos Business School). The Director of the EDC, Peter Bamkole, has sent students of the EDC to my company several times so they would hear the amazing story of Hi-Nutrients from the horse's mouth. Peter Bamkole himself has also told me that my company is now a case study in that premier institution. Note that, as far as Nigeria is concerned, there is nothing better than the Lagos Business School, the EDC, and the Pan-Atlantic University, as far as business training is the topic. Peter Bamkole believes that entrepreneurs would learn a lot from our story because, no matter how inspiring the stories of Microsoft, Apple, and Facebook are, they are all foreign companies. The case of Hi-Nutrient is refreshing because it is an indigenous company that has its head office right here in Lagos, Nigeria.

I learnt a lot about poultry farming in general at Olubisi Farms, and at Ola Farms and Trading Company (especially with the presence of Dr. Olufunwa, who was at hand to answer many of my questions). I learnt more about how to efficiently raise livestock in a modern world. I saw evidence of the miracle of bio-engineering and became a true apostle of 21st century agriculture. I witnessed how day-old chicks became full-grown broilers within six short weeks; I understood why some other chickens, based on what they were fed and their species laid healthy and large eggs every day for close to 320 days nonstop. I saw how a chicken that was sick and so close to death was made to start jumping around and eating ravenously, just by a quick injection by a veterinary doctor who knows his onions. I saw all these, but never had the real opportunity to do what now basically defines my work, premix manufacturing; until I got to Bio-Organics Nigeria Limited, which later became Bio-Organics Nutrients Systems Limited.

I don't know whether to say I got my job with Bio-Organics while still a Master's degree student of the University of Ibadan, but it does seem that way, because, the MD of the company was the one who promised that he was going to employ me, based on our interesting interaction on the grounds of the University of Ibadan, as earlier related. When I eventually started working at Bio-Organics, it was very exciting. At Bio-Organics, we were basically dealing with vitamin fortification. Vitamin fortification entails adding essential vitamins to manufactured food and feed products. Today, when you pick a malt drink or any other soft drink, you may see on the label that it contains such and such vitamins: these vitamins are produced by companies like Bio-Organics, and are usually supplied to the bottling companies as concentrate. All they needed to do was to add the concentrate at some point in the production of their drinks. Naturally, adding concentrate is not arbitrary but based on a specific ratio. This ratio is determined by the Nutrient Research Council, which is based in the United States of America. We may indicate, for instance, that, for every 1000 litres of Maltina, the bottlers should add certain quantities in kg of the nutrient concentrate we supply them.

The practice of vitamin fortification of manufactured food products was in response to new guidelines given at the time by the National Agency for Food and drugs Administration and Control (NAFDAC), under the leadership of its most popular Director General, Professor Dora Akinyuli, who later became Nigeria's Minister of Information. Before Dora Akunyili was appointed to head NAFDAC by former President Olusegun Obasanjo, there was no regulation and standard regarding the issue of vitamin fortification. There was neither sanction nor approbation for substandard products.

Many Nigerians think that NAFDAC was created in 2001, and that late Professor Dora Akunyili was its first Director General. This impression is understandable because, before Akunyili's time, NAFDAC was virtually unheard of largely due to ineffectiveness.

As far as counterfeit and adulterated drugs were concerned, Nigeria used to be a very dangerous place. The problem of fake drugs was so severe in those days that countries like Ghana and Sierra Leone officially banned the sale of drugs, foods, and beverages produced in Nigeria. It was the Ibrahim Badamosi Babangida (IBB) administration that began the formation of NAFDAC, which was created to replace a similar agency then known as the Directorate of Food and Drug Administration and Control. The formation of NAFDAC could not be completed until 1994, when General Sani Abacha was in power.

One of the factors that had literally forced IBB to establish NAFDAC was the case of 150 children, who suddenly died as a direct result of taking paracetamol syrup which contained a dangerous chemical known as diethylene glycol. The uproar over the deaths of those innocent children went round the whole world and IBB had to do something. But the agency that existed then was more like a paper tiger. It was until Dora Akunyili was appointed Director General that NAFDAC began to bite. NAFDAC attacked unscrupulous drug manufacturers, drug importers, and drug counterfeiters. NAFDAC did so with such viciousness that these illegitimate businesses collapsed as she became a personal enemy of the players in that sector who had been profiting from the old order. She became the target of several assassination attempts, which all failed to take her out of action.

Although largely concerned with drugs, NAFDAC also took an interest in food, especially manufactured beverages. Therefore, to improve the health of Nigerians, the guidelines for vitamin fortification was given. That was why one would often see the logo of a human eye on some products like flour, sugar, and vegetable oil. Salt also had to be iodized to prevent goitre. The statistics is that this vitamin fortification guideline alone injected over ₦200 billion into the industry at that time. This fortification was not just for humans; but also for feed for livestock. Bio-Organics was ready to reap from these guidelines because, at the time, it was one of the foremost premix manufacturers in the country. Importation was still rampant, but Bio-Organics was one of the few companies that had begun to produce locally. Livestock Feeds, which used to be a department under Pfizer before Pfizer sold it off to local investors, was also involved in premix production.

However, Dr. Acholonu, the Managing Director of Bio-Organics, was a chemist. So, being employed made it possible for the company to extend its gains, not just in the human nutrition fortification market, but also in the animal nutrition fortification market. As an animal nutritionist coming from the University of Ibadan, my assignment was to review all the nutrients required by chickens. You will recall that, following my earlier employments, I already had experience working with layers; broilers; and breeders. I had also worked with feed for cattle, fish, and other animals. So, I was able to review everything.

I was able to distinguish myself as an Animal Scientist quite early, and as an Animal Nutritionist too. I was able to add value to the company, while expanding my knowledge base in a very drastic manner. Naturally, my confidence took an upward swing as I saw how the knowledge I was applying was transforming things before my very eyes. I was not just an employee at Bio-Organics: my presence and the knowledge I contributed became solution to real problems. After all, I was functioning in my area of specialty; so, I was able to leverage on my core competence and distinguish myself in the animal industry.

As top pioneer of Bio-Organics, Dr. Acholonu, who was the Managing Director at the same time, had worked with Roche of Switzerland and was a vitamin fortifier of international repute. Apart from Roche, he had worked with the FDA in the United States and briefly with our own NAFDAC. He knew the science behind vitamins and had the contacts abroad and was able to integrate me into his network with the companies. I got to know all the suppliers and the required specifications, both for food and feed. Food is what humans take in while feed is the one animals take in.

At Bio-Organics, we had two divisions. We had the human nutrition division, which took care of customers like Cadbury (we fortified their Bournvita); Guinness (we fortified their malt drinks like Maltina, Malta Guinness, etc.), and several other companies involved in making chocolates, beverages, and yam flour. There was also the animal nutrition division. In this division, we were number one. Through the work of this division, we were able to provide the vitamins required as additives when feed is made for cattle, horses, fish, poultry, goats, etc.

Although I had initially joined Bio-Organics in 1998 as a salesman, I later became the Technical Manager around the time that NAFDAC's guideline came up. As Technical Manager, I was responsible for the formulation of the products' production. I also liaise between the customers and the company. I later added the position of sales manager to technical manager and did both concurrently. My goal was to become the General Manager at Bio-Organics. Many people, including some top customers and friends of the company also believed that it was only a matter of time before that aspiration materialised.

I worked with other staff members of Bio-Organics like Uche Okpalanma, Leye Alayande, I.F. Etuk, Idio and Dr. Ifeyinwa (a vet doctor). Together, we were able to make Bio-Organics a force to reckon with. As at the time, foreign companies were even competing with us. There was Roche from Switzerland, BASF from Germany, Provimi (Calgil) from the United States of America, and others. So, we were the indigenous company at the time that was able to measure up in what we were doing. We were getting big business deals and were able to have a foothold in the human nutrition aspect of vitamin fortification as well as in the animal nutrition segment. Some of our clients included Obasanjo Farms at Ota, which had bases in several other locations across the country. Today, we have Obasanjo Farms at Iseyin, Lanlate, and Igboora. We also have Obasanjo Farms at Owiwi, and another in Delta State. There is yet another Obasanjo Farms at Calabar in Cross Rivers State. Bio-Oganics was doing business with all these farms, and I was the nutritionist they interacted with.

We also have Zartech (the chicken producers), Top Feeds in Sapele, and several other big players. By working with Bio-Organics, I got to know many farms; I also got to know NAFDAC and their operations. But, most importantly, I was able to know the different kinds of raw materials required for producing premixes for humans and animals.

I am happy today that my former colleague, Leye Alayande, is also a very successful businessman and the MD of his own company based in Kaduna – Hybrid Feeds. We all jokingly refer to Leye as a big boy while I am referred to as his boss. When I mildly remonstrate with Leye about this label, he would laughingly remind me that he actually learned a lot from me at Bio-Organics. For the records, Leye was running a PhD programme at the Ahmadu Bello University, Zaria at the time of this writing. Hybrid Feed is doing so well in feed mill business that it is one of the largest feed mills in Nigeria today, after Premier Feed, Grand Cereals, and Olam.

Apart from those already mentioned, my other colleagues at Bio-Organics were Ben Nwachukwu, Gloria, Bimbo, Grace (who was the head of HR), and Oluwole. Oluwole was our production manager but is now the production manager of Agrobamagen, an Israeli company based in Ibadan. Just two years ago, after about two decades in the industry, Bio-Organics Nutrient Systems was completely bought over by an Indian company known as bnsl.

I will restate that nothing will ever change my profound respect for my former place of work, Bio-Organics, and Dr. U.K. Acholonu. I give kudos to the company because it recognises hard work, diligence, and performance. I appreciate the fact that I was given a free hand which allowed me to learn a lot to the extent that I was able to build a successful career.

Dr. Acholonu used to ask:

"Are you working for money?"

Then he would answer his own question by saying that anybody who worked for money could not be successful. He would say that a successful man would not work for money; but would want to first build his career; to get knowledge; and to add value to himself. He would go further and say all these come together to transform into real money. In my life and business, I have found this philosophy to be true because, nobody can take your experience from you, and people would be willing to part with real cash to learn from your experience, if it is considered valuable. This is a fact of life.

Dr. Acholonu was very hard-working while at the helm of affairs at Bio-Organics and I learned a lot from him. Even though my father in the village was also hard-working and did inspire me in the area of hard work, it was through Dr. Acholonu that I first saw how a very educated man could also be very hard-working. He is an excellent example of intelligent people. The place of Bio-Organics is safe in the annals of the livestock industry in Nigeria because, someone with international commendable exposure as him has paid his dues to his fatherland; and nobody can undo what he has achieved. Without him, I definitely would not have been where I am today. For this, I will ever appreciate him for giving me a chance and for believing in me. I will add a caveat and state that, there is no perfect man out there, not Dr. Acholonu, nor myself.

However, this story would not be complete without pointing out some things that went wrong, especially because it explains my subsequent decision to quit Bio-Organics, after I had spent about six years, and I stand to be corrected because they are just my views, and I admit that I do not have the whole picture, nor do I have monopoly of knowledge of the matter.

I was not a shareholder of Bio-Organics, so, I had no right to determine how profits were allotted or how the company was administered. I believe I have a right to hold my own opinion on a matter, even if I was not positioned to do anything about it. I feel that there were lots of human management issues, and the office politics became ineffective. I believe in politics, which, to me, is just an escalated form of human relations. So, when I say office politics, I do not necessarily mean anything dirty; just that human relations was not well managed. It got so bad that

I began to feel that I was not being justly treated. Even some friends of the company felt, at some point, that I was not getting my just due.

I worked with Bio-Organics as if it was my father's company. Our brand of products was known as biomix, and some customers even believed that my name, Bode, was part of that acronym. The irony was that they could not find any other explanation for my level of commitment and rigour in doing the business of Bio-Organics. They claimed to have never seen an employee behave like me before. The only thing that would make sense to them was if I was a part of the company as owner. That was why they made the assumption and I cannot blame them. I was so consumed with passion for the success that it did not occur to me that I was working for somebody. I simply gave my all. It was after I left Bio-Organics that some of these people realised that I was not a shareholder of the company.

As part of my work, I travelled extensively to many places: Owerri, Port Harcourt, Enugu, Calabar, Sokoto, Abuja, Jos, Okene, Maiduguri, Owerri, Enugu, Abakaliki, Kaduna, Ibadan, Osogbo, Benin, etc. In fact, the journeys took me to virtually all the 36 states in Nigeria. I worked tirelessly as if I was a shareholder in Bio-Organics, even those who interacted with me in those days can attest to that. Because of that experience, I always tell my members of staff that the way you did another man's job will not be very much different from the way you would end up doing your own. You cannot get used to mediocrity in the employ of an entrepreneur and suddenly become diligent when you set up your own company. That is against the law of nature and nurture, and it would never work. If you train your mind to accept shoddy effort and thrive in mediocrity, it will come back to haunt you and deny you the unleashing of your full potential. On a lighter note, the management used to tell us that, if I had not been rewarded with what was commensurate with my efforts, then God Almighty would reward me Himself. I thank God for that prayer because it is coming to pass in my life. God Almighty is indeed rewarding me today.

It is hard for me to begin to blow my trumpet in terms of how seriously I took my work at Bio-Organics. I believe that my immediate boss' reluctance to let me go when I resigned is the best objective evidence that I was highly needed in that company. Since the company was not my father's own but a corporate business, simple deductive reasoning will tell any honest analyst that I was not doing badly at Bio-Organics. That is the only explanation for the strenuous efforts my boss put in to stop my resignation. For instance, when I resigned, the management promised to buy me a brand new car that I could give the official vehicle I was using to my wife. When that did not work, I was told that my salary would be doubled. The management did everything possible to induce me to stay; but, by then, the damage had been done: I had already decided that I would rather hustle again on the streets of Lagos than work in a place where my rights would be denied me routinely.

The first major thing that made me to number my days at Bio-Organics was an incentive that I was entitled to, which I was deprived of. Even my enemies, let alone my friends, would readily admit that I am a gifted marketer and salesman. Many describe me as a go-getter, while some call me a bulldozer. I know what the people refer to, and I know that, once my mind is locked on a target, I do not take no for an answer. I have gained great and amazing victories through this attitude of pretending to be deaf until I have my way. I would also be lying to myself if deny the fact that God has blessed me with the ability to connect. I was so good in marketing. Dr. Acholonu even considered me a trailblazer. That tag was apt because I was able to break into new markets that had proven impenetrable in the past.

I was the one that broke into Benin for Bio-Organics and opened an office there. In fact, at one time, I secured a supply contract of ₦5m from Ojemai Farms. The owner of Ojemai Farms is Chief Johnson Arumeni, who is also the owner of Arik Air today. When I secured that contract and told the management about it, they bluntly refused to believe me. Like an unabashed Thomas, they told me that, except they saw a cheque of ₦5million from Ojemai Farms, they would not be ready to hear me verbalising things that seemed beyond my pay grade. Shortly after that challenge, I brought the cheque of ₦5million and was able to collect a 10% bonus (five-hundred thousand naira) that I had been promised. This was better than cocaine, in terms of the intoxication it caused in me. I was fired to do more and went literally berserk in my sales drive. But again, the management made another promise, which would be fulfilled based on verified performance.

Only two persons were to qualify for this very special incentive. I would simply state that I got to know that I was qualified, but was not allowed to enjoy the promised incentive, which was a two-week vacation in the United Kingdom. The way I got to know that I was qualified for this is a story for another day, but it happened exactly as I have stated. Since I am human, you can imagine the level of betrayal I would have felt over this breach of promise. It seemed to me that I was good enough to work and perform miracles on behalf of the company, but not good enough to enjoy the promised vacation in London. The fact was that the promise was voluntarily made and if redeemed, it would have spurred me on to more productivity. If I was not a patient man, this was where my relationship with Bio-Organics would have ended. I held the management ultimately responsible for this huge upset but later realised that it may have been the result of an oversight, or egregious deceit by the company. I let that matter ride and continued working.

There was something already brewing at Bio-Organics, and it was only a matter of time before it would rear its ugly head. Like George Orwell would have phrased it, "some animals were more equal than others." This situation created uncertainty and was a source of psychological stress for me. There were some people who were not treated strictly according to the rules because they seemed to have special access to the top management, and this privilege was displayed in full view. I did not mind this unprofessional practice and would have ignored it forever, but it soon gave birth to something that almost broke my heart. At the time, I was the only staff of Bio-Organics that had a Master's degree certificate, and was also the final authority in animal nutrition at Bio-Organics. This was not because someone was admiring my height but because I was the most knowledgeable in that area that even the management deferred to me. But when an HND holder was made General Manager of Bio-Organics ahead of me, I felt so bad that I could not hide my displeasure. I actually confronted the management over the issue. This was sometime in 2002.

Dr. Acholonu, in response to the issue on behalf of the management, was not only brilliant, he was also astute. And I would say he was humble too because, instead of brashly brushing my concerns aside, he actually admitted that I was treated badly by the management. It was during this confrontation that I even reminded him about the UK trip that I had been denied, even though I was qualified. The man tried to meet me halfway on behalf of the company. I would never know why Dr. Acholonu did what he eventually did, but, I would like to believe that God was in the matter. After accepting my complaint that it was justified, the management could have placated me in a number of ways: I could have been given a fat bonus; my official car could have been changed; a future reward could have been promised or even tendered a serious apology to mitigate my hurt feelings and end the matter. I loved the company and; I know I would have accepted an apology because that would have been refreshing, and would have given me hope. In fact, there was nothing that would have stopped the management from even sending me on a vacation. I know I would have appreciated that a lot and would have been placated. But something very remarkable and very special was done.

Dr. Acholonu on behalf of the management, decided to spend over ₦680,000 (the equivalent of over ₦5m today), to send me to the Lagos Business School. Interestingly, I did not immediately know the value of what Dr. Acholonu did for me until some of my church members who knew about these things told me that attending the Lagos Business School was many times better than going for any sponsored vacation to London. According to these friends and mentors, if I could consolidate on the gains of attending the Lagos Business School, I was going to be positioned to go to London at will and do so countless times. I could not wait to find out what those people meant.

What was it about the Lagos Business School that made it better than an all-expense paid trip to London, where I had hoped to see Trafalgar Square, London Bridge, Buckingham Palace, and other exciting places I had heard about?

Indeed, I did not know much about the Lagos Business School, but I decided I was going to find out before too long.

CHAPTER 11

ON THE PATH OF DESTINY

Sometime in 2014, I found myself attending a conference inside the United Nations building in New York. The conference was organised by the African-American Business Forum and I was part of a presidential delegation of Distinguished Young African Entrepreneurs that had been invited to be part of that gathering. The Nigerian delegation included notable personalities like the then Minister of Finance, (Dr. Ngozi Okonjo-Iweala), then Minister of Agriculture (Dr. Akinwunmi Adesina), Emir of Kano (Mallam Sanusi Lamido Sanusi), and international business mogul, Alhaji Aliko Dangote among others. But for me, the high point of that UN visit was the fact that, before the end of the conference, former United States' President, Barack Obama, who was the then incumbent president, joined us. The sight of Obama within shouting distance seemed surreal, and I could hardly believe that what I was witnessing was not a dream.

Obama and I under the same roof! I had to pinch myself to be sure that the experience was real. I soon recovered from my shock and had a great time at New York before returning home to Nigeria.

When I settled down to consider my trip, I could not help but think about how I had managed to become part of the presidential delegation from Nigeria, which was what gave me the opportunity to see Obama. Of course, the reason was that I was the CEO of Hi-Nutrients International Limited, and Hi-Nutrients had been listed among the 50 fastest growing companies in Nigeria. As stated earlier, the ranking was done by the Tony Elumelu Foundation, in collaboration with an international organisation simply known as AllWorld Network. Apart from Hi-Nutrients, there were 49 other companies that were qualified for the award: some were well-known, others were less popular, but the common denominator was that each one of them had recorded not less than 100% annual growth in the year under focus. This led to Tony Elumelu featuring Hi-Nutrients in his book, *Success Factor*.

There was no way I would have been the CEO of Hi-Nutrients if I had not set it up in 2004 under dire circumstances. I knew in my heart that the possibility of setting up Hi-Nutrients would have been slim, if I had not attended the Senior Management Course 19 of the Lagos Business School. Chances were that I would have moved from one job to the other or, I may even have continued to hope for a better tomorrow and remained at Bio-Organics.

I had attended the Lagos Business School, and there were things I learnt that changed my scope. Someone has rightly observed that "knowledge is power." While this axiom is generally true, it can also be true to the extent of creating such phenomenal change that the person with the knowledge becomes transformed into a very different individual.

Before I attended the Lagos Business School in November 2002, there were things that I thought were possible and some that I felt were simply impossible. One of the things I truly believed was impossible was to set up a business without cash. However, before I finished my Senior Management Programme, I had a change of heart. Professor Patrick Utomi (then Dr. Patrick Utomi) succeeded in convincing me and my colleagues that what a person needed was an idea. As long as there was a very good idea, money would show up. We were taught to regard good ideas as having more value than money.

We were also taught to understand the fact that, with a business plan, there was no amount of money that was too large to be put together by investors. The key was the business plan. The business plan had to be based on an idea; and the idea could not just come from nowhere: the idea must be based on the experience and knowledge of the prospective entrepreneur.

Even before I attended the Lagos Business School, I already had an idea. In fact, this idea was implanted in me long before I started to work with Bio-Organics Nigeria Limited, which, around 2002, was renamed Bio-Organics Nutrients System Limited. The idea in my mind was there before I graduated from the University of Ilorin; in fact, the idea was there before I went to the University of Ilorin because it was part of what convinced me to go to Ilorin in the first place. Professor Joseph Bolarinde Obebe was the one who had planted that idea in my mind. Every other person and every other experience only polished the idea and gave it more substance. The idea I refer to is that, for me to be economically emancipated, I needed to set up my own business; I needed to establish in the same way Chief Olusegun Obasanjo had done. This idea remained in my mind like unpolished diamond until it connected with the requisite knowledge at Lagos Business School. When that knowledge collided with the idea that I had carried like an interminable pregnancy since 1988, there was an explosion. The first casualty of this explosion was my employment with Bio-Organics.

I returned from the Lagos Business School sometime in May 2003. I was a well informed man by then, even though the colour of my skin did not announce this fact, neither did my height warn anybody that I was like dynamite that had been rigged, that was waiting for the trigger that would make it explode and rock the world, beginning from somewhere in Lagos. I would be wrong to attribute this trigger that unleashed the giant in me to a single event. The fact is that there were several collaborating events that finally gave me the push I needed to get on the path of destiny. The first was the appointment I thought I deserved, even before going to the Lagos Business School. Like I recently told a friend, if I was immediately given the position of General Manager of Bio-Organics when I returned from the Lagos Business School, rather than thinking of setting up my own company, chances were that, I would implement the knowledge I had gained within Bio-Organics itself. This would have made me a cutting edge General Manager because I learnt quite a lot to make me one. That did not happen. It did not take long when the old feelings of discontent harassed me to return, but I did not know how to deal with the situation.

Then one day, I sat under a tree outside Bio-Organics corporate office. I must remark that the shade of a tree is a wonderful place of repose because, many great ideas have hit men before while they were sitting under a tree. For example, Sir Isaac Newton, the English physicist, astronomer, and mathematician, is said to have discovered the law of gravity while sitting under an apple tree. Newton built the first practical reflecting telescope in 1668, but he is more famous for his work on the laws of motion, optics, gravity, and calculus. In 1687, he published a book titled *Philosophiae Naturalis Principia Mathematica* in which he presented his theory of universal gravitation and the three laws of motion. The story is that, while Newton sat under that famous apple tree and was thinking about the forces of nature, he got a paradigm shift and extended human knowledge drastically when an apple fell and hit him on his head. Newton wondered why the apple had not gone up instead of coming down. He immediately concluded that a force was responsible for pulling the apple downwards. To think that rocket propulsion and many other sophisticated inventions depend on this discovery is just wonderful. I was not trying to imitate Sir Isaac Newton that hot afternoon; but I would admit that I also ended up with a massive paradigm shift that changed the course of my life.

What triggered me into my entrepreneurial journey that fateful afternoon was the human traffic of Bio-Organics members of staff that were returning from lunch break. Colleagues among them would wave at me and I would nod back at them. I remember I was munching on a piece of bread and a local snack popularly called *akara*. I guess it was the incessant greetings of the subordinates at the office that finally got to me. As each of them passed by, they would pause very briefly and greet me with the traditional "Good day sir" or any other acceptable variant. The greetings became so much that I started to feel irritated. Then I asked myself if this was how I wanted to spend the rest of my life receiving greetings from staff members of Bio-Organics. I asked myself if this was what my life was really all about. Something inside me said that I had to do things differently and change the course of my future. Life could not just be about being greeted with respect by junior staff or my appreciation of their courtesy, notwithstanding. There and then, I decided that I was not working with Bio-Organics any longer, but would set up my own company. That was the future I wanted for myself. The ingredients that brought about this sudden reality had everything to do with the six months I had spent at the Lagos Business School.

That is why, today, I blame Professor Patrick Utomi for making me what I am today, but I do not intend to take him to court. I believe that, as gentlemen, we can settle the matter out of court. But, really; he is to blame. Of course, I also blame Peter Bamkole and Dr. Juan Elegido (now Professor Juan Elegido and current Vice Chancellor of Pan-Atlantic University). I also blame Professor Albert Alos, who was Vice Chancellor of LBS at the time I did my programme in 2002.

It was while I was at the Lagos Business School that my eyes were finally opened to the business world. I learnt many important things but one of them was how to successfully manage a company or an enterprise. We treated practical cases of both local and foreign companies. We also did analysis of both successful companies and companies that had failed. We were told, based on critical analysis, why a company had to be liquidated and why the other one was acquired, and why the next one has continued to expand and is set to keep expanding; all factors being equal. We were made to understand that luck played little or no role in success and in failure. There are things that successful companies do; amazingly, all successful companies have similar traditions. The same is the case for companies that collapsed: definitely they did not do something right, and no amount of prayer or fasting or wishing was going to change their situation. We got to realise that one could avoid several pitfalls in business by learning and taking heed to the lessons of those that had gone before. Lagos Business School has solid information about foreign companies and even their inner workings. When you hear the things that are taught there, you will wonder how they got the information. All the practical examples of actual companies went a long way to equip me properly.

We were also taught about marketing, financing, and how to source capital for a new business or for a business at the point of expansion. We learnt about how to write business plans and the various parameters a typical business plan should consider. As far as business is concerned, there is a serious need for focus, mission statement, vision statement, and what the entrepreneur intends to achieve. We were even taught how to register a new company.

In manufacturing, we were taught what is known as GMP; that is, Good Manufacturing Practices (GMP). Other things were quality control, operations management, negotiation, general ethics, and ethics of business. There were legal implications for some actions some people take without thinking twice, and we were told how to avoid such actions.

It was not everything that was taught at the Lagos Business School that seemed achievable, but I can report that, if a businessman lives by them, success would be the end result. For example, we were taught that, to run a standard company, you must have a mentor or some mentors. One easy way to do this (and the main objective is to subject yourself to accountability), is to have a board of directors. For you to succeed in business, there must be a person or a group of persons you report to. It is just the way it is. This may not make sense at first, but the people who have studied business have also studied human nature: without being held accountable, there is the risk that a bad decision can be taken, spending may be indiscriminate, danger signals may be ignored, and necessary counsel may be absent. In fact, there are many other reasons. People like me who have tried it know that there is a way you run your business when you have no one to report to, and there is another way you run it when you have to report to someone. Some people (even my colleagues at Lagos Business School) did not fully accept this lesson. To them, it felt like allowing someone else to poke their noses into something that was none of their business. I know that is not true. I have been saved and blessed simply because I have a board of directors who know about every key decision I take and who can ask any question and expect a lucid and immediate answer. When I err, they even scold me.

There was the issue of mitigating risk in business. It was one important lesson I learnt and do believe has caused my modest success today. We had several lecturers at Lagos Business School, but it was Professor Pat Utomi himself that taught us this very subject of mitigating risk, and the best way to do this is to allow other people invest in your company. In this way, when you make profit, you share; and when you make loss, you also share the pain and the loss, so that you would not have to bear it alone. The psychology of being associated with others is even an advantage on its own and it will take a special kind of selfishness and greed to deny yourself that advantage just because you do not want to share profit with others: that is a myopic way to do business, and all successful businessmen know that.

To drive home his point about mitigating risk, Professor Pat Utomi gave an analogy, after insisting that it is better and wiser to share by allowing others to come and invest in your company. He added that holding on to 100% shares was like holding on to a cock. Then he would asked us to compare the quantity of meat in a whole cock with that of the thigh of a cow. In Professor Pat Utomi's analogy, the cock is the result of singular effort and the cow is the expected result of combined effort. His point was that, even if, after sharing a whole cow with others (investors), and you get a thigh, you will still have more meat than the business illiterate who insisted on doing it alone and ended up with a whole cock for himself. This analogy has always been at the back of my mind. It was what opened my eyes such that, by the time I started Hi-Nutrients, it was easier for me to seek people of like-minds that I could bring together to share from the risks and the profits. Up till this moment, I believe in sharing: I believe it is the only way to grow.

The thing that Pat Utomi said that made Bio-Organics no longer an exciting place to be, happened not too long before we were scheduled to conclude our Senior Management Programme. One day while lecturing, he paused and said that he has seen all of us in the class and that he wanted to see us, in a year or two, running a successful company of our own. He said that we would be foolish if we still went back thinking that, by being employed, our employer was doing us a favour. He said that some of us had outlived our usefulness in our respective companies. That was when it dawned on me that I had already spent 5 years at Bio-Organics. Actually, one of the requirements for being enrolled into the Senior Management Programme was to have worked for five years. So, this was why Patrick Utomi knew that all of us have spent at least five years in employment; and that was why he talked to us the way he did. His challenge should be taken in context because it does not apply to all and sundry. I guess it was the digestion of Pat Utomi's words that caused my near violent outburst as I sat under the tree near my workplace that afternoon. But how was I to proceed?

As we were taught, the first thing was to conceptualise the end game. I got direct inspiration in that regard. I decided that I wanted to achieve three things with the company I was going to set up, and that I wanted those three things achieved within twenty years. At that time, there were 14 companies in Nigeria that manufactured premixes, or at least engaged in premix importation as traders. I could have decided to set up a livestock farm or do one of many other things in the agricultural value chain, but I decided that I wanted to become the 15th manufacturer of premixes in Nigeria; in spite of the tall order that was. I said to myself that my premix was going to be different from others. It was going to contain higher nutrients, and that was what gave birth to the name of my company, Hi-Nutrients International Limited. I decided that my premix was going to be the very best among the rest. If a person wanted the best premix, I must ensure, within twenty years, that the person would buy from my company.

As for my second goal, I decided that I wanted my company to have an international status. As Sales and Technical Manager of Bio-Organics, I related with different companies. Some of these companies were multinationals. I could see that they conducted their business with a certain panache. So, I wanted my company, in less than twenty years, to also join this special group. I liked the way they behaved. There was something different about them. I wanted to be a multinational someday; and that was why, after the "Higher Nutrients" concept, I thought of adding "International" to the name of my company. So, what I now decided was to name the company "Higher Nutrients International Limited," and that would have been the name of my company today, but my lawyer advised that it should be made catchier by hyphenating the Higher and the Nutrients into a new compound word Hi-Nutrients. My lawyer's advice was based on the advice he himself had received from the Corporate Affairs Commission. As for my third goal, I decided that I wanted my company to be listed in the stock exchange.

There was another goal. Although I did not give it a duration of 20 years to be accomplished, It was a goal I had set earlier. I told myself that I would love to write two books in the future. The first would be the story of my life. The story would be written in such a way that Nigerian youths and everyone with a poor background could learn from. The second book would be a book that would chronicle my experiences in business and serve as a reference material for students of business and agriculture.

Leaving Bio-Organics was not going to be easy. First of all, I could not just stop coming to work and claim that I had resigned: that would be unethical and would raise suspicion, damage the relationship I had built for years, and even be beneath my training and belief system. So, I had to depart without any acrimony. In case somebody is thinking that I had stashed enough cash in the bank to provide a soft-landing for myself, that was far from the case. I remember that, at that time, the total amount of cash I had in my bank account was around a hundred and twenty thousand naira. Apart from that, I was also due to collect my savings which I had been contributing as part of staff cooperative scheme and gratuity. There was an interesting thing that actually happened to that money. It was huge and it had been contributed sacrificially over years. The amount was ₦975,000 which the management refused to hand over to me because it was kept in trust for us. I am sad to report that, up till today, that money has not been given to me. I must quickly state that it is possible that this breach was as a result of an oversight; but at the time it happened, it was like a malice. This was only one of the sad things that happened in the build-up to my quitting Bio-Organics.

The first step I took by way of legitimately and peacefully disengaging from Bio-Organics was to have a private conversation with the management team. It was during that first interaction over this issue that I reported that I would be leaving the company. Then I asked to be allowed to proceed on leave. But due to the habitual reluctance of the company to allow performing staff members to go on leave, I had accumulated up to six months of leave and wanted to take advantage of that as an intermediate period to prepare for a new chapter in my life. After telling the management that I wanted to leave Bio-Organics, I was not only disallowed to embark on my six-months leave, my official vehicle was also withdrawn. If that was meant to make me stay back in the company, it had the direct opposite effect. All the stubbornness and willfulness in my nature, coupled with the knowledge I had garnered in life, faith I had in God, my self-confidence, the fact that I had a right to my six-months leave and also a right to quit a company I had been working with, cumulatively conspired to cause me to cast my decision in stone: come what may, I was going to leave Bio-Organics.

Out of displeasure over my attempt to leave the company, the management reluctantly approved a two-month leave. I knew that a quarrel with my boss would not help my reputation, and I was willing to manage things as peacefully as I could. So, I accepted the two-months leave but knew that it was not going to change anything. Knowing that there was a policy that required giving the company at least a month's notice before quitting, I spent one month out of the two-months leave under the radar and then suddenly sent in my resignation, to be effective at the end of the second month, and to fulfill the condition of my one-month compulsory notice. Things got nasty after this but I found a way to submit my resignation letter and avoided any meeting. It was when I eventually showed up that what I had already mentioned above ensued.

When it dawned on them that this boy that was brought from the campus of the University of Ibadan had made up his mind to quit, they promised to double my salary but I did not budge to the request of staying back. I was even promised a brand new car, that I could give my wife the official car; still, I refused to budge. At that point, there was nothing the management could have done to change my mind. Only at a gun point would I have agreed to stay at Bio-Organics. Perhaps, this was why my gratuity and cooperative scheme savings which had been kept in trust by a collective decision of staff members of the company were not paid to me. In the same manner, this was why there was a breach of tradition of the company which was that, after five years, a person leaving the company was eligible to leave with their official vehicle – at no cost.

After trying to induce me, the management warned me about a possible bleak future; followed by being appealed to as a child. At some point, I was asked if I wanted my wife, Bukky, and the little girl, Deola, to go hungry. I retorted that they would not go hungry. This was after I was told that they liked me and really did not want me to leave.

I resigned from Bio-Organics because I was disappointed. I had thought that, after returning from Lagos Business School

(LBS), things would change. But no! I simply could not bear the thought of coming back from LBS and still keep reporting to someone with a HND. I had hoped that, as I was coming, the *status quo* would change. If that had happened, perhaps I would not have resigned. The people that moved the company, apart from the MD himself, were myself, Uche (who studied Home Economics), Dr. Ifeyinwa (a veterinary doctor), Leye Alayande, Ben Nwachukwu, Ajayi and others. This was the reality at Bio-Organics, but the power structure, as represented by the organogram, did not reflect this reality.

Because my car was withdrawn against company policy, because my money was held back, and because there was bad blood and tension within staff members over the same issues that I had complained about, my disengagement from Bio-Organics was not as neat as I would have wished.

The grounds on which I left Bio-organics notwithstanding, I could vividly recall some quite smooth times. One of those times was when I got the five-hundred thousand naira bonus which I believe I had earlier mentioned. After getting the ₦500,000 bonus from the ₦5m deal I sealed with Ojemai Farms, I decided to buy a car. Buying a car had been my dream for a long time and, at last, this was an opportunity. I could not wait to get into my new car. But I made the mistake of telling my elder cousin, Yomi Oyinloye. He was my mentor and role model, and I should have known that mentors and role models have their way of influencing a decision – they tell the bitter truth. So, I mistakenly carried my exciting news to Yomi Oyinloye (who is now Rev. Yomi Oyinloye and the Director of Home Missions for the Foursquare Gospel Church) and told him that I wanted to buy a car.

The first thing Yomi Oyinloye did was to point out that I had an official car. He wondered why I wanted to buy a car when I had an official car – with an official driver. I countered and told my brother that what I had was official; but that I wanted a personal car: my own car. I wanted a car registered in my name. He looked at me. He knew the influence he had over me and decided that he was not going to argue with me for too long. Almost imperiously, he said I should take ₦50,000 out of the ₦500,000 and bring him the balance of ₦450,000. He said he was going to buy me a land and that I was going to build my first house with his support and the support of Rev. Jide Taiwo, and Mr. Lawson, a nearby builder who had a block industry.

I regretted my decision in opening up to my elder brother, but I had no choice than to comply with his instructions. I lamely went to do as told and the sweetest part of this story now is that I ended up building a four-bedroom bungalow in Ogun State. It was a wonderful achievement and I am immensely proud of the leadership, love, and firmness of my mentor and elder cousin, Rev. Yomi Oyinloye.

While I was building that house, word got out and eventually came to the ears of my MD, Dr. Acholonu. My other colleagues at the time were buying cars. They probably did not expect anybody to be able to build a house; so, the story was that I had embezzled money from Bio-Organics which I used to build my house. I was not the accountant of the company; I therefore do not know if my accusers meant that I embezzled the money spiritually. In any case, the matter got so serious that my credibility got on the line. Apart from the person who propounded this case of embezzlement, the gossip around it was too dazzling to be ignored by others. Soon, I was being looked at as a thief. I will always be grateful that the management stepped in decisively.

I was invited and interrogated about the rumour. It was then that I explained to the management how everything about the house I was building had started, and the role my older cousin had played, and the sacrifice I was making to raise the building. I thank God that the management used their authority to put the malicious rumours to death. In fact, those who wanted to find their way into tarnishing my reputation were summarily disappointed. So, I will always appreciate the management of Bio-organics.

For years after leaving Bio-organics, I looked for an opportunity to pledge my loyalty to the company, make them see me as a former employee and not as an enemy or a wayward child. The opportunity came when the father of Leye Alayande, my former colleague at Bio-organics, died in 2016. As long as I was healthy and within Nigeria, there was no way I would not attend Leye Alayande's father burial. I was so pleased to see the management and members of staff of Bio-organics at the event. On their part, I am sure they were proud because no matter what I had achieved, everybody knew that I was cooked and trained by Bio-Organics. We all greeted and exchanged pleasantries. That was how we were re-united. As far as I am concerned, the past is solidly behind us.

In fact, I met the top management staff, Dr. Acholonu at the 2018 Alumni Day event of Lagos Business School. This opportunity for another reunion was not wasted. We talked about the past and took pictures. Also, he told me how proud he was that I was doing well. That day, Thursday, 15th November, 2018, was one of the best days of my life. May God bless Dr. U.K.A., as he was fondly referred to by all senior Bio-Organics staff members in those days.

To be fair to Dr. Dele Oyediji, President of Feed Additives Manufacturers of Nigeria (FESMAN), I must add that he also played a role to stand by me during the attempt by malicious fellow employees of Bio-Organics to besmirch my reputation. Dr. Oyediji is the pioneer Registrar of the National Institute of Animal Science (NIAS) and one of a few key elders in the agricultural sector in this country who has played a role in raising the professional standard of animal production in Nigeria. He would always remain my mentor. Somehow, he got wind of the unfounded allegations of embezzlement to undertake my building project. But Dr. Oyediji believed in my integrity and stood by me. I will never forget the way he put his own reputation on the line and vouched for my integrity. Almost comically, he told whoever cared to listen at the time that I was from Ekiti State. He said that Ekiti people are not thieves and that I could never steal from anyone. I am touched anytime I recall this bold defence from Dr. Oyediji.

The first three years after leaving Bio-Organics were the toughest years of my working life. At last, I had done what I wanted to do: I had quitted a company where I was guaranteed a salary of ₦54, 000 at the end of every month, apart from possible bonuses. After leaving, it was time to face the consequences of my decision. One was if I had forgotten that I was no longer a staff of Bio-Organics, the fact that I no longer had a car and a driver brought the issue rudely into my consciousness. It is one thing to hustle for years and then become a car owner, but it is quite another to have a car at your disposal for years and then suddenly have to cope without it.

Once in a while, I got invited to different institutions to deliver lectures. In September 2018, I was invited as a guest of the Enterprise Development Centre, Lagos Business School, Lagos, to speak on a segment known as 'Sharing with the CEO.' Before then, I delivered motivational lectures at various universities across the South-West of Nigeria. In all these lectures, I had advised young businessmen and students. One common thing I told them was that their character was the only cheque that they had. If they lost their character, it was equivalent to losing a cheque. And in that case, nobody would like to help them and they would be treated like leprosy.

After leaving Bio-Organics, the only asset I had was my character. Some people would later tell me that the reason they decided to help me was that, among other things; I never had the habit of asking them for bribes (euphemistically or plainly) when I had business dealings with them. My transparency was so refreshing that they saw me as an odd fellow. I did not know what these people were talking about because, to me, I was only doing my job and did not believe that I should cheat anybody just to make extra cash. As a salesman, I believed in sales commission and that was my right, as far as sales was concerned. I did not believe in taking advantage of customers to defraud them in whatever guise. I was told, after leaving Bio-Organics that I would get help. Some were so committed to helping me that they actually said, even if I brought packaged refuse to them, they would buy. There was a groundswell of opinion that I had served my former company and that I deserved to be supported in my attempt to set up my own company.

The first thing I immediately started doing after leaving Bio-Organics was to visit farms and find out what they required. Using my vast network of contacts, I would try to meet their needs and get a commission on every successful supply. That was how I was moving from farm to farm and then to product manufacturers, trying to connect those in need with what they wanted. I was using motorbikes to move around during this time because, although I needed a car, I simply could not afford one. For the first two years as the MD of my own company, I had no car. This is one of the reasons I feel bad when I see people who just buy very expensive cars once they begin a business. Of course, I do not mean those who are trying to set up a transport company or who require a vehicle as part of the necessary investment for their business; I am referring to those who refuse to endure the inconvenience of operating without a vehicle and choose to unwisely buy a vehicle too early in the life of the business. Apart from the possibility of affecting the business by increasing the overhead cost, this early vehicle purchase by young entrepreneurs may actually have other side effects, like creating distraction.

In my case, I was not in a hurry to buy a car. Rather, I saved all the money I could, I knew I had taken a very great risk and that I had to be very careful so as not to fail. I was ready to spend money, but only on things I believed would later make a meaningful impact in my life. For example, in spite of the situation I was going through – without a job and with a great need to raise cash and start something big – I still managed to go for a Master degree in Business Administration (MBA) at the Lagos State University. Such was my commitment to education that I was ready to get it at all costs. Many people admire my marketing skills today and consider me a maverick when it comes to that endeavour. They may not know that, apart from my natural predisposition, I also had to acquire formal knowledge so as to sharpen what nature had already endowed me with. I went for the MBA in 2006.

Despite all my efforts, I was unable to raise sufficient cash to do what I needed to start doing, namely premix manufacturing. This lack of sufficient cash was not going to be a problem. With what I had been taught at the Lagos Business School about how to source for finance, I created a short list containing the names of ten persons that believed in me, who had the financial capacity and may be willing to invest cash into my new company to give it life. Based on LBS lessons also, I wrote down my business plan. In my class at the Lagos Business School (SMP 19), there were bankers and financial experts, and I was able to get a few of them to take a look at my business plan, with a view to having them advise me on how to perfect it. The few experts I contacted looked at it and assured me that I was good to go. It is interesting to note that I was not the only one who could not cope in paid employment after attending the Lagos Business School. Apart from myself, up to five of my SMP 19 classmates also quitted their jobs and established their own companies.

Shortly after creating the list, I began to approach them one after the other. Without going into details, I would simply state that, at the end of my exercise, three persons responded positively. However, there was not a single person out of the ten that said I was crazy for asking them to be investors in my new company. I received moral support, even from those who, for one reason or the other, declined support. Of the three that indicated willingness to support my new company, two agreed to give me cash. The support of the third person was as unique as it was interesting. This third supporter, Dr. Pension Smith, is the owner of Capsfeed in Ibadan. He said he would support me by helping me to import required raw materials from outside Nigeria. For those who do not understand my kind of business, the support of Dr. Pension Smith may appear like a small matter; but I knew it was not. It was huge and had serious positive implications. Incidentally, this same Dr. Pension Smith would later play a key role that took my company to a whole new level. So, the history between me and this man is that, although he has not invested in my company with cash, he has been used by God to help me make more money than I can quantify.

The plan with Dr. Pension Smith was simple: he would be bringing in the raw materials I required at his own cost while I would be paying him gradually. Eventually, he was the one that imported my first set of machines, even though I part-paid him ₦4m for that. The balance of ₦3m was paid by supplying him enough of my products to offset the amount. Finally, I was able to clear my debt with Dr. Smith.

The first person that gave me cash to start up Hi-Nutrients gave me a loan of ₦4.5m. That person was Dr. Femi Faniyi. At the time I was setting up my company, he was already a customer. Dr. Femi Faniyi is the owner of Good Health Farm. The second person that gave me cash was a woman I referred to as Mama Sabina in deference to her age. Her name is actually Mrs. Olopade, the wife of Engr. Olopade. It is the name of her company that is Sabina Pad. Mama Sabina loaned me ₦5m. Interestingly, when Engr. Olopade later heard that the young man his wife helped was the same young man who he had been hearing about, he decided to add another ₦5m. Mama Sabina had told her husband how I had been helping her with my knowledge of the livestock industry, so, he did not want to be left out of the effort to help me. This case is an example of how people hold you up when you also do not mind doing the same for them. I felt blessed to be so treated by this family. At the end of the day, I had a total of ₦14.5m from the Olopades and Dr. Faniyi. This was how a poor boy, armed with faith and business knowledge alone, was able to raise ₦14.5m within two months.

With the money I had raised simply by presenting my business plan to people who knew me, trusted me, and believed that I had the capacity to deliver the claims in my business plan, I was able to rent a factory. It was also from that money that I was able to do a down payment of ₦4m for the machines that Dr. Pension Smith graciously imported for me. Out of that amount also, I was able to deposit ₦5m into our ECOBANK account, as part of conditions for qualifying for a loan of ₦17.5m, which I was able to secure. With the amount from ECOBANK, I was soon able to bring in raw materials on my own so as to relieve Dr. Pension Smith the burden and risk of helping me with that aspect of the business.

I did not start premix manufacturing quietly, though. I did some advertisement. As a businessman, I understand the value of publicity and, through the past 14 years, I have spent tens of millions of naira on publicity alone. I see effective publicity as a veritable marketing tool. To kick-start operations in my new factory in 2007, I organised an event to launch the factory. That occasion was chaired by my father in the industry, Chief Folorunsho Ogunnaike of FOLHOPE Farms, who had supported me over the years. Chief Ogunnaike did something very interesting during the occasion. After taking the microphone from the MC, he cleared his throat and began to talk as though he wanted the guests to donate money, as is sometimes done at occasions. He told the guests that it was time to launch the new factory, but what he had in mind was not cash donation. By the time the man was through with his unique concept, he had secured supply contracts for Hi-Nutrients International Limited worth ₦20m. I will never forget this crucial support, which helped to give us the needed momentum.

I remember that Chief Olusegun Obasanjo was represented by then Managing Director of Obasanjo Farms (Dr. S. O. Ajayi). It was one of the most important days of my life as an entrepreneur because, after that day, I became an actual manufacturer. Before then, I had to get orders and fulfil them by depending on other companies. But those days ended in 2007. That factory has since been vacated for the new ultramodern factory located near Lagos, but, many thanks to Mr. P. M. Oritsharemi for those days of production.

I must mention the immeasurable support I received from several customers during those early days. One of the ways those who wanted to support me did was by paying me for my products as soon as they were delivered. The usual practice in the industry was for a supplier or manufacturer to wait for a month before payment. Nobody would take it lightly to be told to pay earlier than a month, but these people who took my success as their personal business, went out of their way to support me in this way. Akinsateru Farms was one of such clients.

Another company that also helped me rise quickly was Bendel Feed and Flour Mills. The man at the helm of affairs was Mr. Ogbogodo, who knew me when I was working with Bio-Organics. Fortunately, he had seen my commitment, so he decided to give me a chance. He asked the quality control department of Bendel Feed and Flour Mills to test my product. The nutritionist in charge of this process was Mr. Dick Obasoyo, who I owe a debt of gratitude for honestly reporting his findings. Mr. Dick later told me that, after several experimentations, they discovered that my premix was actually better than the one they had been buying from a South African company. I was very pleased and encouraged.

After that order of patronage from the MD of Bendel Feed and Flour Mills, I got a Local Purchase Order (LPO) of ₦3m from the company. When that first deal went fine, the MD directed Bendel Feed to thenceforth buy nothing less than ₦5m worth of products from my company every month. Apart from that, he directed that I must be given a cheque the very day I bring the goods. Only God knows how I valued this sort of support and only He will repay these helpers. They took my success personally. I shudder to think how differently things would have been if I had ever been caught engaging in fraud while I was working at Bio-Organics, or if I had tried to take advantage of these people by demanding for tips and bribe.

Bendel Feed and Flour Mills eventually closed down. It was bought over by Pastor Chris Oyakhilome of Christ Embassy Church. The place is being renovated now and I am waiting for them to conclude that renovation project. As soon as they start operation, I intend to go back and revive the relationship. I hope they will respect the history between us by restoring our business relationship. The good thing is that it is very likely that they would do so, especially because, the former head of Bendel Feed – who had helped me – has been contacted to serve as a consultant to the company. The man is now an associate Professor at Ambrose Alli University, Ekpoma, Edo State.

There was another man that helped me. He was the General Manager of Top Feeds at Sapele at the time. I used to relate with him like my elder brother. That was how I related with my customers. I would call some my mummy, and some my daddy, and some uncle, or brother; depending on their age. It was my way of showing both respect and love, and this gesture was well-appreciated. This man who used to work as GM of Top Feeds (Mr. Frank) eventually left to start his own company, known as Rainbow Feeds. In his case, he left virtually every transaction of the company under me. He asked me to supply everything he would require to operate, and to even source for things I did not produce. Such was the man's trust in me. I was free to source for the things he required, add my little commission, and supply him. He was happy with me and was content to support me in making money. I thank the people but their support should be seen from another point of view. Apart from the actual cash transaction with them, their acts of kindness also made me to have hope. I was so grateful to God and was encouraged that He had ignited such miracle of goodwill from several people. My psychological disposition was very good as a result of these things.

The first year after setting up my factory, I was able to declare a profit of a few millions. The next year, it was many more millions. The third year, the profit rose by 70%. It was after that third year that I was able to share profit with Dr. Femi

Faniyi for the first time. Before then, however, Mama Sabina and her husband, Engr. Olopade, had taken their leave. The 3-year waiting period before sharing profits was in line with what we were taught at the Lagos Business School. Because Dr. Faniyi was willing to wait that long, I appreciated him and made him Chairman of the Board of Directors of Hi-Nutrients International Limited – a position he held until 2013. As a farmer himself, Dr. Faniyi was not only using my products but was also deploying his influence to convince sceptical persons to buy. He convinced them by simply telling them that he was using the same products himself and was getting good results.

Back in 2008, one of my church members introduced me to Mr. JID Dada, who was then the Managing Director of Grand Cereals. For those who may not know, Grand Cereals is a subsidiary of UAC Nigeria Limited. I later got to know that Mr. Dada was from Ekiti and hailed from a village just a stone throw from mine. He was very instrumental in my relationship with Grand Cereals/UAC. Grand Cereals later conducted trials on my new products and discovered that the quality was not only up to their required standard, but that the price was actually lower than those of competitors. After giving them two heavy punches in the area of quality and price, it was only a matter of time before they succumbed under the influence of the dual benefits they stood to gain in doing business with me. Eventually, they gave me a trial order worth several millions. It was the highest LPO I had ever got at the time and, for them (Grand Cereals UAC), it was also the first attempt to depend on a local supplier for this sensitive product. So, I was very determined to prove to Grand Cereals that I loved the concept of high quality products just like they did.

By the grace of God, I was able to deliver the trial order to UAC and did make some profit, but that was not the strategic goal because I knew it was only a trial order. It was if I passed their test that something better and bigger would come. I remember that it was from the profit I made from the Grand Cereals' trial order that I was able to pay off an outstanding ₦2m debt to Dr. Pension Smith. This UAC trial order opened the floodgates a few years after – the very floodgates that spewed enough water to convey the ship of Hi-Nutrients across the seas, unto international shores.

Bode at 6 years old

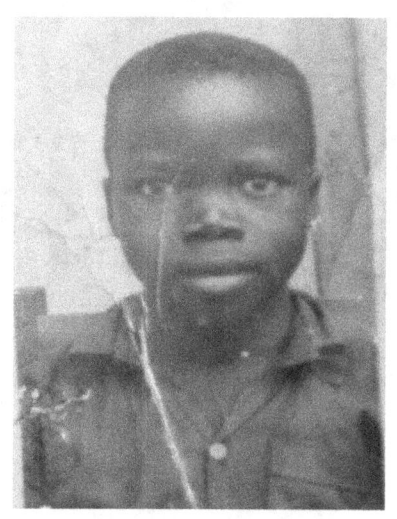
At 11 years old

My parents at their wedding in 1955

Pa Adetoyi John Peter (My father)

With family at Ido-Ekiti, 1975

With family at Ido-Ekiti, 1975

Elder Gabriel Popoola Adetoyi
Eldest son of the family

With my mum in Warri, 2016

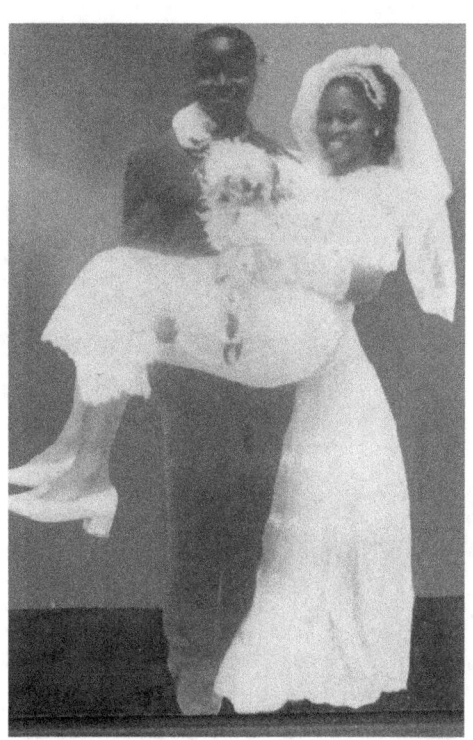

My church wedding at RCCG, Ilorin, Kwara State, 2001

My traditional wedding at Sawmill area, Ilorin, Kwara State, 2001

My family, 2016

My Children, 2012

My wife and Children, 2018

My Son, David Adetoyi, 2018

My daughter, Adeola, 2018

My wife, Bukky, 2018

My Uncle, Elder Olaniran Oyewopo, 2018

My Sister, Mrs. Alice Odia, Warri, Delta State, 2018

In front of Oore Awosowoye's house (1810-1860)

My Brother and Mentor, Prince Ade Abolarin, 2018

With Professor Niyi Osundare

With the Oore of Mobaland, HRM Oba James Adedapo Oladele Popoola, 2018

Receiving the Entrepreneurship of the Year Award, from HRM Oba Oladele Popoola, 2014

The house where I was born and brought up at Oke-Afin, Ile-titun compound, Otun-Ekiti

My first house at Lambe, Akute, Ogun State

With Alhaji Yakassai, DMD Grand Cereals and Mr. Mebude, Jos, Plateau State, Nigeria, 2018

With Bukky and Prince David Adetoyi, 2018

My childhood friend, Dr. Tunde Olofinbiyi, 2018

Hi-Nutrients Early Days and Products

Hi-Nutrients by Neovia logo after merger and aquisition, 2018

Hi-Nutrients Hi-Mix® layers, flagship product patented in 2005. NAFDAC Certified for Nigeria livestock feeds

Salt block for cattle

Hi-Nutrients stand at Nigeria Poultry Show, Abeokuta, 2018

With a staff at Nigeria Poultry Show, Abeokuta, 2018

Hi-Nutrients by Neovia stand at International poultry Show, Abeokuta, Nigeria, 2018

With Sales and Technical Team of Hi-Nutrients by Neovia at a poultry exhibition, 2018

Attending to customers, 2018

Hi-Nutrients first office (middle floor) 18, Shonola street, Ogba, Lagos, 2005-2007

With Sales team at Hi-Nutrients by Neovia Head Office, 2017

With staff at Entrepreneurship Award at Otun-Ekiti, Ekiti State, 2014

Posters of Hi-Nutrients patented products 2005-till date

Business Colleagues, Bosses, Mentors and Professional Associates

At Enterprise Development Centre (EDC) graduation Pan-Atlantic University, Lagos, 2011

With Dr. Gbenga Oluyemi
Vivax Ltd. 2018

With Dr. Buka, Director VMAP NAFDAC

With Francis Toromade Tee Square Atlanta, Georgia, 2018

With Professor Omitoyin, UI, 2018

With Felimar and Chief Onigbinde, Atlanta, USA 2018

With Mrs. Udidi Nwueli, Founder Leap Africa, Sahel Consulting, OAU, 2018

Late Layi Oyatoki, MD, Grand Cereal Limited, 2017

Leye Ayande,
MD Hybrid Feeds

With Professor G.M. Babatunde at Landmark University Omu-Aran, Kwara State, 2016

Professor Atteh (left); Prince Adetoyi (Centre) and Dr. Dele Oyediji at Nigeria Institute of Animal Science Conference, Ilorin, Kwara State, 2018

At Standard Organisation of Nigeria, (SON), towards livestock development in Nigeria, 2018

Dr. Ayoola Oduntan immediate past President of Poultry Association of Nigeria

With Ibrahim Ezekiel (National President Poultry Association of Nigeria)

With Uche Opalama, former colleague at International poultry Show Abeokuta. Hi-Nutrients by Neovia Stand

With Dr. Peter Bamkole, Director EDC, Lagos State, 2018

With Rev. Yomi Oyinloye, Lagos, 2018

With my former boss, Dr. U.K. Acholonu at Lagos Business School Alumni Day, 2018

CHAPTER 12

MERGER AND ACQUISITION

On 28th August, 1963; Rev. Dr. Martin Luther King Jr. ended his seminal "I Have A Dream" speech with the catchy statement: "free at last; free at last; thank God Almighty, we are free at last." That statement is one of the best climaxes in any speech ever given by man.

While it would be wrong to suggest that I had gotten to the climax of my life in 2018, I would say that the year actually marked a mini-climax of some sort. In June 2018, I could have easily repeated the very words which Dr. Martin Luther King Jr. employed in ending his most memorable speech. After decades of struggling to achieve economic emancipation and fulfilling my childhood dream of becoming a wealthy man, including 14 years as CEO of my company, and a cumulative period of over twenty-two years working on the job, I was ready to say: free at last, free at last, thank God Almighty we are free at last.

The events that led to the mini-climax of my life varied. First, there was good news, but after sometime, the news wasn't so good anymore due to a combination of external factors. Things started to get bad and began to get worse at a point in time. For quite a while, there was no improvement. In fact, it was when things were about to get out of hand that a sudden twist turned my situation around and brought about a wonderful result, the full effect of which is still unfolding, even as at the time of this writing.

First, it was the large UAC contract of 2013. Before that contract, I had begun to implement some smart ideas to increase the market share of Hi-Nutrients International in order to reduce cost of marketing and other overheads. What I began to do was to sign supply agreements with certain clients that have confidence in us. These were clients who were very satisfied with us and were even ready to recommend our products to others. As CEO of Hi-Nutrients, I believed that signing supply agreements as exclusive supplier with certain companies for a certain number of years would lock down such customers, and at the same time give them some advantages like discounts and scheduled deliveries. This sort of agreements would further allow us some predictability in our finances and increase our capacity over time. I signed a couple of these agreements, and it has made business easier and more productive.

By 2013, our business discussions with UAC was at an advanced stage. This was about five years after successfully delivering their initial order. But, before we got the supply order, we had to present our supply agreement with some of our big customers just to prove our viability in the industry. However, UAC had no reason to doubt us, having tried us earlier and not found us wanting. After considering the matter, UAC also wanted some predictability in their supply chain and so, decided to give us the opportunity to supply the premixes.

In years past, UAC used to produce its own premixes from individual vitamins. But the fact that they needed to import these individual vitamins and do a lot of other things was becoming a distraction to them, even though they had a facility to blend the individual vitamins into premixes. To do things more smoothly, there was a need to order for large quantities of these vitamins and space had to be created to store them before eventual use. However, the sheer quantity implied that some of the products may not be used before their expiry dates, resulting in losses.

To prevent such losses therefore, the idea of outsourcing that aspect of their production process came up. It would be a win-win situation for UAC to allow a company that solely focused on premix manufacturing take the burden off them so that, they could focus on their primary assignment of feed production, using the premixes from the supporting company.

As a company committed to getting the best for its customers, UAC/Grand Cereals did not just initiate discussions with Hi-Nutrients as a way out of this quagmire, it also contacted several other premix vendors and gave all the vendors the opportunity to make a pitch. That was how Hi-Nutrients was selected and given a portion of the total premix requirement.

After concluding discussions, a detailed Memorandum of Understanding was signed between UAC/Grand Cereals and Hi-Nutrients International Limited. Part of the terms of this MoU entailed that some staff of Grand Cereals would be stationed at the factory of Hi-Nutrients to ensure that the quality of their product was not in any way compromised. That was how thorough they were. The supply contract we got by way of kick-starting this MoU was for the supply of products worth hundreds of millions of naira, to be delivered within a period of one year. This was too good to be true, but there was a condition that we needed to meet in order to activate the deal and actually begin production.

To protect Grand Cereals in case Hi-Nutrients failed to meet up with its part of the bargain, the supply contract from Grand Cereals needed to be backed up with an equivalent amount in cash, which will serve as a sort of guarantee by Hi-Nutrients. This amount was to be placed in a bank agreed upon by both parties. The idea was to get Hi-Nutrients to deliver and to protect Grand Cereals in case we did not. The bank had instructions to pay Grand Cereals this amount in case Hi-Nutrients failed to deliver the order. This was the best way to protect both parties in the MoU, which was fair and in tune with international best practices. The only problem was that Hi-Nutrients International Limited did not have the sort of amount required by the MoU, and it needed that amount in order to fulfil its obligation in the biggest supply contract it had ever secured. The time was set for this amount to be paid, and the clock began to tick.

I was now faced with the greatest financial challenge I had ever encountered in business. The interesting thing was that I had to surmount that very challenge in order to make the greatest profit I had never made since I became a businessman. If there was ever a bitter-sweet news, this was it. I thought long and hard but only succeeded in wasting hours and then days: there seemed to be no way out. By this time, I had finished building my house and had lived there for many years. I, therefore, thought about using the house as a collateral for a bank loan; but, the challenge with that house was that it was located at Lambe, near Akute in Ogun State, and would not impress any bank as a collateral for the kind of amount I was hoping to borrow. I had left that house two years before then when my bankers came around to see where I lived. Those bankers and a few business friends were the ones who had insisted that I could not stay in such a place, in view of the kind of business I was involved in. So, I moved to a rented apartment in Omole Phase II. I remembered the things they said that day, so I knew that no bank would even be interested in going to inspect my house at Akute for the purpose of giving me the type of loan I dearly needed. Seeing that there was no harm in trying, I approached a bank for a loan using the house as a collateral, but the bank turned down the request.

After thinking more seriously, I decided to talk to Dr. Pension Smith. This man knew me, trusted me, and was doing business with me. He had helped me in the past. He could help me again. Dr. Smith was ready to do anything to support me. I remember how he had introduced me to one of his friends. This farm owner was apparently a VIP, but I had no way of knowing who he was at the time. His farm was located at Ogbomoso, but he himself lived in Ibadan. The reason I was introduced to this farm – which was managed by the son of the farm owner – was to deal with a situation of high overhead and other inconsistencies frustrating operations at the farm. At that time, the farm was spending an average of ₦750,000 per week as overhead. But when I came in, I was able to use my experience in the industry to bring down the weekly overhead cost to ₦300,000 without compromising anything. The son of the farm owner was so impressed with my performance that he told his father about me. Then one day, the curious farm owner told his son to bring me to him.

I was so shocked when I discovered that the farm owner was none other than Senator Rashidi Ladoja, the former Governor of Oyo State. After exchanging pleasantries, Senator Ladoja thanked me for what I was doing on his farm and said his son had told him that I was the young CEO of my company. He then asked if there was anything I wanted him to do for me. Having been taught to be content and not to take advantage of people, I told the Senator that I was fine and did not need anything, and that I was well paid. The man was impressed by this statement. In bidding me goodbye, he said that, since I said I did not need anything for now, I should come and see him the day I needed something; and it was on that note that we parted. These were some of the things that Dr. Smith had done for me in the past. If he did not have absolute and abiding confidence in me, I doubt it if he would have introduced me to the farm of his VIP friend – someone with the status of Senator Ladoja. So, as regards the loan I was seeking for the UAC contract, I was convinced that Dr. Smith would help and I approached him with confidence.

After listening to my very exciting story, he was happy for me. But more than that, he was willing to help. However, for some personal reasons, he could not play the role I would have wanted him to play and he explained everything to me. This would have been a low point in my search, but I recalled that it was this same Dr. Smith that had introduced me to Senator Ladoja's farm before the Senator himself eventually asked to see me. Just then, a bold idea hit me and I decided to present it to Dr. Smith without much ado.

I asked Dr. Smith if it was possible for him to ask his friend to help me. Both of us knew the friend I was referring to. The advantage I had in relating with Dr. Smith was that this was a man that believed in me completely. There was no iota of doubt in his mind that the paper I had shown him to prove my LPO with UAC/Grand Cereals was genuine. The kind doctor would have still believed me, even if I forgot to bring the LPO along. Such was the level of trust he had in me. So, I decided to leverage on that by asking him if he could seek the help of his friend on my behalf.

I was pleasantly surprised when Dr. Smith exclaimed and said he had just recalled something. He told me that while they were at the club a few days before that day, Senator Ladoja had spoken about me in glowing terms and said that I was a good boy. Dr. Smith then said the most important thing I was hoping to hear: that Senator Ladoja himself had told him that he had earlier told me to come and see him if I needed anything. With that recollection, there was nothing stopping him from going to Senator Ladoja with my request, since the man made the offer himself; more so, the business was genuine, and neither Ladoja nor Pension Smith had any reason to withhold help from me. So, Dr. Smith asked me to give him until the following day because he planned on seeing Senator Ladoja at the club. On this note, I returned to Lagos prayerfully.

When Dr. Smith called me later the following day and asked where I was, I told him that I was in Lagos. He said I should start coming to Ibadan immediately because Senator Ladoja wanted to see me. Pension Smith asked me to come along with the financial statements of Hi-Nutrients International Limited, and other documents that would show what we had been doing for the past years. I did not need to be told to bring the LPO along since it was the main thing. I also got a detailed description to Senator Ladoja's house.

When I met Senator Ladoja the second time, things had changed a little. The meeting was more formal than the first one because a serious matter was at hand. The Senator asked for the LPO from Grand Cereals and I gave it to him. He looked at it for a while, and then handed it and other documents I had brought over to a financial expert that was also in the meeting. I was told that I would be contacted after two days. Obviously, the Senator needed to review my company so as to make the most intelligent decision on how best to help me. As expected, those two days were the longest in my life.

On the third day, I received the call I had been waiting for and immediately left Lagos for Ibadan. When I got to Senator Ladoja's residence, I prayed that God would take me to a new level in life and in business. I knew that Senator Ladoja could commandeer the money I needed or guarantee a loan to secure it, but my biggest hurdle was his will. I knew that he did not need the deal. If he was willing, the money was not going to be an issue. So, I fervently prayed that he would be willing.

As simply as he could, Senator Ladoja told me that he was interested in playing a financial role in the UAC deal. My heart raced with nearly uncontrollable excitement, but the man was not done: he added that he had seen what my company was doing and was especially impressed with our bookkeeping culture. We had a very commendable paper trail that, it was so easy to review our operations as a result of this. On a lighter note, he added that, although he was impressed with the way I was running my company, I was still a very poor man and that it was expensive to be poor; and that he was going to help me.

But before my excitement will go unchecked, Senator Ladoja said that he had a bit of bad news. My heart stopped momentarily and then began to race furiously. I had come so close. 'What was it now?' I asked myself.

The Senator allowed me a few seconds to prepare, and then dropped the bomb. He was going to provide the required money on the condition that I made him the Chairman of the Board of Directors of Hi-Nutrients International Limited. I came to understand that, as a businessman himself, the Senator did not just want to help and leave me alone: he was actually interested in the success of Hi-Nutrients and was willing to provide remote leadership by helping me with broader issues and giving advice where and when necessary. The best way to position himself to help me in that manner was to be chairman of the board. So, it was easier for me to invite him to invest in Hi-Nutrients.

I swallowed the clear message from Senator Ladoja without carelessly betraying my emotions. I was almost 45 years old at the time and was no longer a kid. I knew that as an adult, one had to be realistic about issues in life. So, I did not know how to respond. I just remained silent.

Normally, one was not expected to immediately respond to these kinds of issues. I asked for time to think about the offer, and left Ibadan for Lagos. But the clock did not stop ticking. I must confess that I tried to look for alternatives, but none was forthcoming. At least, none was going to materialise before the Grand Cereals deal expired.

How would I forgive myself in years to come if I lost the Grand Cereals deal because of a bad decision? Then, I knew I had to be careful. I believed in counsel. The Bible says that, "in the multitude of counsel, there is safety." I asked some trusted people for their advice and I got varying opinions. Some thought it was a good idea while some did not think so. At the end, I made my decision based on the training I had received at the

Lagos Business School. I remembered what Professor Pat Utomi had taught us and actually warned us about. If I insisted in doing it alone, Hi-Nutrients would remain a cock and I could have the whole cock to myself. That cock, however, would not be able to fulfil the stiff terms UAC had given, and the deal would be lost, as would other similar deals. However, if I wanted to partake in the thigh of a cow, I needed to allow big fishes like Senator Ladoja to come along and do what it takes to turn the cock into a cow so that we could all share it.

I therefore decided to cooperate with Senator Ladoja than lose the biggest opportunity I had ever had. I was going to make Senator Ladoja the Chairman of the Board of Directors of Hi-Nutrients International Limited. The only person I needed to convince was my wife, who was both a shareholder and a director of the board of Hi-Nutrients.

I told my wife about my decision and encouraged her to believe that everything was going to be alright. After all, Senator Ladoja had assured me that he was not interested in running the company or poking his nose into its day-to-day affairs. He was only interested in occasional annual or bi-annual reports, apart from doing all he could to support the growth of the company.

I eventually accepted the offer. Senator Ladoja played his mandated role and guaranteed a loan for the required amount from one of Nigeria's third generation banks. After that, UAC released the final contract and I was able to procure raw materials from foreign suppliers. This local content drive of the UAC must be commended because it has helped to provide jobs in Nigeria, and to cause businesses like mine to thrive. Talking of patriotic companies in Nigeria, UAC is one of them; especially in view of the fact that they had limitless options, if they had wanted to deal with foreign entities across the whole spectrum of their operations. At the end of the year, our profit looked so good and we were able to share profit. It was one of the best moments in my life as a businessman. As a result of the deal, the profile of Hi-Nutrients International Limited improved dramatically and things were never the same again. It was obvious that Hi-Nutrients performed creditably because, rather than cut down our quota over time, Grand Cereals kept increasing it until we became their key vendor. We proved reliable, were producing to standard, and meeting their expectation. Grand Cereals was very concerned about the issue of consistency in availability, the issue of meeting up with their specifications, and the use of high performing potent vitamins, among others. Apart from its main plant in Jos, Plateau State, Grand Cereals had other production facilities in Kano and Onitsha. We basked in the euphoria and got more clients, which allowed us to increase our business activities. Unfortunately, the good times did not last long.

In 2015, Nigeria began to witness one of its worst economic recessions that created many problems for businessmen, including myself. The economic downturn actually began to set in later in the year. It became official in the economic report of the first quarter of 2016 when the economy saw a negative growth rate. One of the problems this recession caused was a sharp and unprecedented fall in the value of the naira which directly affected the exchange rate. Given that the raw materials Hi-Nutrients imports for producing premixes are dollar-denominated, this fall in the value of the naira impacted negatively on the company. Cost of procurement went up sharply, resulting in a number of unpalatable reactions from the local market, which had already contracted.

The problem was that, when this recession started, nobody knew that it would last for a period of fifteen months (covering five consecutive quarters), but that was what eventually happened. In fact, as late as August 2018, the Statistician-General of Nigeria and CEO of the National Bureau of Statistics reported that Nigeria was yet to recover from the 2016 recession. The recession which was so deep and so protracted came at the wrong time for me as a CEO. The economic recession robbed us of the gains of the UAC deal we had secured and turned our finances up-side-down. Things got so bad that we began to borrow just to stay afloat.

I tried to apply all the tricks I had been taught at the Lagos Business School to see if things would improve and I would be able to turn the situation around, but nothing really changed. To the best of my knowledge, I did my best. In fact, in doing my best, I sought for knowledge wherever I could find it. In pursuit of knowledge, I could remember my trip to the United State in 2008 in order to know how to successfully run a company at an international seminar hosted by Michael Gilbert when my company was over four years old. I did not want my company to die but, with the economic recession, it was appearing that it may die after everything.

Before I left the United States, Michael Gilbert gave me a book he had authored and asked me to use it as a guide for my business. He advised me to relate with the book in the same way the pastor of a church would with the Bible. The title is *The E-Myth Revisited: Why Most Small Businesses Don't Work And What To Do About It*. At the time Michael Gilbert was giving me that book, it had already sold more than one million copies. This should not be surprising because, Michael Gilbert was known as the world's number one small business guru at the time. I do not know if he still retains that status.

My encounter with Michael Gilbert was remarkable in many ways that it changed the course of my business. That trip was one of the most consequential trips of my business life and the reason for this is the significant knowledge that I gained from that encounter.

There were some specific things Michael Gilbert taught me during the three-day seminar and during the business clinic, which necessitated my interaction with him. The first thing he taught me was to see my business as my life. The second thing he said was that I should always nourish my business like a human body for optimum performance. Michael Gilbert also advised me against remaining in my comfort zone. He said I should be bothered when everything seemed rosy and juicy. I must confess that I found that counsel quite fascinating. The normal line of thought would be to work and hope that things would get quiet and predictable and nice, but Gilbert's advice was counterintuitive: he said I must learn to leave my comfort zone as soon as I notice that everything seemed ok. I was also told to try to do things differently from the way others do; especially, competitors who offered the same services or sold the same products.

Another thing that Michael Gilbert stressed was the need for staff training. He said that it would be unfair to blame staff for incompetence when they are not first trained to be proficient or knowledgeable. He noted that the attempt to train my staff, including myself, would open up opportunities for meeting people, increase knowledge, and provide answers to problems. He also stated that any entrepreneur who thought he knew it all would not subject himself to training, and that doing that might lead to the death of his or her company. One other interesting thing that Mr. Gilbert told me was not to hire people I could not fire when the situation warranted. "Never sell on credit" was also one of his rules of business. According to him, selling on credit was partly responsible for the death of some businesses.

He further warned me to manage scarce resources. He said that my ability to manage scarce resources will lead to the survival of Hi-Nutrients International Limited. According to him, I should consider my staff as my family members. This would enable them to deliver their best and be very loyal.

He assured me that the investment would eventually prove worthwhile because it would come to a time when my staff members would begin to see me as their father or their mother. This was not to mean that I should sacrifice discipline and general enforcement of rules and regulation. According to him, the best way to instill discipline is to be firm, consistent, impartial, and never emotional.

For seven years after meeting Michael Gilbert, I tried to follow his rules. In fact, my strict compliance to his rules earned me some enemies who felt offended with the way I handled things. Fortunately for me, I had seen the positive impact of my actions and was still hopeful that things would get better. In my private time, I was able to convince myself that what Hi-Nutrients was going through was not really a result of bad business practices. The problem was an external one, created by a change in political leadership in my country, and a shift in economic policy, which the global market was reacting to negatively. I dared to believe that things would get better. In the meantime, I had to pay the bills, and it was not the easiest thing to do when products were not being sold; when customers could neither place new orders nor pay for old ones; when there was no motivation in buying more products since it was clear that they would be sold at a great loss. The company I established 12 years previously was showing signs of imminent death.

A Nigerian bank came to our aid at the time, but interests on the loan we got from them continued to mount. Yet, I continued to run Hi-Nutrients with boldness and courage. After all, many bigger and older companies had folded up. I refused to close shop because I believed that the external factor responsible for the recession would not last forever. I kept taking risks. One particular risk I took was to accept a loan from Meristem Finance at 35% interest for a period of just six months. Even as I recall this, I wonder what would have happened if not for the miracle that occurred a few months after I had taken the loan. During this period, I was running from pillar to post just to ensure that Hi-Nutrients remained in business. UAC/Grand Cereals had renewed our supply contract, but the gains were redirected to financing loans and buying raw materials to produce products and sell at a loss. Hi-Nutrients was literally passing through the valley of the shadow of death.

At this point also, Senator Ladoja, being human, was beginning to show signs of fatigue. I would have felt the same way if I were in his shoes. But I must commend the man because he did not pull out of Hi-Nutrients at that juncture. If he had done so, that would have provided the final blow to cause the company to crumble. He held on but became shy of further financing.

To make matters worse, the Managing Director of Grand Cereals (Mr. Layi Oyatoki) became sick and was flown to Germany. This man was the main facilitator of our business relationship with Grand Cereals, after JID Dada introduced us to him. Although some persons liked to refer to me as Mr. Integrity, the MD of Grand Cereals was even more qualified to be called Mr. Integrity than I was. He had awarded Hi-Nutrients the supply contract based on merit and did not want the issue to muddle up with anything suggesting otherwise. He, therefore, warned me that, as penalty, he would end the business relationship between Grand Cereals and Hi-Nutrients if he ever learnt that I had given any sort of cash to any of his people. This was the best way to do business – to allow shareholders to get maximum benefits of business relations which their company formed with others, while staff members remained content with their salaries and bonuses. Nevertheless, not many people believed in that school of thought. No wonder, Grand Cereals staff and management remain ethical in their operations up till today. This tradition is actually in line with the core values of UAC itself, which takes pride in its commitment to corporate ethics. Like JID Dada (former Grand Cereals Managing Director), recently said, UAC is so committed to ethics that they would not make a claim they would not justify. He also said that, before many others began to do so, UAC was among the first companies that implemented a corporate governance tradition, which required employees to sign an undertaking at the beginning of every year asking that they be fired if ever caught collecting bribes. It was such a strong tradition that Layi Oyatoki was trying to ensure that it was not breached in my case.

While all this was going on, I did not know that the God I serve and to Whom I belong, was working behind the scenes to splash me one of the most pleasant surprises of my life. The linchpin of this miracle was Mr. Thiam Bayella. I had known Thiam Bayella for many years before this miracle I refer to. The last I knew about him before that time was that, he was the African Director of an American company known as Novus. Novus was a player in the agricultural sector that was involved in the manufacture of individual additives for the industry. The Nigerian agent of Novus is Norgem Nigeria Limited. I had been doing business with Norgem for years; in fact, I have a very good relationship with the Chairman of Norgem, Mrs. Nworga. I recently told a friend that I regard Mrs. Nworga the same way I regard my own elder sister, Mrs. Alice Odia. The current Managing Director of Norgem Nigeria Limited is Mrs. Nworga's daughter, Amaka, with whom I also have warm relations. As part of customer relations and confidence building, Mr. Thiam Bayella used to see me once in a while when he came to Nigeria to check on their agent, Norgem Nigeria Limited, but because I was one of the major customers of Norgem, this visit by Bayella was not unusual. So, I had known Bayella for quite a while. He always made sure I had enough raw materials from Norgem Nigeria Limited, some of which I traded and some of which I used for our own premix production.

As God would have it, Thiam Bayella had left Novus and had started working with a French company known as Neovia. Meanwhile, I had no idea that this was the case until one day when things wanted to get out of hand. I was not in the best mood on that particular day because I was still riling from a bitter experience I had. I will not be able to go into the details of that experience which involved a British national who was working with an international company, and with whom I had done business for many years, dating from when I was still working at Bio-Organics. This was a man I held in high esteem, whom we had steady and incremental business together. He was a man over the years, I would say has been considered a family friend. He was someone I could trust. But, my experience with him proved that absolute trust is dangerous.

Whether rightly or wrongly, most Africans grow up with the notion that white men are generally intelligent, honest, but irreligious. I have grown up to find out that the belief that white people do not take religion seriously is false. The second idea that white people are generally intelligent is correct, but only partially. Like every other race, the white race has its own share of stupid people. On the issue of honesty, it is true that you will find many white men who are quite honest, who detest dishonesty, and who will generally honour their word. This is as a result of good upbringing, and not as a white gene that predisposes white men to virtue. In a nutshell, it is not every human being with a white skin that subscribe to these ideals. Generalising is always a wrong thing which I paid heavily for about white men. The price was high and might have well involved the loss of my deal with Neovia. I just imagine what would have happened if I had refused to get out of my prejudiced mindset about white men in general.

The British national I am referring to was in some difficulty at some point and he pleaded with me to help him by linking him up with some people he knew I had such links with. He explained that, with the links, he would be spared from a potential messy situation that could affect his economic fortunes and change his standard of living for the worse. But if he had access to these people, he would not have needed me to link him up with them. We were in a hotel in the United Kingdom when he actually prostrated before me asking for my help. I am a Yoruba man and, to us, prostration is nothing but a sign of respect and submission. This British man, who had lived long enough in Nigeria to understand the meaning of his gesture, obviously wanted me to know that he was at his wits end. He was the first and only white man that have ever prostrated before me.

I complied with his request, not just because of his dire situation, but because he was a friend. However, for doing this, I had my fingers burnt. Only in retrospect did I get to realise that his breach of trust was premeditated. In order to activate the arrangement I had gone into with this British man, we needed to sign a Memorandum of Understanding. But this man brought out every trick to ensure that the signing was delayed. At some point, signing the MoU became a non-issue. I was actually fooled into believing that it was a non-issue because this man began to comply with our verbal agreement, and the terms and conditions stated in the unsigned MoU. After lulling me to sleep, I begin to understand that this Briton did not intend to uphold his end of the bargain. I wish I could give details of this experience because it caused me so much pain and great financial loss. I felt so stupid and careless because what was involved in this understanding was not less than ₦3b worth of business annually, from which I could have earned as much as ₦250m or more. I recently told someone that the mistake I made by going ahead with the contract without signing the MoU that would have defined our deal, was the worst mistake of my entire career as a businessman. I am ashamed to admit that I actually did this, even after attending the Lagos Business School and the EDC. My action was very unbecoming of a graduate of those prestigious institutions. I acted below my level of intelligence and what was partly responsible for this carelessness was the idea I had been groomed with; that white men were basically honest. On the other hand, the idea was also groomed into us that black men were basically dishonest. Both ideas had proven patently wrong in my experience. I believed this is why Senator Ladoja pointed out that my weakness is being an incurable optimist and too trusting. So, the Briton took advantage of me.

While I was still trying to recover from the pain of being burnt because I had trusted a white man, I received a call from Mr. Thiam Bayella. I remember that I was on Iwo road in Ibadan that day, still trying to do the little I could; but the handwriting on the wall was that, except something monumentally positive happened, the days of Hi-Nutrients International Limited were numbered. To be frank, things had become so bad by this time that Hi-Nutrients was finding it very difficult to repay loans, even as other loans matured. It got so bad that it was only a matter of time before the company would go under.

So, at a time, when I did not want to hear anything about white men in general, Mr. Thiam Bayella told me on the phone that he was no longer working with Novus but was now working with a French company called Neovia. Moreover, Bayella said that his new company, Neovia, was interested in investing in Hi-Nutrients through a merger and acquisition deal. This meant only one thing: I would need to sell some of the shares of Hi-Nutrients to Neovia, and Neovia will pump in money and become part owner of the company.

On any other day, what Bayella told me would have been a good and even highly exciting news. After all, I had deliberately set up Hi-Nutrients International Limited to make it attractive to prospective international investors, and this was in perfect alignment with my goal for the company. You will recall that I had three key goals, one of which was to ensure that my company became a multinational within twenty years of its establishment. In fact, I had deliberately launched a bold propaganda campaign in 2014, using the opportunity of the 10th year anniversary of Hi-Nutrients. I wanted to tell the world that Hi-Nutrients had come of age. I wanted to make a statement, and I spent over ₦12m to make that statement.

The venue of the 2014 anniversary celebration was the new ultra-modern factory of Hi-Nutrients, to which we had relocated from our first factory, located at Ogba. A few months before the 10th year anniversary celebration, Hi-Nutrients International Limited had been selected as one of the 50 fastest growing companies in Nigeria by the Tony Elumelu Foundation, in conjunction with the AllWorld Network. With the momentum gained from that international award (validated by the fact that AllWorld Network is chaired by Harvard Business School Professor, Michael Porter), I made arrangements to ensure that our 10th year anniversary did not pass by quietly. I was determined to make some noise, which I succeeded in doing.

All the banks in Nigeria were represented at that event, the Director General of NAFDAC was there in person; the Director General of the Standards Organisation of Nigeria was there in his personal capacity; the federal government of Nigeria was represented by a Director in the Federal Ministry of Agriculture; several foreign companies that were stakeholders in the agricultural sector were also at the event. In fact, Huvepharma sent their representatives all the way from Belgium to that event. I also used the event to launch raw materials for premix production worth ₦700m.

One of the reasons I decided to use the 10th year anniversary of Hi-Nutrients to launch raw materials was that some of our competitors were engaged in a campaign of calumny against us, claiming that we did not have enough raw materials and did not even have a factory. This claim was preposterous, but still, I did not want to take chances. I could have held this event at the Sheraton Hotel or any other hotel or facility in Lagos. My decision to hold it right on the grounds of our ultra-modern factory was strategic. I wanted my competitors and all the stakeholders in the industry to see for themselves that Hi-Nutrients was the major player. I displayed raw materials to the guests at the event and the reaction was swift. Even before the end of that event, things had begun to swing. I also felt that, there was a need to show some of our big customers that there was no need for them to continue to import things we could comfortably produce. After all, we have the raw materials to do so. I was keen to display our massive capacity so that, just in case some of our big clients were attempting to include importation in their business plan, they could have a rethink.

The strategy worked. I recall that it was shortly after our 10th year anniversary that Impextraco Belgium came to Nigeria, as a result of the direct fallout of that 10th year anniversary. A young man known as Oladipo Kayode was the person that started Impextraco in Nigeria in early 2015. Interestingly, Kayode had worked briefly with Bio-Organics before that time. He worked with Bio-Organics from October 2012 to around February 2015 before starting Impextraco in Nigeria. He is today the West Africa Representative of the company. Kayode has openly admitted that Hi-Nutrients was a stabilising factor for Impextraco when they started here. Indeed, I was one of his first key customers and I know that I did a large order with Impextraco in 2015. I actually gave Kayode my first order when we met in Atlanta, United States. Basically, Impextraco imports individual vitamins and minerals, and other additives used for premix and feed manufacturing.

Kayode later told his bosses at Impextraco that I was credit worthy and that they should not hesitate to give me anything I wanted. He said I was in charge of the industry. Such recommendations were moving around industry circles to the extent that, anytime I went for international conferences, some participants would be referring to me as the biggest premix manufacturer in Nigeria. The point to note is that, this was all post-2014 – specifically after that remarkable 10th year anniversary. Neovia would later confess to me that it was from such sources that they got to know about the true status of Hi-Nutrients as the leader of the premix industry in Nigeria. Of course, they had to conduct a thorough investigation to confirm that kind of second-hand information.

I also used the 10th year anniversary event to give loyalty awards to some special clients who had patronised us and stuck with us over the years, apart from distinguishing themselves by the sheer volume of business they did with us. The award was titled, Best Supporting Partner Award. All our top 25 clients were qualified and all of them got the award.

I recall that the anniversary lecture was delivered by my friend and mentor, Mr. Abiodun Toki, who is a friend of my former Managing Director, Dr. Acholonu. Mr. Abiodun played crucial role in our training while I was working at Bio-Organics. Up till this very day, I remember how wonderful, meaningful, and inspiring that anniversary lecture was. Abiodun Toki played a significant and crucial role in my training because it was his company that consulted for Bio-Organics in all matters of staff training. He personally told me that he began to take interest in me because I often did excellently well during appraisal tests, which his company conducted periodically for staff members of Bio-Organics.

It was after that 10th year anniversary event that the table finally turned full swing, as far as the fortunes of Hi-Nutrients was concerned. We began to dominate the market in a new way. Most of the major users of premixes decided to begin to do business with Hi-Nutrients. This was how Hi-Nutrients secured not less than 50% of the premix market in Nigeria, cementing its position as the leader. With that happening, I knew it was only a matter of time before some smart investor would come knocking. But when this dream was beginning to come true, I was in the worst possible mood.

Given the fact that Thiam Bayella was a fellow African, I could open up to him as a brother, while I refer to the white man as an outsider. I told Bayella not to mind all these white men who claimed that they wanted to come and invest in Africa. For some reasons, I could not explain the situation with the Briton to Bayella, but the negative effect of that experience was clear in my conversation with him. I told Bayella that white men only related with blacks when they needed to tap some information; but after that, they treated you like scum. Bayella disagreed.

After listening to my harsh words, Thiam Bayella knew that, except he got through to me, the intended merger and acquisition between Neovia and Hi-Nutrients International Limited was going to be dead on arrival. I was the alpha and omega, as far as Hi-Nutrients was concerned. I was the only person who could decide the future of the company and if for any reason, I refused to sell the controlling shares of Hi-Nutrients, there was nothing anybody could do about it.

So Bayella calmed me down and tried to talk some sense into me. For starters, he assured me that Neovia was a credible company with an international reputation. Neovia was certainly not trying to get information from me with no intention to do real business. Bayella also assured me that Neovia had actually been operating in Africa for over 20 years through export and local affiliates. They had no reason to do anything that would besmirch their image and damage the reputation they had built for so long. I later got to understand that the reason Neovia was interested in Hi-Nutrients was because they wanted to rapidly develop their own brand of premix, known as Wisium, which is an international premix brand already present in more than 50 countries of the world. The idea was for the Wisium brand of premix to complement the already recognised technical know-how of Hi-Nutrients' Hi-Mix® brand, so as to provide an innovative product tailored to the specific needs of the Nigerian market.

Bayella averred that Neovia was quite serious about its interest in Nigeria and Africa as a whole. He made me to understand that the proposed deal was real and that I could trust him. He reminded me of the support I gave to him by patronising Novus products through Norgem Nigeria Limited. He further explained that he had no reason to reward me badly by leading me up the garden path and introducing me to a company with questionable integrity. He said he was the African Business Development Director of Neovia and that, whatever he was claiming, I could safely take to the bank.

It was not that I was not interested in a merger; I guess my mindset was so poisoned by the experience with the Briton already referred to, so I wasn't thinking straight. Looking back, I can hardly believe the amount of prejudice I had developed against white men in general, based on the bitter experience with just a white man. People should learn not to stereotype because it is not only dangerous, but also counterproductive. Now that I know Neovia as a real, good, and credible multinational company, I cannot imagine what my prejudice would have caused me. I prefer not to even think about it.

To further convince me, Bayella said that Neovia was different. They were ready to come to Africa; develop our country and help us leave a legacy for our people. He said that God had put me in a position to do something that would be good, not just for me as an individual, but also for my country, Nigeria, and even for Africa as a whole. He passionately urged me to join him and make the merger work. In trying to persuade me about a deal that was, frankly, for my good and the good of my company, Thiam Bayella was not frantic; he was clearly determined not to allow me to make a bad decision. In his view, turning down Neovia was not only going to prove a bad decision but also a horrible one. Thiam Bayella went on to say that the successful merger of Neovia and Hi-Nutrients would transform Nigeria.

The least I could do after Bayella's presentation was to agree to think about the matter. I certainly had not agreed to go ahead with the merger, but I had become open to the possibility. So, I did not deceive Bayella by telling him that I was game and ready to roll: I simply told him that we would continue the discussion the following day.

Shortly before this slow-motion miracle began with that fateful call from Thiam Bayella, my wife and two others had categorically told me about seeing a vision where I was in the midst of some white men. So, I went and told her about my conversation with Bayella. First, I told her that it seemed the vision she had shared with me was becoming a reality. She wondered what I was talking about and I told her about my phone conversation with Bayella. Instead of asking further questions, my wife simply went on her knees and began to offer a prayer of thanksgiving to God. She thanked God for confirming the word He had already told her. Like I stated, she had seen a vision of me working with white men and had also related the vision to me.

When she rose up from giving thanks to God, she said I should go ahead with the merger and assured me that Neovia were the people she had been told about. The sign was that it was the foreign company that was going to call Hi-Nutrients, and not the other way round. I had been making efforts to get an international investor, but the vision my wife had categorically showed that it was the investors that called Hi-Nutrients. Since that condition had been perfectly fulfilled, my wife was 100% sure that the merger of Neovia with Hi-Nutrients had received divine approval even before it was officially initiated by that call from Thiam Bayella.

When Bayella called the second day, I told him that I had decided to give the merger deal a trial. Bayella did not like the idea of a 'trial' deal. He retorted and said that the deal was not a trial but very much a reality. He was eager to make me see that this deal was not about anything other than business expansion for Neovia and business development for Hi-Nutrients. Nobody was trying to play games here. Bayella did not know that I was having a jaundiced view due to an experience I was still recovering from. As long as the owners of Neovia were white men, Bayella needed to work extra hard to make me see and accept obvious things.

I eventually acquiesced to Bayella's argument and asked him to tell his company to send a letter of intent to Hi-Nutrients. Things were now moving from semi-formal to purely formal, because a merger and acquisition deal was a highly complex business procedure that had to be well managed. I knew that, and Bayella knew that too.

At last, my dream was coming to pass, and the most interesting aspect was that, it was coming to pass at my worst moment. I could not help but notice the irony. It was also exciting to note that I was over six years early in the fulfilment of this dream. Not wanting anything to go wrong, I therefore, decided to be as thorough as possible. First, I needed to speak with the Chairman of the Board of Directors of Hi-Nutrients, Senator Rashidi Adewolu Ladoja. There were some chairmen of Boards of Directors that could be pushed around. This sort of people served at the whims and caprices of the company owners; but Senator Ladoja was not in that class. Not only did I personally respect him as a Nigerian political leader who had served the nation as a senator and as a governor, I actually loved the man enough to have adopted him as my father. So, I needed to handle his feelings with care. I also needed to be sure that he was with me as I approached a key milestone in my life.

Part of Senator Ladoja's credentials for earning such a special place in my heart was the fact that he appreciated me when I did something for him and even offered to help me. You will recall that I first met Senator Ladoja only because he had asked to see me. And he had asked to see me because of the good report he had received about me from his son. Some other person would have acted differently, but this man chose to thank me in person to the extent that he asked me if there was anything I wanted him to do for me. I consider such a person a rare gem and have always held him in high esteem. To add to this, there was the fact that he secured a huge loan from a new generation bank to enable me to seal the deal that changed the fortunes of my company. Now that there was talk of a merger, I needed to carry him along. I was so happy that he accepted the idea without much scruple, and was even excited about it.

Senator Ladoja was so impressed that I was able to pull off such a thing and he wondered what Neovia had seen in Hi-Nutrients. We later did some analysis and came to the conclusion that, apart from being the market leader, Hi-Nutrients' brand of excellent products must also have been a factor. It was also a fact that I had a lot of international travel experiences. By this time,

I had already patented and registered up to 12 products, all of which were doing well in the market. I was also an opinion leader in the Nigerian livestock industry as a whole. It was viewed that all these must have been taken into consideration because no foreign company would make such a move without thorough investigation.

Having secured the green light from the Chairman of Hi-Nutrients' Board of Directors, I replied Bayella's letter of intent and requested that the merger and acquisition process should commence. Shortly after that, I got an official letter from Neovia proposing a timetable of activities that would culminate with the merger of Neovia and Hi-Nutrients and the acquisition of the latter by the former.

The nature of a merger is based on trust and on effective resilient communication; nothing less would do. Since I had never gone through the process of a merger before, except theoretically through the analysis available in case studies, I decided to reach out to people I knew would be able to help by way of advice. There were some people that I already knew would have to play an active role in the merger and acquisition process. Persons like the company's accountant, the company's lawyer, and even Dr. Gbenga Oluyemi, who had played a role in my first visit to France almost ten years before the merger process was initiated.

Dr. Oluyemi is a fellow of the College of Veterinary Surgeons of Nigeria. He could not only speak French fluently, but also had been in the industry for donkey's years. As far back as when I was still an employee at Bio-Organics, Dr. Oluyemi was a competitor of Bio-Organics already because, he was involved in premix production through a company known as Shepherd Nutrition Limited. Since the early days of Hi-Nutrients, I have been doing business with Dr. Oluyemi, who later became the Nigerian and Ghanaian agent of a French company known as Rhone Poulenc Nutrition Animale. Rhone Poulenc produced the raw materials required by Hi-Nutrients and other companies for premix production.

After graduating from the university, Dr. Oluyemi worked briefly with the Ondo State Ministry of Agriculture before he went ahead to work as a farm manager in one of the largest poultry farms in Nigeria at the time. That was in 1982 and the farm had over 100, 000 layers. Then he went to the International Laboratory for Research in Animal Diseases in Nairobi, Kenya, for a joint experiment with the University of Glasgow, Scotland. It was the result of that experiment that Dr. Oluyemi presented to the Federal University of Technology, Akure, for his Masters' degree thesis. Interestingly, by obtaining his Master's degree at FUTA in 1986, he became the first Master's degree graduate of that school.

After lecturing briefly at FUTA, Dr. Oluyemi was employed by international drug manufacturer, May & Baker. This employment was based on the work he had done at the International Laboratory at Kenya, and his connection with the University of Glasgow, which sponsored the research. He became the Product Manager of May & Baker and retained that position until 1991, when he was promoted to become the first Divisional Manager in charge of the newly created Animal Nutrition Division of May & Baker.

While at May & Baker, Dr. Oluyemi witnessed and even partook in several merger and acquisition deals, which explains my decision to make him a core member of the team I put together to oversee the merger of Hi-Nutrients with Neovia. First, May & Baker was bought over by Rhone Poulenc Nigeria Limited – the same French company that Oluyemi later served as agent to, for both Nigeria and Ghana. Actually, it was the animal nutrition department (and every other aspect of May & Baker not directly related to pharmaceuticals) that was bought over by Rhone Poulenc Nigeria Limited, which later became

Rodia Nigeria Limited. It was when Rhone Poulenc became Rodia that he exited the company and began to work with Shepherd Nutrition.

In 2001, Dr. Oluyemi founded Vivax Limited and I was able to work with him when I founded Hi-Nutrients International Limited because I knew that Vivax was the agent of Rhone Poulenc. Knowing he had seen it, all, there was no way he was not going to be part of the merger talks, especially because of his experience with the French. To show how much confidence I had in Dr. Oluyemi, I insisted on his going along with me to attend my very first meeting with the CEO of Neovia in Abuja. I remember we worked together until 2am on the eve of that meeting, preparing slides for the presentation that was to be made to Neovia. Drawing from his experiences, he was able to correctly anticipate the sort of questions that would be in the heart of a typical French investor, and we were able to scale through that meeting unscathed.

Dr. Oluyemi was literally on fire, as far as the merger deal was concerned. He recently confessed that he was so committed because, in interesting Neovia to merge and acquire Hi-Nutrients, I had succeeded in achieving the exact thing he had wanted to achieve years ago which he could not. I was so touched by this man's honesty and sincerity, and was better able to understand why he had taken the merger and acquisition of Neovia and Hi-Nutrients personally. Dr. Oluyemi's dream for his professional career was, in his own words, to attract foreign DNA into the Nigerian business environment. He felt it was his duty to help me in making that a reality. Better than others, he knew the impact this would have on Nigeria and on Africa as a whole.

The timetable I had received from Bayella contained what I would like to refer to as a programme of activities. One of the key issues in the programme of activities was the due diligence exercise, which was going to cover six areas, namely: Legal, Tax Accounting, Human Relations, Information Technology, and Industrial. I soon got to realise that foreign investors generally took the issue of tax very seriously. Fortunately for us, we were not wanting in that area.

Mr. Alarapon, my banker, was the first person I called. After verbally telling him about the conversation with Bayella and what was about to happen, I forwarded him the letter of intent. When he saw the letter, he called me back and basically told me that God had answered our prayers and that this merger deal actually meant the end of struggles for Hi-Nutrients International Limited. Mr. Alarapon knew what he was talking about; since there was really nothing about Hi-Nutrients that he did not know. He was an insider in the company and I remember the circumstances that had brought us together.

In 2010, Mr. Alarapon was the branch manager of the Ijebu-Ode branch of Stanbic IBTC Bank. The main reason I opened a bank account at that branch was that, I had some customers in the area that I supply products. At a time, I felt that it was better to have a bank near them so that our financial interaction would be more convenient for all concerned. Shortly after he began to manage the branch, Mr. Alarapon sat me down one day and tried to know how he could be of help to me in my business. First of all, he made me to understand that he studied Agricultural Economics in the higher institution and that, by virtue of his knowledge and his understanding of the agricultural business in general, it was not every banker that could support me. For a banker to work effectively with me, such would need to understand commercial banking as well as understand certain aspects of the agricultural business. He explained that, as a player in the agricultural value chain, my company, Hi-Nutrients International Limited, actually stood astride both the agricultural and manufacturing sectors.

Mr. Alarapon took a look at my LPOs and realised that I had some big customers as patrons. There was Obasanjo Farms, there was Rainbow Feeds, and even Amo Byng. He then offered to help me. At the end of what I would call intensive discussions, he influenced his bank to open a credit line of ₦10m for me, and that was nothing short of a lifeline at the time. I later improved upon this modest beginning and was able to get a credit line running into hundreds of millions of naira. In fact, in less than two years, I used the ₦10m credit line opened by Stanbic IBTC Bank to do a turnover of over ₦500m. Since that time, he has not stopped supporting Hi-Nutrients. In fact, I am aware that he actually put his job on the line for my sake in order to secure that first ₦10m credit line. The man was so ready to help me that he told his superiors that if I failed to pay back, he should be fired. Fortunately, I did not default, and there was never a need for Mr. Alarapon to lose his job.

After hearing what I had to say about the interest of Neovia in acquiring Hi-Nutrients, Mr. Alarapon was unabashedly excited. He actually said that, if successful, the deal with Neovia would make things a million times easier for Hi-Nutrients, and I knew what he was referring to. Since 2010 when we initially made contact, there was virtually nothing about the financial situation of Hi-Nutrients that Mr. Alarapon was not privy to. He knew that, even at that moment, we were virtually on life support. The offer of investment from Neovia could not have come at a better time. I was not just calling Mr. Alarapon to tell him about the possible merger and acquisition deal, I had called him because I needed his advice on how to proceed. Without missing a beat, he asked me to talk with one Dr. Toye Sofayo who was the Managing Director of Toye Sofayo and Associates Consultants. He said that Dr. Sofayo was based in Lagos and could come and see me if I was ready. Mr. Alarapon and I agreed that I should speak with Dr. Sofayo first on phone, after which he agreed to come and see me.

When Dr. Sofayo showed up in my office, the first question he asked me after we exchanged pleasantries was how well I knew Neovia. Before his visit, I had already gone through Neovia's website to understand what sort of business they were engaged in. So, I told Dr. Sofayo some of the things I had read and complemented that with the many things Thiam Bayella had told me about the company. I also told Dr. Sofayo about the positive implications of the merger for me as an individual; for my country, Nigeria; and for Africa at large. I added that I felt comfortable with the idea of the merger and would like to go ahead. Besides, I had secured the permission of the Chairman of the Board of Directors of Hi-Nutrients and could count on his support through the process.

After listening to my response, Dr. Sofayo said that, for us to move ahead with the process, we needed to set up a team he tagged the Hi-Nutrients Merger and Acquisition Team. He said that the issue of a merger and acquisition was so complex and multifaceted that it could not be done by a single individual or even a single firm. We talked about a legal expert on the team and I tried to assure Dr. Sofayo that I had a company lawyer. While he did not doubt me, he said that, for the merger and acquisition process, my company lawyer may not be enough to constitute the legal team. It was his view that I needed a lawyer with specialty in commercial law. For tax matters, I also needed a specialist, but Dr. Sofayo was a tax consultant and could deal with the tax issues that the process would throw up. Apart from legal and tax experts, we also needed a chartered accountant and an expert in human relations, who will produce a Human Relations Policy for Hi-Nutrients. Dr. Sofayo also explained the due diligence requirements under the headings of information technology and industrial matters.

At the end, we constituted a merger and acquisition team comprising myself (as Managing Director of Hi-Nutrients International Limited), Dr. Toye Sofayo, Mr. Adekunle Frank Alarapon, Dr. Gbenga Oluyemi, Barrister Ayodeji Acquah, and Henry Odiachi. Henry was our accountant at Hi-Nutrients. The only stranger in the group, as far as I was concerned, was Dr. Toye Sofayo. As already stated, I had known Dr. Oluyemi for years before this merger and acquisition deal came up. I had also known Mr. Alarapon for at least seven years before that time. Barrister Ayodeji was my company lawyer and we had been working together for some time. As for Henry Odiachi, the accountant on the team, our history is an interesting one.

I first met Henry at Bio-Organics. He was employed in 1999, just about a year after I made my own entrance. To cut a long story short, my relationship with Henry was so solid at Bio-Organics that, when I left in 2003, he began to offer me freelance accounting services as early as 2006. It would seem that, by this date, his spirit was already at Hi-Nutrients International Limited, even though his body was still at Bio-Organics. The body eventually joined the spirit in 2009, when Henry became the Financial Consultant of Hi-Nutrients. Henry has remained the head of the accounting department since that time. The best evidence that I trust him as much as I trust his intellect was the fact that he was included in the merger and acquisition team. As I have been stating, my key goal for Hi-Nutrients, *ab initio*, was to ensure that it ended up as a multinational company. The offer from Neovia meant the fulfilment of that long held dream and there was no way I was going to trifle with such a thing. So, Henry enjoyed my utmost confidence and trust: and that was why he was on that team.

As a person, I value the opinion of others. This is perhaps because I realise that I do not know it all, in spite of my desire to know it all and my keen interest in gaining knowledge. So, I always take advantage of insight from qualified persons whenever the opportunity presented itself. Sometime before the offer from Neovia, I had met the renowned Nigerian lawyer and civil rights activist, Mr. Femi Falana (SAN). I am proud to claim him as my mentor, brother and homeboy because, for those who do not know, Mr. Falana is from the land of professors and achievers – Ekiti State. I met him at the French embassy where I had gone to do some paper work in connection with a trip I wanted to embark on at the time. Although it was a short meeting, Femi Falana later told me that, within the fifteen minutes of our interaction, his opinion about me was cast in stone. He said he quickly concluded that I was a cerebral fellow, an achiever, and an employer of labour. The man was very happy when he saw the deep and abiding passion I had for Ekiti State and its development. We maintained contact since that first meeting and I felt it would be right to inform him about the impending merger of Hi-Nutrients with Neovia. Femi Falana is a lawyer of international repute and a Senior Advocate of Nigeria: I knew that his counsel would come in handy.

When I informed Falana about the offer from Neovia, he was not only excited, but was also committed to the issue that he told me to seek his counsel whenever I needed it with the promise that he would not collect a dime. He said he liked me as a person and liked what I had achieved in bringing a multinational company to Nigeria. In fact, when I later took some political pamphlets to him to intimate him of my aspiration to contest for the position of a Member of the Federal House of Representatives, he wasted no time in discouraging me. He said I should rather focus on the merger and acquisition with Neovia, with the assurance that a successful merger was far more crucial and beneficial than the seat of a Member of the Federal House of Representatives in Nigeria's National Assembly. I kept Mr. Falana in the loop of the merger talks by going to his office to brief him once in a while.

To provide back-up for my in-house accountant, I also worked with Wale Onigbode, whom I had known for years. Wale is the Managing Director of Calyx Finance House and has been a helper, a mentor, an inspiration, a brother, and a friend, for years. I cannot forget a time when this man was so interested in my success that, after giving me a loan and noticed that I was having difficulty in paying back, he went outside the rules of engagement and told me to take it easy. He would give me time to do things at my pace, always telling me that he knew that I was going to succeed and would soon be in a position to pay with ease, if given time. Such understanding from a financial expert is not only unusual but was also unheard of: but Wale Onigbode treated me that way. Only the God I serve will reward him and people like him, who are the real secret of my meteoric rise. My belief is that God positioned those people for my benefit. There was nothing I could have used to secure their favour at the time they extended it to me. It was simply a miracle.

At last, the merger and acquisition team began to work. We met twice weekly to analyse issues and delegate new tasks. Things moved forward from both sides of the divide until June 2018, when I can say we actually crossed an important bridge. A few things still need to be sorted out, but, the merger is a done deal today. The story would, however, not be complete, without a mention of the contributions of the accounting genius known as Layi Oyatoki.

The fact was that, like in the case of Mr. Femi Falana, I also worked with an outside consultant in the person of the former Managing Director of Grand Cereals, Mr. Layi Oyatoki, even though Layi's participation was more active. The role Mr. Oyatoki played in the merger and acquisition of Hi-Nutrients and Neovia was very crucial and more or less, one of the most important. But it was not just that alone, he did more; but for reasons beyond my control, I cannot divulge the particular role he played. All I can say is that, without Layi Oyatoki's contribution, the merger would have turned bitter in my mouth after I had signed the papers ceding Hi-Nutrients' shares to Neovia. Layi was the one who advised me on some of the parameters I needed to use in completing a very critical merger-related task. But I was not surprised about Layi's ability in playing a role at this international level. Even the former Managing Director of Grand Cereals, Joe Dada, has openly said that Layi Oyatoki was one of the best accountants he had ever encountered in his 35 years career. According to Joe Dada, unlike most accountants who seemed to have a streamlined view, Layi had a business mindset; he had a way of looking at issues from a broader perspective than one would find in an average accountant. Layi was not average in any sense at all. He was in a class of his own. He was a thinker; an engineer of some sorts in the world of accounting.

Unfortunately, it feels so sad to report that, in spite of what he did in pushing this merger and acquisition in the right direction, Mr. Layi Oyatoki, my brother, friend and helper, did not live long enough to see the deal concluded. Layi was snatched away by the cruel hands of death in April 2018, after battling with a health condition that ravaged him for a year and caused all his true friends real pains, shock and distress. For those who knew him, Layi Oyatoki was such a great guy. His former boss, Joe Dada, recently confessed with sombre and forlorn looks that he always thought about Layi. That was the sort of person Layi was. His loss is one of the greatest losses many of us who knew him have ever endured. The man, Layi, like Daniel in the Bible, certainly had an excellent spirit. Layi's death has only added to the mysterious reality many people have come to accept: it does seem that exceptionally good people do not last long in this world.

Layi had gone and left a great vacuum that can never be filled. I believe that even UAC and Grand Cereals Limited are feeling the pinch of Layi's departure. As a Christian, my only consolation about the painful and unexpected death of Layi Oyatoki is that God knows best. God knows why Layi had to leave us at the height of his powers and at a time when his star was set to shine brighter than ever. By way of honour, I hereby dedicate the successful merger and acquisition of Hi-Nutrients International Limited by Neovia of France to the memory of Mr. Layi Oyatoki – a great man who lived a great life and positively affected the lives of others.

Furthermore, the new man at the helm of affairs at Grand Cereals now is Alhaji Murktar Yakassai, a highly intelligent man whom I trust to take Grand Cereals to the highest level.

CHAPTER 13

BUKKY: MY DEPENDABLE INTERCESSOR

My success story is incomplete without acknowledging the constribution of my wife, Bukola. She has been the secret of my success in many ways than one. Today, it is my settled opinion that, in spite of the challenges, the ups and the downs, and the fact that she is not perfect, coupled with the fact that she did not marry an angel in human form, Oluwabukola Florence Adetoyi and I were meant to live as husband and wife. I believe that I was made for her, and that she was also made for me.

You will notice that, all through this book, my friends and I were not the type of guys that saw ladies as fair game, to be hunted and haunted, used, and then dumped. I am forever grateful that I had very good upbringing. I did not allow myself to be distracted by the youthful exuberance that deceived young men to believe that, in order to prove their virility, they had to waste their time having flings with women.

I proposed marriage to Bukky during the wedding of her closest cousin, Ayo. The process through which I had the courage to do that shows the power of God's providence in linking lives. But this was not because she was desperate for marriage, or because I was too handsome to be kept waiting. Indeed, we did have a long relationship running from our days in Otun. But we did not really have close intimacy in Otun, until when I started visiting Bukky's house in Ilorin while still a student of the University of Ilorin.

Bukky did not accept to marry me because I was rich. At the very time that she agreed to be my wife, there was another man in her life. If we attempt to compare social standing at that time (which, honestly, we shouldn't), the man actually had an edge over me. While I was working in Bio-Organics and was receiving a salary of ₦13, 500 (not a bad amount at that time), he was working with Chevron Petroleum Company, which was one of the best places any young man could work in Nigeria at the time, Bukky must have loved and respected me to have agreed to be my wife, but there was another factor that I must not fail to recognise in order to give a well-rounded narrative.

I have come to accept the reality that Bukky is a praying woman. She picked up this very helpful habit from her father, who could only be described as a prayer warrior. Before Mr. Atolani died in 2005, he seemed to have lived his life praying – and then doing other things if there was time left after prayers. His was not a usual case. He prayed many nights in a typical week, and one could only wonder at what time he had the opportunity to sleep. He would pray from midnight till daybreak and still be the first to wake up. Unfortunately for Bukky and her sisters, the man did not like the idea of seeing them sleep beyond a certain hour in the morning: so he would wake them up for frivolous assignments like going to get him a cup of water. And if he noticed that they were still groggy and planning to return to bed after that first task, he would come up with another equally needless task, and yet another, until he mercilessly drove the sleep out of their eyes.

Bukky and her sisters became early risers as a result of their father's grilling. When Bukky gradually transmuted into a prayer warrior herself, this already ingrained habit of rising early became consolidated and served as a boon to her new-found hobby. Today, she routinely attends prayer vigils and still carries on her daily assignments the subsequent day without missing a bit. I am not complaining because her prayerful life has impacted me positively to the extent that I have learnt to actually seek her intercession whenever I find myself in a crisis.

When I proposed marriage to her around late 1999, I had no idea that Bukky was already in a very close but still platonic friendship with her co-worker at the company that made the very popular and highly successful BAGCO super sack. She had secured the job with the company after concluding her HND in Accounting from the Kwara State Polytechnic. This friendly relationship was already many months old and was nearing maturation by the time I made my move.

About a year before I would ask for her hand in marriage, Bukky's co-worker, Kunle, had moved in for the kill and enacted a relationship with her, which only had one purpose in view – marriage. Kunle was a decent young man whose intention to make Bukky his wife was neither criminal nor impertinent. Like myself, he had every right to this intention, and, from all indications, he was sincere. In fact, things began to build towards a possible marriage between the two, even though Bukky was just holding out and waiting for divine confirmation. That was her style, as I have come to realise. The will of God is very critical in every step she chooses or declines to take. But Kunle was building to a climax, and their relationship was growing day after day. As evidence for this, Bukky's elder brother, Lanre, knew Kunle; her paternal aunt in Lagos also knew him. Several friends on both sides knew them as very close friends. Because of their strong Christian background, everybody expected that, for them to be unabashed about relating openly only meant that they were considering marriage. Besides, these were days when morality still formed part of the fabric of the society; not these days when nothing seems to matter.

According to Bukky, she was just about to accept Kunle's proposal for marriage – after months of ardent prayers, night vigils, and fasting for direction and confirmation – when I suddenly ambushed her at Ayo's wedding and audaciously asked her to be my wife. It seems that, by that time, Kunle had left BAGCO super sack and was already working with Chevron. Bukky knew that I was working with Bio-Organics and, still, she wasted no time in agreeing to marry me instead of Kunle. Before that time, Bukky and I used to meet at her aunt's place. Anytime I went there, under the shadow of my friendship with her elder brother Lanre, it was Bukky herself that served me refreshment. But we were more like siblings. To fully unravel the mystery behind Bukky's decision to choose me instead of Kunle, we must return to her prayer life.

Naturally, people who pray a lot also like attending prayer meetings. Bukky had attended a prayer meeting for about a year before I proposed to her. It was at that meeting which was anchored by one Pastor Kalejaiye of the Redeemed Christian Church that the Pastor's wife came up with a prophesy which impacted on her life. A prophesy is supposed to be a kind of supernatural information received from God and then shared with a group through a specific member of that group – usually the pastor – or a member of the group gifted with a gift known as the word of knowledge.

At some point when Pastor Kalejaiye's wife was speaking to the group of young people who had gathered for the meeting, she seemed to have walked close to where Bukky was seated, but not addressing Bukky directly. She prophesied that someone was going to receive a marriage proposal from a person that was not a stranger. The case would be so shocking because that person proposing would be well-known and definitely not a stranger. The prophesy instructed that this proposal was not to be declined because it was a divine arrangement. Bukky's cousin, Ayo, was also at that meeting but neither Ayo nor Bukky ever thought about me for a second.

Incidentally, it was shortly after that prophesy at the youth programme that Kunle had made his move. This move by Kunle brought some confusion to Bukky, especially because it came after her encounter at the prayer meeting and seemed to suggest that Kunle was the man in question. However, the prophesy stated categorically that the person would be a very close person, known for a long time. As far as Bukky was concerned, she did not think that Kunle could be described as someone she had known very well for some time; at least, not to the degree she felt the prophesy had emphasized. She had just met Kunle at BAGCO and he just happened to be a co-worker.

Being a wise and courteous lady, Bukky did not just chase Kunle off – neither did she accede to his request – but she spent the period praying and asking God for direction. After intense prayer for confirmation from God, Bukky did not get any clear response. This only propelled her to intensify her prayers. Up until the day I waylaid Bukky at Ayo's wedding, there was no answer from God about Kunle.

Shortly after my proposal to Bukky, right at the venue of the wedding, I asked for her date of birth which I did not know before then, in spite of our acquaintance for so long. She told me she was born on the 22nd of December and I nodded. I expected her to have asked for my birthday also, but she did not. So I asked her why she had not also asked me for my birthday. Perhaps just to satisfy my demand, she proceeded to ask, and I told her that my birthday was 2nd of February. She later confessed that she had thought that I just wanted to get her a birthday gift; but that was far from it, at least from God's point of view.

Under terrible tension caused by the fact that she had just got to know my date of birth, Bukky ignored the fact that her cousin, Ayo, had just married his bride. She called him several times that very day of his wedding, moments after facing my tribunal. She needed to talk to someone, and there was nobody better than Ayo to share her dilemma with. Although she was very close to her elder brother, Lanre, it was too early to bring such a matter to him. She felt safer in that instance with Ayo, who would listen to her but not scold her.

As at the day of Ayo's wedding, this was the summary of Bukky's situation: in spite of getting a clear prophesy about a year ago concerning her marriage and the circumstances that would help her identify her divinely ordained husband, she now had two men asking for her hand in marriage. As if that was not enough, by asking and knowing my birthday, her confusion got multiplied because she already knew that Kunle was born on the 2nd of February. Getting to know my birthday now meant that she had received a prophesy about a coming marriage proposal, but the two men who had asked for her hand in marriage after that prophesy were both born on the 2nd of February.

Talk about original confusion and here was a genuine case of it. But the Bible says that God is not the author of confusion; He is rather the author of peace.

If Bukky had never prayed in her life before, she definitely prayed this time around. When she met Ayo a week after his wedding on this matter, there was nothing Ayo could say other than that she should pray harder. If not for the prophesy that Bukky had received before meeting Kunle, no one can predict what would have happened and how she may have handled his proposal. There was a real possibility that I might have come a bit too late: Bukky may eventually have become Kunle's wife. What prevented that development was Bukky's absolute faith and trust in God. The prophesy she had received was clear: the man that God would bring to her as future husband would be someone she already knew very well. Bukky wasn't ready to make approximations and guess her way out of the dilemma she had found herself, in an issue as delicate as choosing a life partner. She wanted 100% confirmation and nothing less. So, she waited and continued to pray.

While praying one day, Bukky got the revelation that cured her confusion and allowed her to move safely into my outstretched arms. Even before meeting Kunle, she had been asking God for a sign she would use to determine her husband whenever he showed up. After sometime, she was given a date as a sort of sign, but she forgot about that date. It was only after realising that both Kunle and I shared the same birthday that she recalled that date, which she had thought had to do with the date of her wedding, when it had been initially given to her.

God reminded Bukky that, based on her request for a sign, He had given her a date which was 2nd of February. That date was not her wedding date, as she had supposed, but the birthday of her future husband. Even though both Bode and Kunle had partly fulfilled the requirement of the first revelation (which had to do with the day of birth), it was only Bode that had fulfilled the requirement of the second sign, based on the prophesy of Pastor Kalajaiye's wife. Bukky was told that she was indeed destined to meet Kunle, but was not destined to marry him. The prophesy she had received from Mrs. Kalajaiye was to prevent her from marrying Kunle, which would have been a mistake, from the point of view of divine knowledge.

With this fresh and powerful understanding, Bukky wasted no time in giving me the green light because the same ministration from Mrs. Kalajaiye had urged her not to delay but to accept the proposal whenever it came. In fact, the ministration had specifically added that the man that would be her husband would be a child of God, sent to her by God, and that she was not to unduly stress him through an unnecessary delay. This was how detailed the instructions were that led to our becoming husband and wife. And that is only part of the story.

On my part, I can truthfully state that I also received direction from God before going to propose to Bukky, even though I must confess that mine was not as spectacular as hers. I cannot pretend that I pray as much as my wife, but I take God very seriously and would not want to do anything against His will, let alone marry a woman without His clear approval. So, I prayed about the matter of having wife for some time. I had a youthful life devoid of rioting and, while working at Bio-Organics, the thought of settling down began to nudge my mind. I remember that, as soon as I got the Bio-Organics job, I rented a one-room self-contained apartment at Ojodu. This was the first time I would be having the privilege of doing such a thing. It felt good to hold the keys to an apartment where I was absolutely in charge.

So, I was now gainfully employed, I had a place to call my own, and I was mature enough to want a female company for a permanent relationship. I continued to pray about the matter, but, Bukky was the last person I thought I would marry.

How could I marry Bukky, when she was more like a sister to me? If I was in Canada, for example, and there was a need for someone like Bukky to visit that country, nobody from her family would hesitate her staying with me and expect that nothing would happen. Such was the innocence of our interaction. The only difference between me and Lanre – as far as Bukky was concerned – was that Lanre had a blood connection with her, and I did not. In 1999, that was about to change.

I was in Bukky's paternal aunt's house one day when I thought I heard God telling me that the woman I was praying for was the one I was looking at right at that moment. I nearly argued with the voice I heard. It seemed brash and brazen for me to think romantically about Bukky. The paradigm shift that was required to relate with her was a woman, instead of as a sister, was not the easiest for me to make. I held my ground and did not immediately accept this leading. It took me time and the whole thing became a struggle.

Bukky was a pretty lady, and I soon began to get excited about the prospects of taking her as my wife. There was no need to begin to get artificial with each other. I already knew Bukky and liked her as a person. I knew she was a godly lady and that she was going to make a good wife; but it never occurred to me that I was going to be lucky enough to be her husband.

Not having enough courage to confront Lanre with my desire to marry his sister, I turned to our mutual friend, Olaitan Alatise. To say the least, Alatise was dumbfounded when I opened my mouth to tell him that I wanted to marry Bukky, the sister of our mutual friend. What I had going for me was that I was not a Casanova. In fact, I was the one that used to urge both Lanre and Alatise to attend fellowship, right from our days at the University of Ilorin. We could all be described as pious men, but I was certainly a bit more religious than the two of them. So, there was no way Alatise would have thought I was planning to have a fling with Bukky. His fear was about something else.

Because we were both friends of Lanre, Alatise was concerned that, if I dated Bukky but our relationship did not end in marriage, that would not be too good and it could create a messy situation. Alatise's candid opinion was that, because of the circumstance, I did not have the luxury of testing the waters. As a young man, it was my right to assess a young woman by drawing close to her for the purpose of eventually deciding if I wanted to settle down with her or not. But, according to Alatise, with Bukky, it had to be a dive. If I dated Bukky and broke her heart by not taking her to the altar, things could get sour between us and our friend Lanre. Alatise wanted to know if I had made up my mind to take the plunge. He made it clear that my intention was both good and safe: if things worked out, I would not be the first man to end up marrying his friend's sister. I assured Alatise that I was good and ready to rumble and he gave his blessings.

Lanre recently confessed that Alatise had seen it coming – my marriage with Bukky. I have not known my friend to be clairvoyant, and I would not deny this information from Lanre, but the fact is that, until things got serious, Bukky was more or less my sister from another mother. And I am glad that things never got funny between us until when it did. I believe that was the best way for it to have happened and thank God for the divine leading given to both of us to enable us make one of the most important decisions of our lives.

I would be lying if I claimed that marriage to Bukky has been without any challenge. We have had times when we quarrelled, when I did not act wisely, when I was too temperamental, and when that feeling of excitement ebbed. But a marriage is judged by its overall taste. When you watch a movie, it is not necessary for every moment to be scintillating. Your opinion about the movie does not depend on the moment by moment excitement but the general perception you have about it. In that sense, I can honestly report that I am blessed to be married to Bukky. Bukky has been a blessing to me. She is a praying woman. She is a person who believes that, with prayer, anything could be achieved. As a matter of fact, I ran into an unexpected hitch just recently. When Bukky got to know about this situation, she encouraged me with the usual words but said that there was nothing that God could not do. I knew what she meant by that. I knew she was suggesting that she was going to pray and that God was going to resolve the situation. I would not say that I did not believe her: I believed, but my faith was not as strong as hers.

According to her faith, Bukky prayed and the situation was resolved. When I went back to tell her the good news, she was very happy but not as surprised as I was. According to her, she already knew that I was going to get the pleasant outcome I was telling her about. I find this type of faith challenging and would like to have it too. Bukky is quite genuine and I consider her an anointed woman. She is everything to me. She is my wife; my sister; my mother and she is my friend. It is not surprising to me that, today, she is the head of the women prayer team in our local congregation. I see her as my backbone and she is part of the secret of my success. I feel I can do all things as long as this woman is around to pray for me. I feel very fortunate to call a woman like Bukky my wife. She is down to earth, respectful, gentle, humble, and absolutely not materialistic. She fears God and seeks His face in everything. She is a very special gift and I treasure her. She gives me rest of mind. There are actually no words to express my appreciation for her.

I travelled to all the states in the south-west and several others in the south-south while working with Bio-Organics, all in a bid to keep up my game and achieve my goals. My extensive travel would have taken a great toll on my family if not because I trusted Bukky and knew she was equal to the task of taking care of the home front. Most of the time, I am away from home. I will ever remain grateful to Bukky for holding the forth all through those days, months and years, while I crisscrossed locations scattered all over the southern region of Nigeria.

As CEO of Hi-Nutrients, my need to travel did not abate. If anything, it intensified. And there was now a foreign component to my travel. Today, the talk in the industry is that I am the most travelled CEO in Agriculture; this may not be far from the truth, going by the fact that, as at the last count, I have visited over 20 countries in the continents of Europe, Africa, Asia, South America, North America, and even Eastern Europe. Since I am not a spirit, it means that, for all the time I was away, Bukky was alone, tending to herself and our kids. This could not have been possible if she was not a strong woman who had already keyed into my vision.

There is something else that is in the background but very critical to all these. If Bukky did not trust and have confidence in me, she would not have allowed me the freedom of travelling so extensively. Such was her trust that, whenever I say I would travel, her next automatic reaction was to plan to pray for me and not to worry about what some other women worry about when their husbands are out of sight. I could not have had my family and my business success without someone like Bukky by my side. It is either one or the other; but certainly not both.

I remember what happened during the last recession in Nigeria, which lasted between 2015 and 2017. Things became unbelievably tough and sticky. Many companies were going under, and some business owners were even dying due to insurmountable business challenges. I tried everything I knew how to do, but nothing was working.

Imagine the kind of situation we found ourselves: we sold a kilogram of a certain product at ₦750 when the exchange rate of the naira to the dollar was about ₦180. How could we maintain the price of that product when the exchange rate rose until it began to hover around ₦502 to the dollar? Yet we went through this situation, and the market was not ready for any price adjustment because the economy was that bad. To make matters worse, foreign competitors took advantage of the exchange rate situation and their access to the dollar, and began to take away our clients. They did not have to make any sacrifice to maintain prices: but we were losing hundreds of millions of naira to do just that. Things got so bad that I actually told Bukky that, from the look of things, I was considering closing shop and relocating to Europe. At least, we could salvage some of our funds and prevent the imminent disgrace of staying on in Nigeria. I was not joking about this idea, but Bukky refused.

At the time, we had over 50 employees, and she asked me to consider their plight. She said what type of story did I want to leave behind? She challenged me to remember my vision, which she was a part of and knew every detail of. I had no place to hide and I could not deny that relocating to Europe or America was not part of the vision I had shared with her. I listened to Bukky but did not feel much better. I could not see a way out of the quagmire the recession had brought us into. I then asked her what she expected me to do, in order to go forward. She seemed ready for my question. She immediately replied me and said we were going to pray. As already stated, prayer, to her, was like a date at the ice cream shop: it was something she loved to do. Bukky is a woman of prayer, she is hard-working, focused, and a genuine family woman. She is the pillar behind the success that God is making me to record today. I took courage from her words and we began to pray.

Because things did not immediately get better, Bukky had to step up her prayer efforts a bit more. This was because it was obvious that I was losing hope and could become hopeless quite suddenly, leading to unpredictable actions. Around that time, Pastor Akin Adekeye, came to my office to pray. It was after a prayer vigil the previous night. During the prayer, he poured a whole bottle of anointing oil on my head and said that God had already answered my prayers. All I needed to do was to be sensitive and wait for the answer. Thereafter, he related a vision he had seen, obviously while praying. He said he had seen some white men surrounding me, and that I was sitting like a chairman in their midst. He said that my company was going international, in line with its name, Hi-Nutrients International Limited. I thanked Pastor Adekeye but did not share his message with Bukky.

However, not too long after that, Bukky woke up one morning and told me that some white people were going to call me. She said that God had seen what we were passing through and that He wanted to rescue us, just like Jesus rescued His disciples when they were sinking in the boat. I was already used to Bukky telling me mysterious things which would later turn out exactly like she had said. Even before she shared her vision with me, Pastor Asaolu Taiwo also got a revelation similar to what Pastor Akin Adekeye had seen. I had no option but to key in. As a matter of fact, there were two additional pastors that had seen something quite similar, all suggesting that I was soon going to be in business with white foreigners. One of these pastors (Pastor (Mrs.) Adeola Mensah) is a senior pastor today and she was my pastor in those days. Her own vision about my eventual business relationship with the white men was declared as early as 2005, when she came to pray in my office. She tapped on the wooden panel and asked if we could hear any sound. When we all looked dumb, she began to declare things that were going to take place soon, one of which was that I was going to set up a factory. All these things have come to pass, to the glory of God.

Again, there was a confirmation from Rev. Jide Taiwo, who, during a Christmas message, made the same statement announcing that, in the future, I was going to work with the white men.

Because of this preponderance of witnesses, I asked God to also give me the revelation and show me what He was showing to others because I was the driver, god showed me. I take God seriously, even though my business endeavour may not allow me to be in church 24/7. So, I asked God to allow the revelation already confirmed by more than three witnesses to come to pass. But I had no idea how that would happen.

Then, one afternoon, I got a call from my friend and look where we are today.

Indeed, this book would become a eulogy if I attempt to fully express the role Bukky has played in my life.

I am so glad that I have a wonderful relationship with all of her siblings, especially my long-time friend and professional colleague, Lanre, who is the second born of the family. Before Lanre, there was Dele, the first born in Bukky's nuclear family. After Lanre, there is Lara, Bukky's immediate elder sister. Bukky herself is next in the ranking after Lara, followed by her younger sister, Shola, and, finally, the last born of the house, Kayode.

Bukky is not only industrious; she is also productive. We are blessed with four children (one is now of blessed memory), but she seemed to have obeyed the Western tradition of ladies first. Our first child is Deola, and she is in Canada today as a student in one of their universities; our second daughter, Toluwanimi, was lost through a ghastly motor accident; the third child is also the first son, and his name is David. He likes to introduce himself as Adetoyi David Jesufemi Adewale Toluwani. David turned 14 in May of 2018 and is still in secondary school. David has said that he wants to study agriculture and even major in animal science. He has also said that he does not mind coming to work with Hi-Nutrients International Limited after school after he must have worked in any related international company.

The last born of the house is the inquisitive and ever restless Daniel, who likes me to check on him every night just to be sure that he has fallen asleep. These days, he even pretends to be sleeping just to see if I would actually check on him. In all, Bukky has succeeded in holding the home front gallantly while I go out and fight for the good of the family. Without her, things could have fallen apart. I will ever remain grateful to her and pray that God preserves this woman of value for me.

CHAPTER 14

NEAR DEATH EXPERIENCES

There are notable experiences I have had that would have ended in death, if not for the mercy of God and His divine intervention. I would like to state these experiences for posterity. It is my way of showing gratitude to God and my acceptance of the fact that living up to 50 years is not a right but a privilege.

The first time was in 2001. I was an employee of Bio-Organics Nigeria Limited at the time and was returning to Lagos from a trip to Owo in Ondo State, where I had gone to pay a business visit to Joff Ideal Family Farms. In those days, my MD, Dr. Acholonu, used to rely on me when he needed to go on a trip and needed some cash urgently. Fortunately, I had the right customer in Owo for such immediate cash and I was able to get some substantial amount for my boss. But due to the urgency of the situation, I had to return to Lagos that very day. Those were days when there were no convenient and affordable money transfer. So, I had to take the cash with me in the official car and my official driver drove the car during the trip.

As we were approaching Asejire, a town near Ibadan, a trailer driving by our side of the road suddenly swerved towards us and my driver lost control of the vehicle, sending us speeding helplessly into the Asejire dam that was filled with water. As the vehicle rushed uncontrollably towards the dam that would have swallowed us both, we heard onlookers screaming so loudly; and I thought that I was experiencing my last moments in this world. But miraculously, the vehicle ran into the path of a tree that was somewhere near the road. This was odd because there were only two trees there: it was one of the trees that stopped our car. Still, the car was thrown off balance due to the speed with which it was coming that it somersaulted. When we recovered from the whole incident, we discovered that the trailer had also tumbled and was lying up-side-down. That accident was a near miss.

The money I had collected from Owo was eight hundred thousand naira, and this was a time when the exchange rate was exactly ₦100 to the dollar, meaning that that amount was equivalent to about ₦3m in today's naira. That money was in our upturned vehicle, which had been seriously damaged. Conscious of the danger of making the first responders know that I had such a huge amount with me, I started asking for my clothes. I kept saying that I wanted to take my clothes in the upturned vehicle. Seeing my interest in my clothes and my indifference to my kiss with death, some of the first responders chided me, saying that I should be grateful to be alive and stop asking for my clothes. But I politely insisted and was able to retrieve the cash, which was inside a plastic bag. In fact, it was one of the onlookers, who did not suspect anything, that threw the plastic bag at me. I hugged this plastic bag and made everybody around believe that I was finally happy to have my clothes back. Nobody suspected that the plastic bag contained money. My driver sustained some slight injury but I think I got a rather serious hit on my back during the accident. Up till today, I still feel an occasional sharp pain around my scapula, which is a fallout of that accident, in which my life was providentially preserved.

The first responders were soon able to take us to a certain hospital located at Iwo road. As soon as I was admitted and given a bed, I quickly considered my options and threw the plastic bag containing the money under the bed. The location of the bed was such that it would have been very difficult for anybody to approach the cash without attracting serious attention, especially from me. News of the accident filtered into Lagos and into Bio-Organics office before the end of that fateful day, but there was no way to send delegation until the following day. The delegation eventually sent by my MD was led by one Mr. Charles Obi, who was the head of all the company drivers. After seeing my condition and expressing sympathy, they extended greetings from my MD over the sad incident. Then Mr. Charles remarked that it was obvious that I had lost the money I had gone to collect at Owo. Someone else added that life was more precious than money and that, 'when there is life, there is hope.'

I agreed with them about life and hope but told them that I had not lost the money. They were surprised because they had seen the condition of the car, which was a complete write-off. It was obvious that the accident could have been fatal. At that point, I told Mr. Charles to check under the bed and bring out the bag. When he did that and saw that it was the money, everybody was amazed and relieved. My boss could hardly believe his eyes when that money was eventually handed over to him in Lagos. As far as he was concerned, the money was gone. This happened in Nigeria where it was not unusual for criminals to pose as first responders at accident scenes in order to rob victims of valuables. As eerie and brutish as this may seem, it happens sometimes. So, the view of my boss was that, because the driver and I had been injured, we would not have been in a very conscious state of mind to even help ourselves, let alone preserve the money. So, he had already given up hope of recovering the money. No wonder, he was pleasantly surprised that we did not only came out alive, but I was able to protect the money.

My brave and honest act made a strong impression on my boss. According to him, it served as overwhelming evidence to convince him that I was a true Christian and a loyal staff. Even after surviving the accident and getting hold of the money, I could have easily stolen it and pretended that it had been stolen. No one would have dared to question my story. But I chose to do the right thing. My boss was so moved that he prayed for me and basically said things that later proved accurate. In his prayers, he said that, for my bravery and honesty, God would help me to establish something greater than Bio-Organics. Amazingly, God answered the prayer.

Just one week after leaving the hospital at Ibadan, where I received treatment, my boss replaced my damaged official car with a brand new Toyota Carina 3.

The second near death experience I would like to document for posterity happened in France, in year 2017. That trip was directly in connection with the merger and acquisition processes that were still ongoing between my company, Hi-Nutrients International Limited, and Neovia of France. I was in Paris when this incident that would have been a tragedy for my family occurred. Unfortunately, it was actually a tragedy for several others.

After a particularly hectic day, I decided to enjoy the sights and sounds of Paris and also have my lunch. As most of my friends already know, I like to post pictures on Facebook when I travel. This is something I am used to. So, after my lunch, I uploaded some pictures on Facebook to show where I had just had lunch. Then I returned to my hotel room.

However, barely two hours later, I began to hear from several sources that there was a terrorist attack in that very restaurant and that several persons had been shot dead. I could hardly believe that it was the same restaurant where I had eaten just that afternoon. At some point, I went on social media and saw several posts asking me to confirm my location and my current condition. Many others who could not reach my line had assumed the worst: they believed I had died in the terrorist attack.

It was much later that people began to realise that, although I had actually been at that restaurant, I had left before the gunman showed up and began to shoot the diners indiscriminately. That was one massive miracle. By just staying longer in that place, I would have died in faraway France, and broken the heart of my family members and friends but God preserved me. I am very grateful to God.

As an addendum to this chapter, I would relate the story of an accident I was involved in during the early days of my company, Hi-Nutrients International Limited. At that time, I did not have a personal car. I was actively engaged in trading at the time, while also trying to raise cash to begin actual premix production. I was on my way to then Bendel Feed and Flour Mills, which was located at Ewu, after Ekpoma town in Edo State. I left my rented apartment in Lagos early that morning and took a motorcycle to the popular Berger bus stop, intending to take a bus to Ojota and from there, to join another bus to Ewu. But, on the way to Berger bus stop, we were almost hit by a car and the motorcycle rider swerved to avoid the collision. It was that sudden movement that threw me off the bike, landing me on the untarred road in an inglorious heap with a painful thud, injuring myself badly in the process. I saw blood gushing out and noticed that my right knee hurt badly. I had hit my knee on the hard ground and was lucky to be able to walk again.

I was immediately rushed to a nearby hospital to receive first aid. My shirt was not only dirty but also bloody; so, after the treatment, I returned home to change. In spite of my health condition, I decided to proceed on the journey. As we started the journey to Ewu, I could only feel slight pains in my knee, which I tried to ignore. By the time I got to Ewu, things were set to get out of hand: my leg had swollen over twice its size and I was in excruciating pain.

When the Managing Director of Bendel Feed and Flour Mills, Mr. Ogbogodo, saw my state, he had compassion on me. He ensured that the cheque I had come for was promptly prepared and given to me. Then he ordered his driver to take me to the airport at Benin. Moreover, he paid for my flight ticket from Benin to Lagos. That was the level of the kindness that man showed me that day, and I can only pray that God would show this man mercy also in his hour of need. I do not know what would have happened if I had returned to Lagos by road. Perhaps I would have become unconscious and fallen into wrong hands or have even died. I will never forget Mr. Ogbogodo for what he did for me.

Perhaps to prevent a recurrence of what happened, Mr. Ogbogodo instructed that I should always be given a cheque anytime I came to supply products to the mill. This was not the norm, but the man extended this special favour to me as a gesture of goodwill because he was touched by my determination to succeed, which was obviously what had led me to press on, even after sustaining a serious injury in an early morning accident.

I will also never forget the help I received from Dick Obasoye, who was then, the General Manager in charge of Nutrition at Bendel Feed and Flour Mills. May God also reward his kindness.

CHAPTER 15

MY RCCG STORY

First of all, I would be correct to assert that Christianity has shaped my life. We grew up to meet our parents as Christians. Both of them were members of the Anglican Church and worshipped at the St. Peter's Anglican Church in Otun-Ekiti. In fact, I attended St. Peter's Anglican Church Primary School and was quite active in several groups. I was a member of the choir and also belonged to the Boys' Scout Brigade. These were some influences our parents exposed us to. Even though they were not rich, they seemed to be contented and generally lived happy lives. My father was engaged in his farming and the sale of clothes, while my mother did petty trading. All my siblings either served as ushers in the church, or were in the choir. My elder brother, Banji, was in the choir also. I remained an active Anglican Church member throughout my primary school. I believe that this helped in shaping me in terms of moral rectitude.

When I got to secondary school, nothing really changed. But through the influence of my elder brother, Gabriel Popoola, I began to attend The Apostolic Church (TAC). Brother Popoola lived in Ido-Ekiti and I spent some holidays with him, and this was how I was introduced to TAC, not to be confused with CAC, which is Christ Apostolic Church. When I got admitted into the University of Ilorin, I joined The Apostolic Church and was also a member of TACSFON – The Apostolic Church Student Organisation of Nigeria. TACSFON was the student arm of TAC and I was very active there even while I belonged to the Ilorin Christian Union, known as ICU.

After graduating from the University of Ilorin, I served in Calabar, Cross Rivers State, and later came to Lagos. It was while in Lagos that Pastor Gilbert introduced me to the Redeemed Christian Church of God. Until Pastor Gilbert's invitation to the RCCG, I was a member of The Apostolic Church and was attending the Palmgrove branch while staying with my elder brother, Lekan, who now lives in the United Kingdom. Due to its proximity to where I was living at the time, the first RCCG branch I attended was Glorious Parish, which was located at Palmgrove in Lagos State. It was in 1995 and I have remained a member of the Redeemed Christian Church of God since then.

It was in the RCCG that I became born again. I also got baptised before the end of 1995, but that was after passing through the Baptismal Class. I remember that I was baptised at the University of Lagos Lagoon. I eventually enrolled for a programme known as Workers-in-Training, after which I officially became a worker in the church. Not every member is an automatic worker; you had to pass through the Workers-in-Training programme to be so designated. I remember that I attended my Workers-in-Training programme with Kunle. There was also Bisi and Brother Obuh, all of whom we still contact one another on the social media.

My close associates and I at the RCCG Glorious Parish were not the usual church members: we were very vibrant. We were so vibrant and passionate that we formed a group known as 'Soldiers for Christ.' We were holding periodic night vigils and later formed the embryo of the drama group of the church. As an individual, I love drama and I became active in the drama group of Glorious Parish.

When I became a Master's degree student at the University of Ibadan, there was a Redeemed Christian Students Fellowship, but it was in need of some re-organisation. Coming with the fiery commitment common to members of the 'Soldiers for Christ' group, I soon found my equals in the likes of Rotimi Oyedele (who now works with Scortia Bank in Canada) and Tunji Olasunkanmi, who is also based in Canada today. Rotimi is now a pastor and did play a pivotal role in the valuation of my company, Hi-Nutrients International Limited, during its merger and acquisition by Neovia. Tunji eventually became a veterinary doctor. While Rotimi and I were Master's degree students, Tunji was in his 600 level, but we had something in common: we all wanted some fire injected into the activities of the fellowship. Fortunately, Tunji had just been elected President of the student fellowship and had the power to make a difference.

We also had the support of others, who, with Tunji, were members of the executive committee of the fellowship. There was Taiwo Lemoshe, who was the music director of the fellowship. Taiwo was fondly referred to as "Pastor T". Some others called him David, with reference to the David in the Bible, who was a musician. Interestingly, Taiwo's twin brother, Kehinde Lemoshe, was a pianist and also part of the music team. There was a vibrant lady in the fellowship known as Ronke; she was so active that she came to be known as "Fellowship Mummy." Later in life, Ronke became the wife of Tunji Olasunkanmi. On my part, I served as the Counselling/ Welfare Director. Rotimi and I, by virtue of the fact that we were running our Master's programme, were well-respected. This respect made it easier for us to offer counsel to the other members, who were mostly undergraduates. I remember that, as we were leaving UI, Tunji Olasunkanmi's tenure as president also came to an end because he too had to leave, and we worked together to install Taiwo Lemoshe (the music director) as the new president of the fellowship.

We used to charter buses every last Friday of the month to the Redemption Camp located on the Lagos-Ibadan expressway for the monthly Holy Ghost service. This service has been a part of the schedule of activities of the larger Redeemed Christian Church of God for decades. It started during the early days of the leadership of the current General Overseer, Pastor Enoch Adejare Adeboye, who was ordained as a pastor of the church in 1975 and became the General Overseer in 1981. Today, the Holy Ghost service is the most popular of the church's activities and it is attended by millions of people from within Nigeria and abroad. Live broadcasts of the service are usually transmitted on TV, Radio and also streamed over the internet. The programme is regularly attended by the RCCG and non-RCCG members, as well as people from other faiths. Apart from the one held in Nigeria, the same type of services are held in other locations in the world, including the U.K. (where it is known as the Festival of Life), the U.S., Asia, and other continents. The average headcount of those who attend the service in Nigeria is over 1,000,000, but the number keeps growing.

To make the Redeemed Students Fellowship in UI more productive and become an avenue for grooming leaders, we introduced a programme to help with career and business development skills. We would normally invite speakers to come and make presentations and encourage the brethren. I remember that Rotimi, Tunji and I used to go to Awo Hall to pray every time, resulting in the hall been referred to as Mount Zion. We would pray for ourselves and also for the members of the Fellowship. We became a positive force on campus. Even the Vice-Chancellor took note of us because our activities helped to reduce cultism on campus and did a lot to uphold the moral rectitude of students. Our activities also resulted in academic excellence because our fellowship members did not engage in time-wasting vices and were able to concentrate on their studies and excel with relative ease. It was a good thing that, we, as leaders, were also leading by example. I am glad that both Rotimi and I, finish our Master's degree programmes with PhD grade.

Up till this moment, the Redeemed Students Fellowship of the University of Ibadan is the largest student fellowship in that school, and that is a source of great joy to persons like me because I believe that, in collaboration with others, we did play a role in making today's reality possible.

When I left the University of Ibadan, I joined Bio-Organics Nigeria Limited. I eventually got a place in a neighbourhood of Ojodu known as Adigboluja. It was off Alhaji Kosoko road. Not surprisingly, I began to attend the Redeemed Christian Church of God, Faith Chapel, which was located at No. ¾ Alhaji Kosoko road, Ojodu. Attending that branch of the Redeemed Church was both convenient and sensible and in line with the vision of the General Overseer of the church, which was to have a Redeemed Christian Church of God branch within 5 minutes' walking distance everywhere in Nigeria. That vision is partly responsible for the fact that, today, the Redeemed Christian Church has over 32,000 parishes in Nigeria, and I am sure that the number would no longer be accurate by now because parishes are being planted every day.

It was at Faith Chapel that I met Pastor Adeola Mensah, who was the senior pastor of that branch at the time. Her husband, Reverend Tetteh Mensah, was also there. One would wonder how a clergy in the Redeemed Christian Church of God would be referred to as reverend, when the General Overseer himself is only called a pastor. The fact is that Rev. Tetteh Mensah was already a reverend in another denomination before he joined the RCCG. So we just got used to referring to him as Rev. Tetteh Mensah and that name stuck with him.

Another pastor at that RCCG branch was Pastor Israel Ogbechie, who now lives in Canada and serves as guardian to my daughter, Adeola. In fact, my daughter worships at the RCCG branch pastored by Pastor Ogbechie. All the pastors mentioned are now senior pastors in the Redeemed Christian Church of God today. Pastor (Mrs.) Israel Ogbechie was Sister Ogbechie when I met her.

I also met Pastor Muyiwa Adeyemo (who was certainly not a pastor in 1998 when we met), Managing Director of Lemurex Pharmacy. There was also Femi Ogunode – now a senior pastor – and others. I remember Tayo Abraham, who became the coordinator of a group we formed known as Covenant Givers' Group (CGG). I remember Tunde Adeleye, who is also now a pastor. There was Pastor Mike Kpolu and his wife, Sister Grace Kpolu, who later played a key role in my life by introducing me to JID Dada of UAC. My meeting with JID Dada later proved significant in my life, business career, and destiny.

Pastor Sunday Adebowale was pastor of one of the churches under Faith Chapel and it was at this time that I met him. There was also Wale Onigbode and Kunle Ojo, both of who later played very important roles in my life. Not only did they give me free financial advice (as financial experts) they actually supported me by giving me cash and also lending me cash at different times. I remember Nike Owolabi, Muyiwa Adeyemo (Lemurex), Sister Funke Taiwo, and her husband, Jide Taiwo. Sister Funke Taiwo was a printer and she helped us during those early days of Hi-Nutrients by printing our documents which we paid for at our convenience. For those who understand the challenges of starting a business, this gesture by Sister Funke had serious positive implications and it helped to preserve my company at its most vulnerable season. To make matters more interesting, Sister Funke's husband, Jide Taiwo, was also supporting us in his own way.

Before coming to Faith Chapel of the Redeemed Christian Church of God – which later changed to Faith City – I had already attended the Workers-in-Training programme of the church. So, I was able to present my certificate as a confirmed RCCG worker, apart from my certificate from the Redeemed Students Fellowship of the University of Ibadan. With these evidence of my activities in the church, I was made Head of Sanitation of the Faith Chapel. We were in a rented facility at the time, but there was a land close by. As people were being blessed and numbers were increasing, it became possible for Faith Chapel to acquire the land and build a structure.

After sometime, a campus of the Redeemed Christian Bible College was situated at Faith Chapel and, with the encouragement of Pastor Deola Mensah, I enrolled at the college. Our principal then was a lady we called Mummy Commy. Her name is actually Comfort Jinadu and she is now a pastor. Before this time, the Redeemed Christian Bible College used to be situated at the Redemption camp and did not have decentralised campuses. Pastor Mrs. Commie Jinadu was the first principal of the new campus of the college at Faith Chapel. In the year 2000, I got my Postgraduate Diploma in Theology from the College.

In 2007, I was moved from Faith Chapel to Faith Tabernacle, which was one of the parishes established by Faith Chapel. Faith Tabernacle was under Area 007 (then headed by Pastor Sunday Adebowale) and it was there that I was ordained a deacon of the Redeemed Christian Church of God. It took up to twelve years of consistent membership before I was ordained a Deacon. I decided to highlight this point just to show that being a Deacon in the Redeemed church is a tall order.

It was also at Faith Tabernacle that my wife was eventually ordained a Deaconess. In 2012, five years after being ordained as a deacon, I was ordained an Assistant Pastor.

I remained an active participant in the activities of the Redeemed Christian Church of God after my ordination. However, as the Chief Executive Officer of my company, I began to be smothered with work such that I could not spend as much time as I would have loved to in church activities. One specific reason was that I travelled a lot – both within and outside Nigeria – and this made me simply unavailable to participate in some programmes. But, wherever I went, I remained an apostle. I was the typical apostle in the marketplace. I was never ashamed to profess my faith when the opportunity presented itself. Besides, I tried to support church's work with my resources, whenever I had the opportunity to do so.

I am glad that, even though we never sat down to discuss and take a decision as a family on what to do, my wife seems to have taken up the slack. She seems to have stepped up to the plate and is now very much engaged in our local parish, which is known as Graceland Parish. On my part, I allow her all the time she needs to play her role. I also do my best to try to support the work of God because my passion is still as fresh as it has ever been. I remain a committed member of the Redeemed Christian Church of God. I love Pastor Adeboye and I'm happy about the impact he is making in the world.

The story of my success in life and even in business cannot be told without mentioning the role played by the wonderful people I met at the Redeemed Christian Church of God. In fact, the first man that invited me to the church, Pastor Gilbert Aimufua, came into my life at a very critical moment. I may not give details of the role he and his wife played, but I would just state that they cared for me physically before attempting to do so spiritually. And it was at a time that, if I had not gotten that physical support, I would have suffered greatly. After Pastor Gilbert and his wife, an army of helpers has been strategically positioned by God to solve and resolve each and every challenge I have come across. Most of these helpers were members and are still members of the Redeemed Christian Church of God. Hallelujah!

CHAPTER 16
POULTRY ASSOCIATION OF NIGERIA

I am a member of the Poultry Association of Nigeria. I am so proud of this association that I consider it a privilege to be numbered among them. The Poultry Association of Nigeria has grown from infancy to become a truly national association and is currently led by Mr. Ezekiel Ibrahim from Borno State, northeast Nigeria. It is my honour and privilege to be the Vice President (South-West) of this association (and concurrently the Chairman of the South-West region also), having served as Ex-Officio Lagos State Branch, Vice-Chairman, and Chairman of the Lagos State Branch. Through its activities, this association has become responsible for creating tens of thousands jobs in Nigeria and turned many farmers into millionaires. Besides, the association is made up of people who are very knowledgeable about the industry. Its members are well-read, and with just a little government support, they have the capacity to feed almost 200 million people of this country and even leave enough for export. However, like all great associations, the beginning was unpredictable, rough, and tough: things were definitely not rosy.

The Poultry Association of Nigeria came into being as a child of necessity. At that time in Nigeria, importation was one of the mainstay of the non-oil sector. Former President Shehu Shagari was in power in 1979 then and the outlook for poultry farmers in Nigeria was quite bleak. Perhaps nothing would have happened to improve the condition of poultry farmers, but, as it sometimes turns out, a challenge may be a blessing in disguise and it was a challenging situation that finally caused poultry farmers to come together and establish the association that has come as far as having a Director General.

The association was formed basically to cooperate with the federal government policy in order to deal with the issue of import license. Otherwise, the other option was for them to close shop. Things were that bad. Just like today, most of the things required for poultry business have to be imported, but to get import license was not the easiest thing to do in those days. Corn was the biggest issue at this time. Almost 100% of the corn used in the poultry industry was imported. This shameful fact was because there was no conscious effort to develop our local capacity to produce corn, in spite of the availability of arable land all over the country. Incidentally, in recent times (as recent as 2017/2018), shortage of corn has been causing problems in the poultry industry. So, by virtue of the fact that corn forms more than 50% per cent of the feed required by poultry, the relatively few players in the industry then chose to come together. By their coming together, they were able to secure import licenses for their members and save their businesses. Interestingly, at the time, a ton of maize was ₦400. But today, it is more than ₦80,000. This goes to show just what has happened to Nigeria and the naira. This astronomical rise in price is equivalent to 20000%. That is to say, the price of a ton of maize has increased 200 times from what it used to be less than 30 years ago.

It is also pertinent to note that the association began in Lagos. Apart from the fact that Lagos was the then political capital of Nigeria, it was also the economic capital of the country, and the most populous state in the Nigeria. It was also the melting pot of the poultry business and livestock farming in general. Due to this historical fact, the Lagos State chapter of the association served as its national body for some time, until, like an embryo, it began to grow by being decentralised into state branches. After initial teething problems, the association got its acts together and began to make things happen.

There were many people that came together to form the Poultry Association of Nigeria. One of these people was late Chief Ladipo Daniel, proprietor of Ladipo Daniel Farms. He was later joined by persons like Chief Olusegun Obasanjo, Nigeria's former president. In fact, the first office of the association was actually located in Chief Ladipo's house. Chief Ladipo out of his magnanimity donated a three-bedroom flat to the association. Not surprisingly, he also served as its first Chairman. During Chief Ladipo's tenure, another founding father served as General Secretary. That first General Secretary was none other than Rev. Dr. Wilson Badejo, former General Overseer of Foursquare Gospel Church. Dr. Badejo was a practising veterinary doctor and his membership and participation in the poultry association of Nigeria in its executive committee shows that the association was never for poultry farmers alone. While serving as the first General Secretary of the Poultry Association, Dr. Badejo was the Assistant General Manager of then Mitchell Farms. So, apart from poultry farmers, there were those who were into livestock in general, poultry equipment sellers, veterinary doctors, premix manufacturers, dealers, and even students studying agriculture in higher institutions. Below is a list of all the chairmen of the Lagos State branch of the Poultry Association of Nigeria, which we refer to as PANLAG for short.

- Chief Ladipo Daniel; Ladipo Daniel Farms.
- Chief Adekunle Oshomo; Esther Port Farms.
- Dr. Samuel Adebayo Olufunwa; Samolus Farms.
- Mr. Olanrewaju Bello; Ibukun Farms and Industries Limited.
- Dr. Folarin Afelumo; Fola Afe Agrovet Services.
- Alhaji Olushoga Olufawo; Solcorp Farms.

- Adedotun Agbojo; Adewura Farms.
- Prince Ezekiel Olabode Adetoyi; Hi-Nutrients International Limited.
- Godwin Egbebe; Akinsateru Farms.

Cumulatively, I can claim to have been a player in the Nigerian agricultural sector for the past thirty years (1988 to 2018). After all, I became an undergraduate student of Animal Production in the University of Ilorin in 1988 and have never stopped thinking about agriculture or actually practising it since that time. But on a lighter note, I can also claim that I have been a player in the agricultural sector since I became old enough to work on my father's farm. That would make me a player with over four decade's experience.

I am always amazed whenever I remember that I often try to give excuses to avoid going to farm each time my father insisted that I should go to the farm to work. I would either suddenly become sick on Saturday morning, or actually escape from home. Alternatively, I would agree to go to the farm, but when I got there, I would tell my father that I wanted to read my books. Even though I had actually read my books, it was nonetheless an excuse. Most of the time, my tricks worked. Those who were already adults at the time I was born would often say that, as a kid, I was handsome, brilliant, and likable but I was also stubborn. But if you press these people to explain why they think I was stubborn, you will discover that my stubbornness manifested when I had made up my mind not to go to the farm. That was when I put all the momentum of my fiery will and passion behind my decision and refused to budge. Now, I am a willing and happy farmer. As someone has said, life is full of ironies.

I first made contact with the Poultry Association of Nigeria (PAN) while I was working at Bio-Organics. I became a member specifically in 1999. Because of my belief in the association, I played an active role, just that I was restricted by the fact that I had limited time, being an employee. I vividly remember that I used to represent my boss and the MD of Bio-Organics, Dr. Acholonu, at meetings. In fact, it got to a point that some of the staffs of the association began to refer to me as second-in-command. They may be right because most times I showed up, it was either to represent my boss, or to do something on his behalf.

For the past 19 years since I joined PAN, I have tried to do my bit in the furtherance of the vision of its founding fathers. I have seen the beauty of what is possible when many good heads come together to try to achieve a common goal. I would not advise any poultry or any livestock farmer for that matter to deny themselves the benefits of belonging to an association like PAN. I have seen PAN, with pleasure, improve the practice of animal farmers in Nigeria.

In early 2004, after strenuous efforts by a committee set up for that purpose, the Poultry Association of Nigeria was able to get the federal government of Nigeria to ban the importation of frozen chicken into the country. No matter how poor the implementation of that ban would have been so far, the fact is that it is a step in the right direction. This step would require only the correct environment to take proper effect and cause a tsunami of progress in the agricultural sector in general. After painstaking efforts and countless trips to Abuja by elders like Lanre Bello (former PANLAG Chairman), Dr. Olatunde Agbato of Animal Care in Sagamu, Ogun State, Chief Tunde Badmus, Chairman of Tuns Farms Osogbo, and Chief Folorunsho Ogunnaike (Former PAN South-west Chairman), they finally cornered the very busy President Obasanjo at the Aso Rock Villa, Abuja, to discuss the issue. President Obasanjo listened to his colleagues in the business and understood their request but declined to approve it, citing the issue of conflict of interest. He was quite blunt about his refusal.

Everybody in Nigeria knows Chief Olusegun Obasanjo to be a farmer, and he felt that the ban on importation of frozen chicken, if implemented may be perceived by some careless persons to have been done in order to favour his personal business. So, he told the PAN elders that were pushing for this ban to pass through the government process, beginning from the Ministry of Agriculture. They would have to lobby all the arms of government on their own, without expecting any help from him. If they succeeded in convincing the other players and the matter came to his table, he would consider the ban.

Left with such a stark reality, the leaders of PAN had to follow the tortuous and arduous process of convincing all the government stakeholders in the agriculture sector of the need to place a ban on the importation of frozen chicken. It is not as if there were no obvious benefits in banning the importation of frozen chicken; but that is the nature of governance. Every government has so many priority issues it would prefer to focus on and deal with such that, sometimes, to get even good things done, one had to lobby government officials, show them the benefits of the requested government action, and apply enough pressure and diplomacy to ensure that the action is taken. This is not just particular to Nigeria as a country, it is the norm all over the world.

To confront both bureaucrats and politicians, leaders of the Poultry Association of Nigeria had an excellent idea. Every product whose importation is not banned in Nigeria is supposed to make its way into the country through the ports or the land borders – except this product has zero import duty – then it must earn the government some revenue through the imposition of import duty. The PAN leaders therefore went to the Nigeria Customs Service to confirm the duty on the importation of frozen chicken. As shocking as it may sound, and in spite of the millions of tonnes of frozen chicken that was being imported into the country every day, there was no single naira that had accrued to the Federal Government as import duty. It was even worse than that: there was no importer of frozen chicken on the record at all. What this meant was that all the frozen chicken that come into Nigeria were through the activities of smugglers. This discovery was a very potent weapon in the hands of PAN leaders, but it was not the only one they had in the arsenal they used to whip the government into submission.

Having established that every imported frozen chicken in Nigeria was as a result of criminal activities which also deny Nigerians the opportunity of getting jobs in the poultry sector, apart from cheating the government by bypassing the payment of customs duty, there were other related factors. In order to evade arrest, it is necessary for smugglers of frozen chicken to disguise the product. The fact therefore that, the frozen chicken cannot be placed in proper storage, thereby exposes them to infectious diseases and even germs due to decay and poor hygiene which immediately presents several health risks.

Fortunately for the PAN leaders, the bird flu epidemic, which had grabbed headlines in 2001, was still very much around the corner, and it was easy to point out to government officials that unscrupulous businessmen from neighbouring African countries and even from countries in Asia and other continents could collaborate with their dishonest Nigerian counterparts to bring in infected poultry, putting the whole population of Nigeria at the risk of bird flu infection. There was also the issue of the use of dangerous chemicals which are used to ensure that the frozen chickens (in spite of being exposed to high temperatures) would remain fresh. Some importers actually used *formaldehyde* – the same chemical that is used to embalm dead bodies – as preservative for the imported chickens.

There was a horrible economic angle to the issue also. Apart from all the health dangers already highlighted, the ban was necessary because, without it, the importers would always be able to sell chicken at a cost much lower than producers of poultry within Nigeria. This will not only destroy the local poultry industry in Nigeria but will also have the necessary consequence of causing practitioners to layoff their workers, which would have further compounded the issue of unemployment in the country. Many people think that the poultry industry is just about chickens, but it is far from that.

Like Dr. Ayo Oduntan told the media when he was the President of the Poultry Association of Nigeria, if the ban on frozen chicken is properly implemented, it would result in, not just hundreds of thousands of jobs, but several million jobs. Apart from that, there will be a huge increase in the demand for maize farmers and soya bean farmers. Also, there are those who engage in the processing of limestone, which is used in the poultry industry. They would also need to increase their capacity by employing much more people. Currently, there are several thousand of women and men who engage in the selling of poultry products, both in open markets and other kinds of markets. Their numbers would have to be multiplied many times to be able to cope with the new situation. Furthermore, hundreds of trucks are used daily to convey both raw materials and finished products for the industry from one end of Nigeria to the other, and the number would also have to increase. This would be apart from the motor mechanics that would be needed to maintain these trucks, the thousands of stevedores that would be needed to load and unload them, and the drivers that would be needed to drive the trucks, together with the assistants that would assist these drivers.

As at 2016, Nigeria was only able to produce 300, 000 metric tonnes of poultry, even though demand is over four times that amount. This is how big the industry is. For those who think this is a joke, the fact is that, in 2014 alone, in spite of the ban on importation of frozen chicken, Nigerians spent over ₦660 billion in the importation of 1.2million metric tonnes (MT) of frozen chicken. The development this money would have given to Nigeria can only be imagined.

Therefore, it would appear that the smugglers were cheating the country on many fronts. They were cheating the government, cheating the populace, and endangering everybody, while enriching themselves alone. If import duty was paid on imported chicken, it will become a source of revenue for the government which will also shore up the price of the chicken to make it similar to what was available within Nigeria. If that was the case, PAN would not mind to receive this complementary help from importers, while it tried to build capacity to meet up with local demand. But by smuggling the frozen chickens into the country, the importers were making a fool of everybody, while laughing to the bank.

With these salient points and CNN showing how bird flu was killing Chinese citizens, it was easy to get the support of stakeholders, and that was how the ban on the importation of frozen chicken was effected. The very sad thing is that, in spite of that ban, the activities of smugglers still appear to be going on unimpeded. In fact, PAN leaders met with customs officials to make them understand the deleterious effects of allowing smugglers to have a field day. The leaders of the association were told that the number of land borders were just too many for customs to man effectively but that the customs service would keep doing its best. There was a positive unintended consequences to this whole issue however.

The volume of smuggling of frozen chicken was what opened the eyes of the PAN members to the extent of demand in the country. Before 2004, most poultry farmers were into egg production, and those that engaged in broilers did so in a targeted manner. Production of broilers was programmed to coincide with festivities like Christmas and Sallah so as to ensure demand. Others were basically contract suppliers who met specific needs of clients like hotels, schools, restaurant chains, and catering companies. But things were set to change.

The information about the activities of smugglers gave PAN members the impetus to go into broiler production, with the assurance that there was ample demand in the country. Those that were already engaged were motivated to increase their capacity. Zartech was one of these; so also was Tuns Farms in Osogbo; and there was CHI Farms. Before 2004, Amo Byng was never involved in broiler production and they were one of those who keyed into this reality to begin broiler production. There were several other farms which went into broiler production after the 2004 ban on importation of frozen chicken. Poultry farmers that were already producing broilers but targeting festivals did not have to wait for festivals anymore. Generally, I would say that the ban had a positive psychological effect, in spite of the clear lapses in its implementation.

Again, through the activities of the Poultry Association of Nigeria, Lagos State Chapter, the idea of poultry estates became a reality in Lagos State. I do not know what is happening in other states, but poultry estates in Lagos have helped to set up farmers who may never have been able to participate in the sector.

A poultry estate is a massive out-of-town land area, carved into individual poultry farms of about one hectare each, all within a common perimeter. It works well because it allows for a lower entry bar for intending poultry farmers. In spite of its drawbacks, the fact remains that these poultry estates have served and are still serving a very key role in the poultry industry. Today in Lagos, there are poultry estates in the following locations:

- Erikorodo in Ikorodu (behind Lagos State Polytechnic);
- Gberigbe, Ikorodu;
- Imota, along Ikorodu-Epe Road;
- Epe;
- Epe (Specially established for graduate farmers);
- Badagry;
- Ajara, after Badagry;
- Ayedoto in Ojo Local Government Area.

There is always the risk that, when one farm is affected by an outbreak of disease, it may quickly affect the others. For example, all the birds in the Ayedoto poultry estate had to be slaughtered and the estate had to be temporarily closed down during the Avian Flu influenza outbreak some years ago. This massive loss was not because all the birds were affected, but as a preventive measure because some birds were indeed infected. It is this kind of loss that is a key disadvantage of the concept of poultry estates. There is also the issue of conflict in the operations of several farmers that operate at such close quarters. These estates will always serve a purpose and I would not recommend that they should be scrapped any time soon, even though their expiry date cannot be very far based on human activity and the need to utilise land for other pressing needs.

It is sheer ignorance for people to think that government has no business in the business of poultry. If not for government participation, how could an individual get access to the massive lands required for poultry estates? Some of the poultry estates in Lagos are as large as 60 hectares and it is clear that, at some points, only government has the clout to make some things happen. The interesting but largely unknown fact is that farmers in Europe and even in the United States receive periodic and emergency help from their governments. Their governments understand the national security component of being able to feed their citizens, so they do not treat the interests of farmers with levity.

For example, the recent occurrence whereby the United States and China began to make moves and counter moves against each other seems like the beginning of a trade war. At some points, because of a particular move by China, wheat farmers in the United States started to face some danger. They were unable to sell their wheat to China and the United States government, in order to keep them in business, bought all the wheat produced by these farmers. The fact is that they may actually choose to dump this wheat in the ocean, give it away as foreign aid, or even sell it to other countries: it does not matter. What matters is keeping the farmers busy and sustaining their businesses. This is the sort of help Nigerian farmers needs from the Nigerian government. We do not want the government to give money to farmers because that is not their role but they should guarantee the purchase of the products which the farmers have suffered a lot to produce. We still have a long way to go, but it is not too early to begin to take the right steps. And as long as these right steps are sustained, things will get better eventually. As it is often said, "Rome was not built in a day." Nigerian farmers do not expect the massive cash injection the US government routinely makes in its agricultural sector, but there is nothing wrong if government takes some small steps. That is all we ask for.

Early in September 2018, some officials of the Poultry Association of Nigeria were in the United States for some training. As reported by the Lagos State Chapter Chairman, Godwin Egbebe, while at the training, there was a breaking news. The United States government had released $200m to support farmers in that country. That amount translates to over 70 billion naira. One can imagine what would happen in Nigeria if farmers could get even a small fraction of such government support from time to time. There would be nothing less than a nuclear explosion in the agricultural sector, with massive employment as an immediate fallout. As someone has claimed, there is no need for government to worry about creating jobs; it should just create the right environment for farmers and they will take care of the rest. Thankfully, more Nigerians are beginning to see that farming is cool. It is no longer the vocation of illiterates and impoverished old men. It is now the playground of highly educated and cosmopolitan Nigerians who deploy knowledge and sophisticated technology to do things differently in order to get outstanding results.

Knowing these things myself and having heard about them, helped me to appreciate the role of government in society at large, and in business in particular. Any sentiments I had against politics began to evaporate. I began to see that, with the right people in government, society could make rapid progress.

Even after setting up my company, Hi-Nutrients International Limited, I did not abandon the Poultry Association of Nigeria although I did not have much time as I would want, especially in the early years of my company, because I had to travel extensively in search of clients and to expand the company's network. In spite of this, I still participated so actively in PAN that, by 2011, I was made Deputy Chairman, PANLAG. I worked with Olushoga Olufawo, who was Chairman at the time. Alhaji Olushoga Olufawo was from the Ikorodu division of PANLAG, while I belong to the Ikeja and Agege division. There are other divisions also: the Epe division, the Victoria Island/Lekki division, the Badagry division, and the Ikotun division. The tradition in PANLAG is for chairmanship position to rotate sequentially from one division to the next. It is also the practice that a chairman and his deputy should not belong to the same division. In 2013, when Olushoga's tenure ended,

I decided to take a break from PANLAG politics. But my break was to be cut short within two years.

Part of the reason for the leadership break from PANLAG, in 2013 was that my company was going through one of its most important seasons since I set it up nine years earlier. In that year, I had the largest order I had never secured before that time, and it was from a reputable company with instant name recognition – UAC Nigeria Limited. The story of my business relationship with UAC had already been told, but I would only add that that relationship was a milestone in itself. So, I was too busy in 2013 to participate in the political activities of PANLAG. However, even the achievements of 2013 were going to serve as a factor in pulling me back into active participation.

The story of Hi-Nutrients began to change in a fundamental way from 2013, which was the first time that those who had doubted my ability to succeed became finally convinced. When Hi-Nutrients was set up, it was the weakest, newest and poorest company in its niche with 14 stable, richer, older, and better-known competitors. It was in 2013 that Hi-Nutrients began to threaten few of these competitors and attempted to unseat them from their place in the ranking of premix manufacturing companies. Some who had watched my activities closely were elders of the Poultry Association of Nigeria, Lagos State branch. At least two of these elders, Mr. Lanre Bello and Dr. Folarin Afelumo, approached me before the 2015 elections and told me to contest as chairman of PANLAG. They had seen the things I had been able to achieve, and it was their informed opinion that, if I could replicate the miracle of Hi-Nutrients at PANLAG, the association would have a new lease of life and be in a position to go places once again.

I agreed to contest for the chairmanship of PANLAG and was a little disappointed when prospective contestants decided to step down for me before the election. In other words, I won the contest before the contest. I began to work with other members of the executive committee as soon as we were sworn in and, before long, tremendous financial growth was recorded.

I was encouraged to become PANLAG Chairman partly because of the success that Dr. Femi Faniyi had recorded as PAN Chairman, Ogun State. Before Femi Faniyi, the average age of PAN Chairmen in Ogun and even elsewhere was 65 years. His ascension was unprecedented, which heralded a new era. I considered that, with me in Lagos and Faniyi in Ogun, it could be a new dawn in the Poultry Association of Nigeria, and I am glad that my team did not disappoint those who had entrusted us with the leadership role.

Dr. Faniyi's style of leadership at PAN, Ogun State, inspired me a lot. I was in touch with him and discovered that he was running the association exactly the way he would run his business. His administration was strategic. He did not just follow the calendar to have only periodic meetings, he utilised his business contacts to garner financial support for the association by engaging them in creative ways and by directly requesting their goodwill gesture. The strategy worked, and Ogun PAN became richer as a result.

I remember that before accepting to become the chairman of PANLAG, I had a heart-to-heart conversation with Dr. Faniyi. I explained my reluctance to him, but he would have none of that. He encouraged me to take the assignment and told me that the elders who wanted me to be PANLAG chairman knew what they were doing. They could only have recommended me because they believed I had what it took to do the job and move the association forward.

Shortly after I became PANLAG Chairman, I organised a stakeholders' forum which had several important players in the industry in attendance. I also secured the cooperation of my own business associates who supported the association financially. I did the little I could to renew the confidence of members in the association and encourage participation through payment of levies.

My assignment was time consuming, but I was enjoying it and combining it with my work seamlessly. As a positive fallout, I knew that my chairmanship would help me to know more people, equip me to manage more people, and, of course, help me in my business. If, for example, I did not know anyone in Badagry before but needed to go and address members there as PANLAG Chairman, one or two customers may want to relate with me because of my position and exposure.

As God would have it, Dr. Ayo Oduntan (Group Managing Director of Amo Byng) became the President of the Poultry Association of Nigeria; as if that was not enough to inspire me, my friend, Dr. Femi Faniyi, became the Chairman of the Poultry Association of Nigeria for the South-West region. As South-West Chairman of PAN, Femi Faniyi was automatically one of the six Vice Presidents of the association at the national level. So says the constitution of PAN, and such had been the practice. What this meant was that, if I looked up, what I could see was a young man as PAN President; if I lowered my gaze just a little, what I could see was another young man as PAN Chairman, South-West zone; and when I looked at myself, I knew that, at less than fifty years of age, nobody could correctly describe me as an old man. So, I was convinced that a new day had come for the Poultry Association of Nigeria, and this went a long way to gear me up to do my very best.

The good thing was that Ayo Oduntan was doing well, Dr. Femi Faniyi was doing excellently well too and I was complementing their wonderful efforts from the Lagos axis, with the support of the vibrant members of the executive committee as well as the other members. In respective branches of the association across the nation, the opinion began to gain ground that it was time for a change of baton from the older generation to the middle-aged generation. Even in branches where elderly men were serving as chairmen, the groundswell of opinion was for them to hurry up and hand over to younger members. They got the message and things began to change very fast. A silent revolution had begun.

On a personal level, I consider Dr. Ayo Oduntan a very rare personality. In spite of the fact that we are almost age mates, I respect him a lot and consider him a mentor and a role model. He is one of those who believed in me, and our relationship is similar to two brothers from different mothers.

Perhaps my personal belief in the leadership of Dr. Ayo Oduntan was what motivated me to make sure that, unlike in the past, PANLAG was not in any unnecessary contention with the national body. We still maintained our priceless independence as Lagosians, but I found ways to douse any needless acrimony.

Sometime in 2017, Dr. Femi Faniyi relocated to the United States of America with his family. Of course, the void his departure created had to be filled as soon as possible, so as not to cause a disadvantage to the South-West at the national level of PAN. I was astonished when some people began to suggest that I should step up to become the Chairman of South-West PAN. One immediate reason for my surprise was that, even at that time, I was still PANLAG Chairman in Lagos State and my tenure was yet to end. What began as whispers soon became audible enough for everybody to hear. It was no longer a secret: some forces within PANLAG wanted me to move up the ladder and fill the vacancy created by the relocation of Dr. Femi Faniyi. Going by the advice earlier given to me by Dr. Femi Faniyi himself that I should not be reluctant to accept the challenge of leadership – especially whenever I was recommended by elders – I decided to accept the challenge and contest to fill the position of PAN South-West Chairman. It's obvious that my decision did not go down well with some association members, including some elders and leaders of branches outside Lagos.

It was during the election that I got to realise that there were two worlds in this world. I got to realise that one could not really know one's true friends until after seeing their attitude during an election. It was during an election that I got to know my true friends and also my true enemies.

Some members and leaders were excited about the prospect of a serving PANLAG Chairman clinching the position of South-West Chairman. They felt that it would balance the equation in many ways because Lagos (that is, PANLAG) was unable to get one of their own as South-West Chairman for quite a while. The opportunity created by Femi Faniyi's relocation was considered now or never by some but others saw the situation very differently. Instead of looking at my contest for the position from the point of view of PANLAG and the corporate interests of PANLAG, some chose to see it as a matter of Prince Ezekiel Olabode Adetoyi and his personal ambition. Thus, the stage was set for a nasty battle of wits between my supporters and my detractors.

In spite of having produced South-West Chairmen in the past, Oyo State was interested in filling the vacant position. Interestingly, even Ogun wanted to fill the slot, in spite of the fact that Dr. Femi Faniyi who had just left the position was from that very zone. Lagos PAN would not hear any of these but insisted that it was their turn and that I was their man. The stiffest opposition to turn a PANLAG Chairman into a South-West Chairman came from Osun State, followed closely by forces in Oyo and Ogun States. As an indigene of Ekiti State and a Lagosian, I had the support of Ondo and Ekiti States. Ondo was also in the bag because, where Ekiti goes, Ondo goes. The good thing was that, even as PANLAG Chairman, I had developed a good relationship with the PAN Chairmen of both Ekiti and Ondo States.

While the tension was building, I received a call from one of the elders from one of the South-West states outside Lagos who invited me to his office. It would be correct to state that this man was just trying to do what he felt was the right thing. I would always respect him for that. He was a true elder who had his eyes on the progress of the association as a whole than on pandering to the parochial sentiments of some individuals.

While in his office, this sagacious elder told me that he had been observing me, not only as a fellow association member and CEO of my own company, but since I was an employee of Bio-Organics. He said he knew that I was a very diligent young man who worked hard to get to where I was. He also stated that he knew how I had taken over Lagos as PANLAG Chairman including the way I conducted my business. Having eulogised me, he stated the bare fact (which my critics did not want to consider) that it was Lagos' turn to produce the South-West Chairman. The man told me in categorical terms that he would not support the emergence of any candidate from any other state other than Lagos, including his own state, and that his stance was in the interest of fairness and justice. He said that Osun State had no moral justification for their opposition to PANLAG because they had produced a National President of PAN in the past. As for both Oyo and Ogun, they had also produced South-West Chairmen. He insisted that it was the turn of Lagos State and added that, because I was an indigene of Ekiti State, my chairmanship of the South-West will go a long way in assuaging the people of Ekiti, who will feel represented and consider my tenure as theirs. The same sentiments would be shared by Ondo State, which was the state that gave birth to Ekiti in the first place.

After receiving this timely moral support from this elder, I summoned the courage to play my own politics at my level and tried to build consensus around my candidacy. With all due respect to other geopolitical zones in Nigeria, the fact remains that the South-West is the melting pot of the poultry business in Nigeria. At least 65% of poultry farms in Nigeria are in the South-West, and whoever occupies the chairmanship position of the South-West automatically becomes a force at the national level. Perhaps this explains why some persons were hell bent on ensuring that I did not step into Dr. Faniyi's shoes.

Before the D-day, I got a call from the Director General of the Poultry Association of Nigeria, Mr. Onallo Akpa, who advised me to take things easy, obviously referring to the political moves being made in the South-West, and on my decision to contest to become the next chairman. Mr. Akpa gave me some words of advice and the tenor of his words suggested that I should be cautious. But I mistook his words to mean that he was suggesting that I should suspend my aspiration. Not wanting to misinterpret him and end up creating confusion in my camp, I asked him if he was saying that I should not contest. I was glad that I asked that question because his opinion would have affected me seriously. Fortunately for me, Mr. Akpa said that he was not asking me to step down but was rather asking me to understand the gravity of the goal I had set for myself, and to tread softly.

When I settled down, I began to do what politicians loosely referred to as permutation. I knew that when the chips were down, Dr. Ayo Oduntan would not oppose me, in spite of any sort of characters around him, and in spite of whatever they succeeded in whispering into his ears. Unfortunately, I knew that I could not count on any vote from Osun State; but I had Lagos solidly and even aggressively behind me. As for Ogun, I knew I had enough backup to expect at least 50% of the vote. What was true of Ogun was also true of Oyo. With my connection to Ekiti and Ondo States, I expected nothing less than block vote in support of my chairmanship from those two. So the outlook was not discouraging.

It seemed I wasn't the only one who had done this objective permutation: my opponents appeared to have done their own permutation also and painfully realised that, except for what insurance companies called an act of God, there was no way I would not win the South-West chairmanship position. I guess this was why they resorted to arm-twisting. Shortly after my permutation, I received unambiguous instructions from some top elders in Ogun and Oyo States. These elders and leaders (names withheld) pointedly said that I should step down for my main contender, Engr. Olateru.

On a normal day, I would have listened to these men. Apart from that, Engr. Olateru was someone I had and still have deep respect for. Not only was he older than me in age, he was also older than me in the industry and had never offended me in any way in the past. More so, our relationship was good and devoid of any rancour. I would have been willing to change course for Engr. Olateru's sake. But the contest for the chairmanship of South-West PAN had gone beyond me as a person. It was not about me anymore. It was about doing the right thing; it was about the will of PANLAG, which I represented; it was about refusing to back down, except under the force of superior argument. It was about democracy, which we all claimed to subscribe to. In my own view, anybody who belonged to a democratic association like the Poultry Association of Nigeria, but did not believe in democracy must be a hypocrite, or a bully, or both. Most of the people who opposed me could not make any objective point except to claim that I was being ambitious. But they did not remember to add that my opponents were just as equally ambitious, and that, as a member of the association, I had the same rights and privileges as other contestants.

When they could not get me to back down, the leaders in question resorted to an appeal. They said that I was a young man and that I should wait for my time. I had already seen the handwriting on the wall and privately taken my stand. As far as I was concerned, the only people that had the moral right to ask me to back down were the very people who had instigated my interest in the first place; namely, the elders and members of PANLAG.

When I stood my ground that the time was just right for me, they proceeded to bare their fangs and warned me of imminent defeat if I did not heed their warning. I knew they were bluffing, but in any case, I had already considered the possibility of defeat and did not think it was the death sentence they were trying to make it sound like. I knew I would have enough goodwill to congratulate anyone who won the election. After all, we all had our respective businesses, and any activity done in the association is supposed to be sacrificial. There was no way I was going to feel terrible for losing an election for PAN South-West Chairman.

I told these opposing leaders that I would rather be beaten fair and square than step down and betray the support and interests of PANLAG. I said that if I lost, I would be the first to congratulate whoever won. Then they knew that the battle line had been drawn and that the issue of who would be the next PAN South-West Chairman was now completely in the hands of the delegates who would vote.

D-Day eventually came and I won the election and became the South-West Chairman of the Poultry Association of Nigeria. It was a keen contest, which was free and fair. Everybody, including those who had been against my aspiration, finally had the incontrovertible evidence that the delegates had exercised their franchise in electing me their new chairman. There was nothing to do but to accept me as such, personal misgivings notwithstanding. As South-West Chairman of PAN, the next logical step, in line with our constitution, was for me to be ratified as National Vice President of PAN. But some people felt that was the place where they could corner me and fulfil that which had been denied them by the electorate.

In a manner I am ashamed to recount, some people converged in Abuja and agreed that they had removed me from being the South-West Chairman of PAN, in spite of a successfully conducted election, during which I had been duly elected. I would not give details of everything that transpired during that period. I must state that, as soon as they learnt of the charade in Abuja, my leaders and elders in Lagos swung into action. They vowed not to allow the robbery of the mandate freely given to Lagos by any person or group of persons, especially because these persons were on the slippery slope of illegality in their attempt. Things were about to get out of hand until I received a call from Dr. Ayo Oduntan. I was happy to receive his call because I knew that he was among those who could resolve the matter. Before the South-West leadership crisis began, I had already asked my Deputy Chairman, Godwin Egbebe, to begin to act in my stead, while I focused on national issues and the South-West region.

Dr. Ayo Oduntan heard my side of the story and confirmed that he was aware of the clandestine efforts to ensure that I did not get ratified as National Vice President of PAN. In addressing the situation, Dr. Oduntan chose to utilise the African method of conflict resolution. He told me that egos were involved in the escalation of the matter. He then appealed to me to use my political sagacity to neutralise the fire by humbling myself to appease some individuals who were indeed powerful and could create problems for me. I listened to Ayo Oduntan because I trusted him. Following his advice, I took the next available flight and did the needful. I was able to appeal to some of these strong men in person and assure them that I would not be a rebel, in case that was what they were apprehensive about. I promised them that I would be amenable to the counsel of the elders and apologised for the mix up. This was how peace was restored, and the coast became clear for a hitch-free ratification process, even though not everyone from the opposing camp came fully on board.

I learnt a lot through that experience and saw aspects of politics I did not know about before then. At its roots, politics is just intensified human relations. It is human relations engineering. I do not know what would have happened if, heaven forbid, I had refused to listen to Dr. Oduntan. I don't know what would have happened if I had insisted on using the power of my mandate to confront the displeased elders. Perhaps, the Poultry Association of Nigeria would have become a casualty of the war that would have ensued.

I would not like to mention names, but I know of some other people who had also drawn out their daggers and vowed that if I was not ratified as Vice President of PAN, they would also do their worst and damn the consequences. The consequences referred to here was apparently the continued existence of PAN, especially, South-West PAN. This was the kind of war nobody would have been able to truly win because, at the end of the day, the association we all cared about would have suffered for it. Anybody who understands the balance of power in the Poultry Association of Nigeria knows that, if the South-West is embroiled in a major crisis, the cohesion of the national body would be negatively threatened to cause it to go into automatic coma. Without the South-West region, the Poultry Association of Nigeria would be a joke.

As far as politics is concerned, I now know that there is time for everything. There is a time to insist on due process, and a time to use the wisdom of humility to find a short cut to the hearts of aggrieved people without judging their motives. Instead of discouraging me from politics, these experiences made me to realise that I could succeed if I chose to engage in politics. I know that listening to elders and being humble were key components, apart from just competence. But the willingness to listen to elders and be humble in human relations were things that came naturally to me. I could be stubborn; but I do not believe in being stupidly stubborn. For example, I would have been manifesting stupid stubbornness if I had refused to accept Dr. Oduntan's advice. I was not stupidly stubborn in the way I listened to him, and I believe that accepting his advice was what contributed to diffusing a potential conflagration.

Eventually, I was ratified as the Vice President of PAN. In this regard, I got the support of Mr. Ezekiel Ibrahim, who is the current President of PAN. Fortunately for me, while he was an aspirant, I had gone out of my way to support him, even against the expectation of some persons around me. In fact, the person at whose expense I had supported Mr. Ezekiel was someone highly esteemed; someone I respect up till today. However, my support for Mr. Ezekiel Ibrahim was based on principles and on the way I saw the issues at that time. There was nothing personal in the matter.

As at the time of this writing, I am still the Chairman of the Poultry Association of Nigeria (PAN), South-West zone; and according to the constitution of PAN, I also double as its Vice President. I do not intend to go beyond this position in PAN but would continue to support its activities and prepare myself for future participation in politics. For now, my focus is on consolidating the gains of the recent merger of Hi-Nutrients with Neovia. I know that Neovia is testing Nigeria and that other multinationals are also watching to see what would happen. In many ways, I realise that whatever happens to the merger of my company – Hi-Nutrients – with Neovia will, in some way, affect the future of mergers and acquisitions in the livestock industry in Nigeria, and even in other sectors of the economy. So, it is my intention to remain focused and ensure that everything goes smoothly.

In retrospect, my experience in the politics of PAN contributed in helping me stay the course in my decision to represent my people of Ekiti North 2 Federal Constituency at the Federal House of Representatives. The vehicle I created for this special purpose was known as BAM – Bode Adetoyi Movement.

CHAPTER 17

MY STINT IN POLITICS

The worst illiterate is the political illiterate. He hears nothing, sees nothing, takes no part in political life. He doesn't seem to know that the cost of living, the price of beans, of flour, of rent, of medicines, all depend on political decisions. He even prides himself on his political ignorance, sticks out his chest and says he hates politics. He doesn't know, the imbecile, that from his political non-participation comes the prostitute, the abandoned child, the robber and, worst of all, corrupt officials ... **Bertol T. Brecht.**

After initially indicating interest to contest for Member of the Federal House of Representatives in the National Assembly of the Federal Republic of Nigeria in the 2019 legislative elections in Ekiti State, I abruptly stepped down. This was in spite of what I would modestly describe as a tidal wave of support for my candidacy from members of my constituents, most of whom were so excited about my interest that they felt it was nothing less than a dream come true. I did not step down because I had any doubts about the clear possibility of success, neither did I suddenly decide that representing my people was no longer worth the time and effort I knew it would demand of me. I stepped down from my aspiration for reasons that would become clear later in the book. It will also become clear that, instead of a termination, what happened to my political aspiration can best be described as a suspension. I am taking time off now, to return not very long from now.

Having fully participated in political leadership at different agric professional organisations, I decided to participate in politics in the larger society to do something that could lead to a better life for the people I cared about. I cannot point to a specific day when I finally decided but I would say my decision was based on various events in my life. These events were not necessarily connected, but they convinced me that, whatever I did in life, I was going to attempt to help people through the platform of government. The only proactive way I know that can lead to this platform is political participation. However, there was the matter of charlatans in politics. Even if to stop these charlatans alone, so-called good men have no option but to participate in politics. I thoroughly believe what Plato said long ago: "the price good men pay for indifference to public affairs is to be ruled by evil men."

The fact is that more than two-thirds of my fifty years on earth have been spent going through financial dependency. I know what it means for an adult to wake up in the morning with no money in his pocket, no food, and no asset to dispose of and raise quick cash. That sort of life creates a painful uncertainty that makes peace of mind difficult. I am glad that no one needs to explain poverty to me. I am glad that I endured a life of abject want and deprivation. I am glad because the painful experience with poverty has enriched my perspective about life and positioned me to empathise with people, and, more importantly, to be a compassionate leader.

I remember when I was still an applicant. I had no good shoes to wear and had to borrow clothes sometimes to attend interviews. One day, my clothes got torn while I was alighting from a Molue bus. Unfortunately, I still had not gotten to my destination and had to decide what to do. If I wasn't such a poor boy by the time, the simple thing would have been to get to the nearest boutique and buy some clothes, while throwing my torn clothes in the dustbin. Unfortunately, I had no such cash. I decided to return home and change to another equally old pair of clothes. It's a pity none of the buses would stop to pick me up because they probably thought I was one of those insane people on the streets of Lagos and I was a graduate by this time. As I recall this, I am close to tears because this is not a condition any human being should have to go through. Lack of money can so degrade a man and make living with dignity near impossible.

For those who grew up with parents that were able to meet their needs until when they started working, these kinds of story would appear fictional. I know it for a fact that there are people out there who use one pair of shoes for as many as ten years simply because they do not have a few thousands to buy a new pair. Even if they have enough money to buy a pair of shoes, the need to preserve that money in order to spend it on things necessary for survival (things like food) will probably not allow them to just go out there and buy a pair of shoes. What is the relevance of a new pair of shoes to a man who struggles to find enough food to eat just to stay alive every day? This kind of poverty dehumanises a man and actually affects his psyche. Like animals in the jungle, this kind of poverty makes a man think of food in the morning, in the afternoon, and at night. I have experienced it in the past. Part of my goal in life is to ensure that as many people as I can empower will not have to pass through that.

In the Redeemed Christian Church of God (RCCG) for example, there is something we do occasionally as a way of reaching out to the underprivileged. This endeavour is tagged "Let's-Go-A-Fishing." We move out of the church as a group with many goodies in several cars and position ourselves at street corners to show kindness to people who have no one to care for them. It was my experience in reaching out to the less privileged through this church programme that inspired me to begin to think of what I could do to give back to the society in a very functional way. Very importantly, I realised that it did not require too much money to give a critical helping hand to those in need. I saw how hungry people accepted the cold rice we would give them and they would eat with such relish and I could not help wondering about their true condition. Some would even keep part of the rice with the intention of eating it later. I decided that I will find a way to help my people. Like the people say "charity, indeed, begins at home." I had to start from Otun, my hometown. As a believer in education and its power to transform lives and families, I decided that my philanthropy would focus on education first before touching other areas. This was how my scholarship scheme was conceived.

First, I discussed the issue with my wife and she accepted it. She said it was a good idea and she encouraged me to go ahead. So we planned to consistently set aside a certain percentage of our annual income for that purpose. We started in 2014 by giving 30 students ₦20, 000 each. This was how Ade Abolarin, a fellow prince of Otun, got involved in the endeavour. Ade Abolarin is from one of the five ruling houses of Otun (the Ileobajeu ruling house) and many people in Otun hold him in high esteem. Like Joseph of old, he is always around the corridors of power and knows the history of Otun so well that he has become an authority on the subject. As a grassroots man, he knew which student was the child of poor parents, and he was the one in charge of compiling the list of beneficiaries. Because I did not visit Otun often, there was no way I could know who and who would be the right beneficiaries. This was why I trusted Prince Ade Abolarin with that assignment. I do not even know the people on the list he prepares, but whatever name he puts on the list gets to benefit from the scheme. The only condition I placed on it was that no student affiliated to me or my family should be on the list.

I was surprised by the effect of the paltry amount I started giving to each of these students. I started hearing some good news from different people, and this encouraged me a great deal. When I considered the fact that it was only ₦20, 000 that I had given each of these students, I was amazed. According to Ade Abolarin and the Oba of Mobaland, my scholarship scheme was the first of its kind in Otun and was making impact beyond what I could imagine. Apart from the amount itself, the scheme brought hope to the people because they were happy to know that somebody from that town was so blessed and had decided to remember them in such a very practical way. There was hope for a better tomorrow, with such sons of Otun on ground.

Many people who were benefitting from my scheme did not know my name because the scholarship programme was done under the umbrella of Hi-Nutrients. Apart from the scholarship scheme, I supported students through the Federation of Otun-Moba Students Union (FOMSU). I supported them with direct cash donations and also by giving them moral support. According to a former president of FOMSU, they were able to rent an apartment in 2016 as their secretariat from the funds I had provided. I also financially supported them in the hosting of the Miss Otun Beauty Pageant and attended the event in person on the 24th December, 2016. It was during that event that I was made the Grand Patron of the Students' Union, and this took place in the presence of the Oore of Mobaland, Oba James Oladele Popoola. Whenever necessary, I give random support to different students who channel their requests under the auspices of the Federation of Otun-Moba Students Union. The Federation of Otun-Moba Students Union comprises all students in tertiary institutions who are from Otun-Moba.

My focus is on education because I believe in the power of education. In this regard, I also bought JAMB forms for 50 students from Ikole Local Government Area. I was doing all these things because I believed that, the more the educated people in the area, the more the chances of some of them breaking out of poverty, and the more people will be liberated, just like I was liberated and was now trying to liberate others. Ikole is not even part of my constituency (Ekiti North Federal Constituency 2) but my scheme touched lives there. I also gave scholarship to 25 Ikole LGA students during the commemoration of the coronation of Oba Ayo Kupoluyi of Temidire town.

Some of my friends believed that I was wasting money, but I believed that I was investing in people. The Bible says that, when you give to help people from the little you have, whatever remains will continue to multiply: and God will answer your prayers. I am a man that believes in God. The Ekiti North Federal Constituency 2 only comprises Moba, Ilejemeje, and Ido-Osi, and I was able to extend my scheme to cover this whole area. Ikole was just an extra. My mission, going forward, is to extend this scheme to all the local government areas in Ekiti State.

Soon enough, people started seeing me as a leader in the community. They started saying that they did not have politicians who cared about them and that, if persons like me were to get elected, I would make a difference. This was after I had sustained my scholarship scheme for years. I wondered within myself if I should consider this sort of call to participate in politics. I kept thinking about these things but did not reach a final decision.

Around that time, Pastor Adeboye said during the Holy Ghost monthly service that it was actually a sin for Christians to be lackadaisical about political affairs. He said that the time for such indifference was past. He urged us to go to our respective villages and register, participate and even go and contest. After that Holy Ghost service, I took time to consider what Pastor Adeboye had said. While in deep introspection, I said to myself that, if Papa Adeboye could be saying this, then God must be in this project.

So, without telling my wife, I went to consult Senator Ladoja. Senator Rashidi Adewolu Ladoja is an astute politician and one of my role models. He is a chemical engineer who had worked with a reputable oil company like Total Nigeria for 13 years. After holding different positions at Total Nigeria, he left there and started his private business in 1985 and has remained a businessman since then. He has ventured into shipping, manufacturing, banking, agriculture, and even transportation. He ventured into politics and had served as a Senator and Executive Governor of Oyo State. Even before I was opportune to meet him, Senator Ladoja had already become a director of Standard Trust Bank Limited, which later merged with the United Bank for Africa (UBA) in January 2007.

As the Chairman of Hi-Nutrients International Limited at the time, there is no gainsaying the fact that the Senator and I got quite close. Because of my hunger for knowledge, I utilised the opportunity I had to interact with Ladoja to learn as much as I could from him. He was not only older than me but was more experienced in business and politics. He had gotten to the pinnacle of his political career by becoming the Governor of his state and there was a lot I could learn from him, especially because I was just about to begin to take the first toddler steps into politics. I dearly needed his advice on how to proceed. If Senator Ladoja had said I should not go into politics, I would have stopped right there. After all, he had played the role of an angel investor at a very critical period in the life of Hi-Nutrients International Limited, and we had been together since that time. I held the man in high esteem and believed that any advice he gave me would be in my best interests.

My interest was to run as a member of the Federal House of Representatives, representing my federal constituency, Ekiti North 2. When I told Senator Ladoja about my intention, he did not ask for time to think about anything but immediately said it was a good idea. He said it was good when one was recognised by his people and asked to step out to lead. He said leadership was easy in such cases. I couldn't agree more with Senator Ladoja. Leadership was indeed easy when the person leading had the support of the led – especially if the people to be led were educated.

Coupled with the spiritual backing from Pastor Adeboye, who had said we should join any political party of our choice and contest for any elective office in the land, I finally had the courage to move. Pastor Adeboye had said we should go out there and show that we were children of God and that we could do politics in a different way. I wanted to do politics and do it in a different way but there is someone whose stake in my life cannot be quantified. That person is my wife, Mrs. Bukola Adetoyi. I had to face her tribunal, and I dreaded the prospects because I knew, from her antecedents, what her response was likely to be. When I eventually told her about my intention to run for political office, she was against it and asked if I had discussed the issue with Senator Ladoja. She was spot on: she knew he was my political mentor and role model in such matters. I did not argue with my wife – neither did I give her any opportunity to discourage me.

I went to Ade Abolarin, who was also my political mentor. I told him about my preliminary consultations and asked for his opinion on the matter. Ade Abolarin told me a lot of things but added that I would need to spend a lot of money if I wanted to run for office. After telling me more things, I asked him the most important question on my mind, which was what the reaction of the people would be when word got out that I wanted to represent them at the House of Representatives.

Ade Abolarin minced no words in assuring me that my aspiration would be totally accepted and supported, not just in Otun and even Mobaland as a whole, but in all the areas where I had become known through my scholarship scheme.

When we got into the details, he said that I needed a structure. He then proceeded to explain that we had two options: we could either adopt an existing structure or build a new one. His advice was that, adopting an existing structure might be the best option. Then he said I had nothing to worry about because I was sellable. That was the same thing many leaders I eventually met kept saying.

When I asked Ade what he meant by me being sellable, he said I was sellable because of the things I was doing and the fact that I was a successful businessman. People knew that I was not hungry, and, as a rule, they were suspicious of persons who had no means of livelihood and wanted their votes to get into political office. The belief of the people was that such poor politicians were going to become rich at their expense by massively embezzling funds meant for community development. I could see the logic and was happy that my antecedents had helped my reputation as a budding politician. Ade Abolarin added that, besides my economic independence, I had shown (through my philanthropy and anti-poverty initiatives) that I cared about the people. They knew I could only do more if given more power and more funds.

Even though Ade Abolarin belonged to another party, he advised me to join the progressives. He was instrumental to the setting up of my structure. It was also Ade Abolarin that introduced Banji Ajayi, another grassroots politician, to me. He is a very brilliant and no-nonsense politician; a go-getter. He used to scold me whenever I tried to bring business principles into political manoeuvring. He would address me respectfully and declare, stern-faced, that even though I am a successful businessman, he would teach me the art of politicking. According to Banji, politicians were like the prodigal son in the Bible. They spent money and did not account for the money they spent because they knew that profit only came when they win an election. And when they lose, they would simply accept the situation and wait for the next election.

Banji said businessmen like me would prefer to spend ₦100 to get ₦150 so that they can declare a profit of ₦50. He said that, in politics, the reverse was the case. It was only when politicians win elections that they could recoup their money: every other thing was a loss. That was why they did everything – spent every naira – to win. Nothing else mattered. Neither was there time for rendering accounts. Banji was part of the structure that Ade Abolarin was already creating, and he was supposed to serve as the Director General (DG) of my campaign organisation. There were others that were supposed to be part of the structure also. Apart from the DG, who was the campaign manager, you had the women leader, the youth leader, and various chairpersons of different committees. I had to learn all these things. So, even though I have temporarily stepped aside from politics, I now know the nitty-gritty of what it takes. If that was all I learnt through my attempt, I feel it was worth it.

When my aspiration began to become an open secret, I got calls from some people who told me that witches and wizards in my village were going to kill me. But I was not that bothered. Pastor Adeboye had once told us that, if God did not allow it, nobody could just kill a person because they felt like doing so. Human life was not that easy to dispose of, he had assured us. Then, while praying, I also asked God to protect me since I was only trying to help my people. Every thought I had was about my people; no other thing but the interests of my people. I am not like Dangote, but I know that, one day, I would surpass Dangote in good works. So, I was willing to share the little that God had given me.

Not surprisingly, everybody in my family opposed my political ambition. Their reason was that they did not want me to die young. According to them (and I understood their point of view), politicians were notorious for killing each other. They said that the game of politics was just too dirty. My counter-argument was that, if politics was a dirty game, who will make the game clean, except those who wanted to use and not abuse politics. I told them that it was the very people who were likely to change the way politics was being played that were also the ones always being discouraged from joining it.

Personally, I believe that, if people are determined, they can change the general impression that politics is dirty. To me, every person in life is a political animal, and there is politics everywhere. Even within a family, there is politics; in the business circle, there is politics. Without politics, one cannot succeed. When one has business acumen and economic power, the next thing that is needed is political power, and these were the two powers I wanted to combine. God had helped me to be in a position to afford the basic needs of life through my business. From that same business also, I am able to pay about a hundred staff every month. So, my main reason for wanting to venture into politics was to serve my people. When you have economic power, and you are able to combine it with political power, you are complete. That is the only personal thing I could have gained – having political power. At the end of the day, I believe that, with both economic and political power, I would have access to the people that matter in this country and be able to use that access to bring good things to my people at home in Ekiti North Federal Constituency 2.

Through this journey, I decided to pitch my tent with the progressives. When the members of the opposing parties in my town heard about the camp I had joined in order to actualise my goal, they chided me and did not hide their displeasure. Anyway, I joined the progressives on the basis of principles.

I started attending ward meetings, senatorial meetings and state meetings. I was a committed progressive and was ready to stick with them. My father had been a progressive. He was an Awolowo follower. That was part of what made me to join the progressives. I like their ideology of focusing on the welfare of the people in general. That was what Chief Obafemi Awolowo was known for: free education and things like that. I respect Chief Jeremiah Obafemi Awolowo a lot and do not feel embarrassed to be called a progressive, while hoping that today's progressives will not betray his ideals.

A look at my manifesto proves where my passion would have been directed. As stated in that document, poverty eradication (not just poverty alleviation) was my key goal. I hate poverty so seriously that I wanted to declare a total war against it in my federal constituency. However, as a businessman, I know that you do not eradicate poverty by lining people up in a long queue and giving each and every one of them an amount of cash. There may be time for such direct intervention, but it can only be a stopgap solution and not a major strategy. My ideas include sound strategies like job creation, which I intend to achieve by providing an enabling environment for businesses to grow, by attracting investment, and by building critical infrastructure. As part of my poverty eradication strategy, I also believe in the short term solution of social grants to provide immediate succour to persons whose situation is too desperate to wait for other initiatives to take effect. Naturally, supporting education to make people self-sufficient was also hot on my plate, apart from doing something significant to support housing, fighting crime to ensure safety and protect investment, and adopting good governance as a policy in public administration.

As is abundantly clear from my manifesto, I already knew what I wanted to do. I drew my manifesto myself because

I already had deliverables. I told the people around me that they should not bother to vote me in for a second term if I did not deliver in four years what I had promised. I knew what I wanted to do for the vocational people; I knew what I wanted to do for students; I knew what I wanted to do for the elderly. As for students, my target was to bring a university to my constituency – either private or public.

As my elder brother, Adewunmi Ajibade, would say, we have many challenges in Mobaland, but one of the major challenges is the absence of a tertiary institution. I completely agree with Mr. Ajibade, who is the publisher of *Eminent Citizens Magazine*, and a founding member of Prime Club, Otun. Indeed, we need a university in that community; or at least a polytechnic. People need to understand the role of a higher institution in the development of an area like Otun-Ekiti.

For example, in a full tertiary institution, you may have up to 1000 members of staff. The chain effect of that alone on the community is enormous. Some of these staff members would be married, and many would have children. They would require lots of houses to stay in and would employ maids, gardeners, and maybe even drivers, some of whom would be from the community. There is a lot that would change, just by the presence of the institution alone, apart from the requirement for building its infrastructure, which will provide jobs for many in the community. As the university or polytechnic grows, so would the community. The staff members would rent houses, buy lands, and build houses: they would require carpenters, bricklayers, painters, and several other artisans. Sand, granite and cement suppliers, and plank suppliers would also become productively engaged in meeting the needs of the infrastructural development.

If you go to Ado-Ekiti today and take away the university and the polytechnic, and you also remove the fact that it has the headquarters of the state, Ado-Ekiti will become like any other community in Ekiti State. That is the truth. If you get to Ikere and take away the College of Education and all the staff there, Ikere would become like any other community in Ekiti State. That is to let you know the role that a tertiary institution plays in the life of a community. So, the major challenge that we have in Otun-Ekiti today is the lack of a tertiary institution. If we have a tertiary institution, all other things would take care of themselves. We have good sons and daughters all over the world but, without a higher institution, we would remain in the same spot: there would be no real progress.

So, my mind is made up to do whatever it would take to get a higher institution in Otun before the expiration of my first tenure. If push come to shove and I need to set up a private university, I have enough contacts to gather up to fifty investors and ask them to put down ₦100 million each, making a total of ₦5 billion. With that kind of amount, a university could be set up with ease. On the public side, I would have been able to use my position in the Federal House of Representatives to make a case for my area. I would make sure my voice is heard loudly and clearly within the chambers of the House for the citing of a tertiary institution in Otun.

With this clear goal in mind, I wasted no time in going to visit the VIPs in Ekiti politics. That was what brought me to Otunba Niyi Adebayo. But before going to see Otunba Niyi Adebayo, I was at an award ceremony where I met the then chairman, Dr. John Oyegun, who also got an award at that ceremony. I was able to meet Chief Obasanjo one-on-one; I was also able to meet Engr. Segun Oni and Dr. John Kayode Fayemi, then Minister of Mines and Power. John Kayode Fayemi has since been sworn in as the current Governor of Ekiti State.

Apart from Ade Abolarin, another grassroots politician I met was Mr. Siki, from Ayetoro in Ekiti State. In fact, it was Mr. Siki that took me to Otunba Niyi Adebayo. Fortunately for me, it was an easy ride. We went to Niyi Adebayo's office at Victoria Island together. Otunba Niyi Adebayo is a level-headed leader with a human heart. I learnt a lot from him. He is as gentle as a dove but very pragmatic; he is very sharp and very articulate. When I met him, he asked me a few questions, but it was only later that I got to know that he was pleased with my answers.

Mr. Oyebanji Abiodun, the present Secretary to the Ekiti State Government, was another consummate grassroots politician I met. He used to be the Chief of Staff to Otunba Niyi Adebayo when he was Governor of Ekiti State. Otunba called Abiodun and told him that he needed to meet a young man who would be under him for a while. As a budding politician, Mr. Oyebanji Abiodun was going to be my direct boss. By the time he read my profile and interacted with me, he said he liked me personally and was seriously impressed that I had achieved so much within a short period of time. He announced to me that he had adopted me as his political son and added that this was something he did not just do indiscriminately. This man taught me real politics. He was the one who now introduced me to more politicians that matter in Ekiti State. Oyebanji Abiodun is the number one loyalist of Niyi Adebayo in Ekiti State today.

I was generally encouraged by meeting these different people. Eventually, Mr. Abiodun took me to Abuja and we began to meet the leaders that matter. I was moving underground. People believed that I was a novice; indeed, I was a novice, but I was using the knowledge I had acquired in business to make things happen. People underrated me, but I could have gotten the ticket if not that I chose to step down.

Some of the elders I met took the display of their support for me to new heights. A remarkable case was that of Senator Olubunmi Adetumbi. He was the one that sewed the BAM attire for me and my team. He was so impressed that he spent ₦400,000 just to make those clothes. They were all monogrammed with the BAM logo. His excitement over my aspiration began the very day I went to see him. I gave him the manifesto of the Bode Adetoyi Movement, through which I wanted to get to the Federal House of Representatives. The man (a seasoned politician) was surprised that a businessman like myself who was just coming into politics already knew what he wanted to achieve.

Apart from those already mentioned (Otunba Niyi Adebayo, Dr. John Kayode Fayemi, Segun Oni, Oyebanji Abiodun, etc.), I also met Baba Bejide, Elder L. A. Kolawole, Baba Atejioye, J.F. Oyinloye and Baba Robinson.

I had already produced 250 copies of my profile and had formed the habit of dropping a copy whenever I visited any renowned politician. Their political colour did not matter to me and the effect of this was like a phenomenon. Some would say they would see me later; some would call me by themselves after reading my profile. Some would wonder why I wanted to go into politics. Their view was that I was doing very well and should continue with my business, which they could see had gone international.

I remember the response of a particular senior friend of mine, Chief Joop Berkhout, Chairman of Safari Books Limited. When I told him about my political ambition, in spite of the fact that Chief Joop was a friend of Chief Olusegun Obasanjo and other notable Nigerian politicians, he refused to endorse my ambition. In fact, he was totally against it. He was adamant that I must continue in my trajectory as a businessman, which had already yielded the critical fruit of gaining the attention of international investors. There was nothing I did not tell Chief Joop about wanting to go into politics for the sole purpose of helping my people: but he countered all my points by reminding me that I was already helping my people through my philanthropic scholarship scheme. When I later suspended my ambition, Chief Joop was one of those that celebrated with relief.

Others, equally impressed, will say they needed people like myself in the politics of our area. They would say I was one of the best materials they had ever encountered. So, everybody was expressing their opinion on my aspiration. At least one person called to advise me. He said he was impressed with me and thanked God that Ekiti had someone like my humble self. I took courage from all of these words of encouragement.

Finally, after getting ample evidence that the train had left the station, my wife succumbed and started praying for me while I launched into the murky waters of politics – a water filled with dangerous hyenas, filled with hippopotamus, filled with crocodiles, filled with assorted breeds of wild aquatic animals. God saw me through, even though I was attacked spiritually. My business suddenly went down during that period. It was so serious that I was distressed. My wife raised some prayer warriors and there were many night vigils. Eventually, my business was restored. That experience helped me to understand the reality of what some people had told me earlier. A few persons had categorically told me not to go into politics because I would be attacked – either physically or spiritually. I could now see that these people knew what they were talking about. But my view has not changed, nonetheless. I believe that, when you want to serve your people, it is a case of no retreat, no surrender. Your situation must be taken like that of a man on a bridge in which a portion of the bride behind him had been blown off. It was a dangerous situation: and the only way out was to keep moving and hope to get to the other side in one piece.

While the build-up to the contest was on, I acquired a large piece of land which I wanted to use to train youths in agriculture. Even as a businessman, I would still carry out that mission. My area is an agrarian area, and I wanted to train young farmers and make millionaires out of as many of them who had the passion for agriculture. I wanted to bring more youths into agriculture. I wanted to show them how they could earn a living through businesses based on agriculture. That was why I got that land, and, by the grace of God, even without going to the Federal House of Representatives, I would still do what I had in mind.

I will be lying if I claim that I have no intention of participating in politics in the future. As a human being who believes in God, I believe that God has His own plans for my life. But until I know otherwise, I will keep my dreams for my people alive and keep reviewing my plans for what I would do, when another opportunity comes around in the future.

I must contribute to my state, which is like no other in Nigeria. It has been said that Ekiti State, though one of the smallest states, has the highest number of professors in the country. Ekiti is, indeed, a remarkable state in many ways. On the 1st October, 1996, Ekiti State was created alongside five other states by General Sani Abacha. The other states were Nasarawa, Bayelsa, Ebonyi, Gombe, and Zamfara. Since Ekiti and the other states were created, Nigeria has not witnessed the creation of additional states. With 16 local government areas and a population of less than 3 million people, Ekiti presents interesting challenges in leadership, and I am ready to be counted among those who will contribute in shaping the small but mighty state, which has produced erudite scholars like Professor Adegoke Olubummo, who was one of the first professors of Mathematics in Nigeria. Ekiti is also the proud producer of Professor Ekundayo Adeyinka Adeyemi, the first professor of Architecture in sub-Saharan Africa.

The fierce independent spirit of the people of Ekiti State was amply demonstrated during the second tenure of former President Olusegun Obasanjo, when they resisted the imposition of a governorship candidate and were able, through the judiciary, to reclaim a mandate, after a three-year battle in the courts. That victory enriched Nigeria's electoral jurisprudence and showed that, no matter how much an election is rigged, there was always a way that things could be corrected. I am proud of this heritage and would not rest until I contribute my quota to the politics of Ekiti. I am glad that I have been baptised, as far as Ekiti politics is concerned. Next time, there would not be need for another baptism anymore. I am now ready to roll purposefully. My love for Ekiti State shall never end. I am part of Ekiti and Ekiti is part of me.

In the meantime, I shall continue to serve the society through my philanthropic scholarship scheme and also through my membership of the Lions Club International, Ilepeju District 404-B2 (040978). As a businessman interested in voluntary service to the community, I found the club as a good platform because even the founder of the club, Melvin Jones, was a Chicago business leader who formed the club after he felt that businessmen like himself should reach out beyond their business environment and address the betterment of their communities and even the world in general. Since 1917, the Lions Club has continued to uphold the tenets of Melvin Jones, who demonstrated his selflessness even from that initial stage by agreeing to serve as the first Secretary-Treasurer of the club under its first president, Dr. William Perry. That attitude is what all the members of the club today have imbibed and are urged to imbibe. Forgetting our personal interests, we seek to engage in unselfish service to others and I am proud to be numbered among such people.

CHAPTER 18

INTERNATIONAL TRAVEL

The joke in my subsector of the livestock industry is that I am the most travelled CEO. In fact, Dr. Ayo Oduntan calls me a globe-trotter. I believe that I have had my share of travelling but have no way of confirming if the assertion about being the most travelled CEO is correct. In any case, as at the last count, I have visited more than twenty countries spread across the inhabited continents of the world, except Australia. I have visited countries in Africa, Europe, Asia, North America, and also in South America.

Some of my international trips were one-off trips to certain destinations (like Morocco, which I hope to visit again), but, in other cases, I have had to return to these countries many times. Even while writing this autobiography, I visited France twice, while still scheduled to go the United States shortly. The interesting thing about my foreign trips is that, if you look closely, you will always find my business interests tied to the trip, except in the case of Israel, which was purely for religious purposes. Even on such trips I would often look around for possible business contacts I could leverage on in the future. I remember that, while in Israel, I was able to find time to interact with the Kibbutz Cooperatives and did learn one or two things that have made me to better understand the agricultural miracle being performed by that small but mighty nation. I saw their focus on communal effort and the massive government intervention that we in Nigeria can only dream about for now.

I have been to France, Germany, Belgium, the Netherlands, the United Arab Emirates, Turkey, and to Qatar. I have been to the United States, the United Kingdom, and also Canada. I have visited Ghana, the Republic of Benin, Morocco, South Africa, Brazil, Ethiopia, Botswana, Malaysia, South Korea, and of course, Israel. But I would only be highlighting a few of the very important trips.

France

My first international trip was to France in 2007. I believe that this early association with the French was part of God's divine arrangement to prepare me for what was going to take place in my life. This is because, 10 years after that trip, a French company initiated the process of acquiring my company. The 2007 trip to France was for a livestock exhibition, organised by livestock farmers and agriculture practitioners in France. This exhibition was held at Rennes, a city in southern France.

I went to France as a businessman who just wanted to explore business opportunities. This was after I had known Dr. Oluyemi for some years as the Managing Director of his company, known as Vivax Limited. In fact, I went on that trip with him. Four of us went from Nigeria. Apart from being the MD of Vivax, Dr. Oluyemi was also the General Manager of Rhone Poulenc Nigeria Limited, which was a French company. The third person on the team was Mr. Raymond Obiajulu Isiadinso, Managing Director of Mid-Century Agro-Allied Ventures Limited, and the fourth person was Mr. Emmanuel Omokwale, Chairman of Dedora Farms Nigeria Limited, Lagos. The team leader was Dr. Oluyemi, who could speak French. This was the first European country I would be visiting and I learnt a lot, even about European culture. I enjoyed the trip, especially because of Dr. Oluyemi, who translated what people we met were saying. His presence mitigated what would have been a very sticky situation of poor communication, with lots of gesticulation and blabbing. We spent about six days on that trip.

Since Hi-Nutrients was established on the 11th of September, 2004, I had always wanted to interact with the manufacturers of the products I was using as raw materials so that I could establish a relationship with them and be able to import these materials directly. That was the whole essence of my going. Before the end of that trip, I established contact with three companies, and this helped me to cut-off middlemen and deal with the companies myself. I made this move as a cost-saving measure.

Ethiopia

I went to Ethiopia as a member of World Fish Trade Association. It was during their 1st Africa Conference and Exhibition. The occasion was used to rally the movers and shakers in the business of aquaculture. I was and still a strong member of Fisheries Society of Nigeria (FISON), and that was why I was selected as a delegate to that conference. This Conference and Exhibition was organised by the World Aquaculture Society. I stayed in Ethiopia for two weeks. The essence of that conference, among other things, was to introduce catfish to Ethiopia. Before that time, Ethiopians only consumed scaly fish like tilapia and others, but were not used to fishes like catfish, which do not have scales. We were there to share our experience with the Ethiopians on how to cultivate African catfish. That conference, as its name suggested, had delegates of aquaculture practitioners from every part of the world in attendance. It was my first trip to Ethiopia and I felt fortunate to be part of the Nigerian delegation.

One notable experience I had in Ethiopia was that I was opportune to visit the ruins of the palace of Queen Sheba, mentioned in the Bible. She was said to have visited King Solomon, the third king of Israel and son of its second ruler, King David. There is no record of any other queen who visited King Solomon, apart from Queen Sheba. The record was that she was so impressed with Solomon's wisdom and splendour that she became virtually breathless and totally awestruck. I saw the ruins of the palace, and my faith in the Bible was strengthened.

I also visited the Church of Saint George at Lalibela. One needs to see this edifice to believe that it is possible for human beings to situate a structure within a rocky mountain. It is simply breathtaking to behold, and there are several of these rock-hewn churches in Lalibela. Lalibela is one of Ethiopia's holiest cities, second only to Axum, which is Ethiopia's holiest city. I believe that the main reason Axum is regarded as Ethiopia's holiest city is because of the Church of Our Lady Mary of Mount Zion.

According to the Ethiopian Orthodox Tewahedo Church, the original Ark of the Covenant that contains the two tablets of stones on which the Ten Commandments of God were inscribed are inside the Church of Our Lady Mary of Zion. Whether this claim is true or not, there are millions who believe it and this is why Axum is Ethiopia's holiest city. Incidentally, Axum is also an important city for Muslims around the world because its Christian king, Sahama, lived at the time of the Islamic Prophet, Mohammed, and was able to provide refuge and protection to some of Mohammed's people when Mohammed was facing persecution from the Quraysh clan. These refugees taken in by King Sahama did not leave Axum in Ethiopia until around AD 628, while many of them who chose to remain in Axum are still there till today.

As second holiest city in Ethiopia, Lalibela is a centre of pilgrimage, which explains why I visited there. Not many people (including Christians) are aware that Ethiopia was one of the earliest nations to adopt Christianity. This acceptance of Christianity by Ethiopia occurred in the first half of the fourth century. In fact, the historical Christian roots of this ancient nation dates back to the time of the Apostles of Jesus Christ. The churches in Ethiopia themselves dated from the seventh to the thirteenth century.

I was able to make some business contacts before leaving that country, which is reportedly the only African country that has never been successfully colonised. The closest that Ethiopia came to colonisation was during the reign of its most popular emperor, Haile Selassie. Emperor Haile Selassie ruled Ethiopia for 44 years (1930 to 1974) but was out of power for the six years between 1935 and 1941, when the better equipped army of Emperor Mussolini of Italy invaded his country and deposed him as emperor. The only thing that saved Ethiopia from actual colonisation was the triumphant return to power of Haile Selassie, who had critical help from Great Britain and was able to defeat Italy and break their hold.

Ghana

My trip to Ghana was to attend a poultry exhibition organised by the Poultry Association of Ghana, in collaboration with the government of Ghana. The idea was to promote poultry production in Ghana. One of the reasons we were invited to Ghana was because Nigeria was the leading producer of egg in Africa. The trip was under the auspices of the Poultry Association of Nigeria, and I was part of the delegation that included members of the executive committee of the association. We were in Ghana for five days. Apart from some government officials, I also had the privilege of meeting the President of the Poultry Association of Ghana. Perhaps that explains why some of the products produced by Hi-Nutrients International Limited are used in Ghana today.

United States of America

I first went to the United States in 2008. The talk in town at that time was that companies were likely to die before their 5th anniversary. I was concerned about this because my company had celebrated its 4th anniversary and was getting close to its 5th. At this time, someone gave me a book written by Michael Gilbert. The title of the book was *The E-Myth Revisited: Why Most Small Businesses Don't Work And What To Do About It*. For reasons I cannot remember, I decided that I did not want to read the book but would prefer to hear from the horse's mouth. I wanted Michael Gilbert to explain to me in camera what I needed to do so that my young company would not die. The same person that had given me the book later told me that Michael Gilbert organised an international seminar and training session in the United States for businessmen twice every year. I should be able to meet him in one of them if I could go to the United States. The training was known as International Business Leadership and Entrepreneurial Seminar, and it normally held at Santa Rosa in Los Angeles, California. I eventually got to know that Santa Rosa was the largest city in California's Redwood Empire, Wine Country and the North Bay, and the 5th most populous city in San Francisco Bay Area after San Jose, San Francisco, Oakland, and Fremont. However, in California as a whole, it is the 28th most populous city.

I took the bold decision and went to the United States to attend the seminar. The 3-day seminar came to an end and then it was time for the business clinic, during which I was able to interact with Michael Gilbert one-on-one. Gilbert told me that, if I could abide by the principles that he had taught over the past three days, there was no way my company would die before its 5th anniversary, even though that was the destiny of many young companies. He added that, if my company actually lasted beyond five years and thrives for a couple of years more, it will get to a point where it would have left the danger zone. Its condition would become similar to a healthy man who may get sick once in a while with malaria or headache, but who would always bounce back after medication and rest.

Gilbert's opinion was based on research by experts which had shown that companies that survived from seven to ten years got to a point where they could suffer malnourishment but could not just die off, except for drastic and unexpected situations. For example, if a company has survived for ten or even twelve years, and the country where it is situated goes to war and is defeated in battle and becomes an occupied territory, this sort of drastic change must affect its fortunes. But short of such things (and natural disasters or civil war), the research was clear on the issue and was quite accurate.

There was an interesting fallout from this first trip to the United States. Since that time, I have never been denied visa by the United States embassy here in Nigeria. The reason for this special status given to me was that, after my training with Michael Gilbert during the International Business Leadership and Entrepreneurial Seminar he hosted, I wrote to the US embassy in Lagos to thank them for giving me the visa that allowed me to go for the seminar. I told them that I learnt a lot and was grateful for the opportunity. I told them I would like to return to the United States to learn more of the sort of things Michael Gilbert had taught me. Incidentally, Michael Gilbert had said that we should keep on appreciating everything we received that we would get what we did not even expect, as a result of that attitude of gratitude. His words have proven true so far: I have never been denied United States visa since that first trip in 2008. I do not even suffer delays. My application is always treated with dispatch. Anybody can choose to learn from my experience. It is no wonder today that my company has a very cordial relationship with the US embassy. In fact, the African Agriculture attaché of the embassy has visited me in my office before. This visit was part of efforts to strengthen the agricultural relationship between Nigeria and the US.

I was in the United States again in 2009 to attend an international poultry exhibition where I spent two weeks. One reason I was always interested in attending international exhibitions was that there was usually free training at such exhibitions, and I was always looking out for opportunities to learn more things so that I can improve my business.

Recently (in 2017), I was an executive student at the A & M University at College Station via Houston, Texas, for a certificate course in Animal Feeds Extrusion. But before going to the A & M University in Texas, I fulfilled a lifelong dream by attending the Harvard Business School, located in Boston, Massachusetts, for a retreat organised by the AllWorld Network, USA. My second visit was to attend an Executive Course on Agribusiness Management (AGB). I must confess that being a Harvard alumni means a lot to me because it puts me in good company. In fact, according to *Business Insider* magazine, if you want to be an executive, a billionaire, or a United States president, it is a good idea to graduate from the Harvard Business School. The reason for this assertion are many but none can be divorced from the fact that the Harvard Business School, founded in 1908, was the first institution in the world to grant a Master's degree in Business Administration. Since then, that school has churned out much of the world's elite, including former US president, George W. Bush, Mitt Romney (former governor of Massachusetts), and Michael Bloomberg (former mayor of New York), who is worth over $50 billion as at 2018. Others are former US Secretary of Defence, Robert S. McNamara, and Walter Hass Jr., former CEO of Levi's, the jeans makers. Even the very popular Stephen R. Covey is a product of the Harvard Business School. Meg Whitman, the Chairman, President, and CEO of Hewlett-Packard, also had a stint at the Harvard Business School, and she is reported to worth an estimated $2 billion today. To continue to mention the eminent persons who passed through the Harvard Business School is virtually impossible and I am thankful to God that, as one of them, I am a worthy alumnus and I intend to go higher.

United Kingdom (England)

My first visit to the United Kingdom was in 2009 to honour an invitation extended to me by Premier Nutrition Products Limited, which is based in Rugeley. This invitation was facilitated by Mr. Ian Atterbury, who was working with Premier Nutrition at the time. Kate Robinson (Ian's assistant) was also involved in facilitating this trip. I had already started importing raw materials from Premier Nutrition long before this trip. Although not formally stated, it was implied in our business agreement that I would be coming to the UK from time to time for training and also to see how they produce premixes. My trips would also allow them to offer me some technical support to ensure that I produced high quality premixes.

Way back in Bio-Organics, we used to import raw materials for premix production from Premier Nutrition UK. When I set up Hi-Nutrients, I actually thought that Premier Nutrition may not want to do business with me; but it was this same Ian Atterbury that reached out to me himself and we started to do business together. Ian was the international sales manager of Premier Nutrition at the time. For those who may not know, Premier Nutrition is actually a subsidiary of Associated British Foods. Apart from Premier Feeds, I also had a relationship with a similar company known as Kempex Holland BV, based in Netherland; and Vitafor NV, based in Belgium. I did business with Premier Nutrition to the extent that, at a point, I became a force to reckon with in the list of their customers.

About five years before this trip to the UK, I had been wrongly denied a vacation trip that would have been my first trip. But my kind and considerate boss had compensated me by sending me to the Lagos Business School at the time. So, those who knew about the Lagos Business School had claimed that, if I was able to consolidate on the knowledge I was going to gain at the school, I would be in a position to go to the UK anytime I wanted. So far the words of these people have since proven true. I have indeed reached the position where I can go to the UK anytime I want to. Apart from that first trip, I have actually been to the UK a couple of times.

Morocco

The World Aquaculture Society conference that took me to Ethiopia was held in 2009 in Morocco, specifically for Africa, and that was why I found myself there that year. The choice of Morocco as venue for this conference was partly because Morocco produces fish. I decided to use that trip to have a few day's rest and was able to do that after the conference. Altogether, I spent two weeks in Morocco – one week for the conference, and the other week to rest and explore the land. It was in Morocco that I saw typical Africans looking like Europeans. Morocco also shares a boundary with Spain. I went to Rabat, the capital of Morocco, and to Agadir. More importantly, I went to Marrakesh. The unwritten rule was that, if you visited Morocco without going to Marrakesh, your trip was incomplete. Marrakesh is a city of leisure, culture and tourism. It is actually the 4th largest city in the kingdom after

Casablanca, Fez, and Tangier. I had camel rides, horse rides, and was generally able to relax.

One evening, I was taken to the house of a family when I told my host that I wanted to have a taste of the local cuisine. The head of this family eventually picked interest in me. This man was so impressed with me that he offered me his daughter. He was ready to allow me to take his daughter back to Nigeria, if only I was interested. The man said he liked Nigeria and I was amazed by such outpour of admiration for my country from a foreigner.

The only option I had to counter the "gift" of my very kind host in Morocco was to tell him that I was married, and that I was a pastor. I added that, in my church, we could not marry more than one wife. That was not the interesting part: what I found intriguing was that the man's daughter was also ready to follow me to Nigeria. That experience was so incredible and funny to me that I would laugh out loud anytime I remember my trip to that North African country.

Moroccans are generally very nice. I will warn anyone planning to go there about a certain tradition they have. The tradition is that you do not refuse food when it is offered. It is a taboo in Morocco to decline to eat food offered to you, no matter how satiated you are, rather to take a little portion in appreciation and then leave the rest.

I truly believe that tourism is an opportunity to learn about different people and their different cultures. This is because I found something nearly opposite the tradition of the Moroccans when I visited Kuala Lumpur in Malaysia. In that Asian enclave, it is a taboo to finish the food that was offered to you. That strange tradition has something to do with the worship of their gods, which is well entrenched in that society. Talk about different strokes for different folks and you find a classic case when you compare Morocco and Malaysia; at least, in the area of how to handle food offered to you. I intend to return to Morocco one of these days. But when I do, it would be with my family. I am sure my readers can guess why.

Kuala Lumpur, Malaysia

My reason for going to Kuala Lumpur in Malaysia was to attend the World Aquaculture Society for the Asian continent. Because I was engaged in the production of premixes for fish, I attended these meetings so as to get the latest information that would help me to stay on the cutting edge of my industry and produce the best products possible. After layer premix, our next most important product was premix for aquaculture; so, I was keen to have all the knowledge I could get in that regard.

My second reason for going to Malaysia was to go and study the agricultural prowess of the Malays. The history is that the Nigerian government gave the people of Malaysia some oil palm seedlings about 40 years ago. My interest was in how the Malays were able to use those seedlings and start from square one to become the number one producer of oil palm in the world. I was curious about such an achievement and wanted to learn one or two things from the Malays.

While there, I went to their Ministry of Agriculture. It was in Malaysia that I first saw a functioning Bank of Agriculture dedicated to farmers only, in Kuala Lumpur. Another thing I saw there was that virtually every family had a small-scale business. Because of extensive training by the government, the products produced in these family-sized small-scale businesses were of high standard and suitable for export. This family-oriented entrepreneurship is part of the success secret of Malaysia: it was the method they used to transform their economy.

Before concluding my trip, I found time to visit a few fish and shrimp farms and was able to learn the art of modern culturing of fish and shrimps. I honestly wish that some of us in the aquaculture industry in Nigeria would muster the courage to venture into shrimps, with massive cage culture fish farms, utilising the large water body and coastline of over 850km we are blessed with.

CHAPTER 19

FISHERIES SOCIETY OF NIGERIA (FISON)

I am sure that my colleagues in the fisheries sub-sector of Nigeria's economy will not forgive me if I conclude my autobiography without mentioning anything about fishery. I also believe that my skipping a chapter on fishery will be most impertinent and uncharitable because I am a former National Vice President of the Fisheries Society of Nigeria. But, more than that, I am part of the exclusive club of Fellows of the Fisheries Society of Nigeria, and I have been a fellow for more than two years. I am excited about the strides I have made and my membership of the very top echelon of this society, which has come a long way since its inception some 42 years ago.

The fact is that fisheries development in Nigeria as a geopolitical entity predates the independence of Nigeria as a nation. As far back as 1914, a Fisheries Development Branch was established by the colonial government (under its Agriculture Department) and headed by a Senior Agricultural Officer. The mandate of this officer was to, among other things, conduct a survey of the industry with a view to determining its potentials. The office of this fisheries department was first located in Victoria Island (around Apese village) before it was eventually moved to Onikan, all in Lagos State.

By 1945, things had become so serious that the colonial government commenced a five-year Fisheries Development Plan. Part of this plan involved expanding the scope of fishery beyond Lagos and Opobo, and saw the establishment of the Panyam Fish Farm in faraway Plateau State, which was then just a province under the colonial administration. A substation was maintained at Opobo and fish culture in inland areas started with stocking of ponds and reservoirs at many places throughout the country.

The 1954 constitution gave fishery a higher stake in the scheme of things, and its administration became decentralised, with the Federal Fisheries Service (headed by a Director) holding things at the centre and supported by the Eastern Region Fisheries Division and the Northern Region Fisheries Division. While the Federal Fisheries Service was under the Federal Ministry of Economic Development, the Eastern Region Fisheries Division was under the Eastern Regional Ministry of Agriculture. Like in the East, the Northern Region Fisheries Division was also under the Northern Regional Ministry of Agriculture.

In 1975, three federal institutes were established in support of fisheries development in Nigeria. They were the Nigerian Institute for Oceanography and Marine Research, located at Victoria Island, Lagos, the then Kainji Lake Research Institute (which is now the National Institute for Freshwater Fisheries Research), located at New Bussa, and the Lake Chad Research Institute at Maiduguri. As fishery continued to develop, there was consequently an increase in the number of persons working in establishments connected to fishery. It was not too long before somebody began to see the need for professionals in the field to come together and have a common voice in order to be recognised and reckoned with. Discussions in this regard began as early as 1972, during the National Fisheries Development Committee Meeting. By 1975, it was resolved that an association known as Fisheries Society of Nigeria (FISON) be formed, and this became a possibility sometime in 1976, which was when the formation of this society dated. At its inaugural stage, the society had 74 members, but that number has grown astronomically today.

In spite of the pomp and pageantry that marked the formation of FISON in 1976, for some reasons not very clear, it took another six years (until 1982) for another FISON annual conference to be held, where Mr. E.O. Bayagbona was elected President. In 1982, Mr. Bayagbona handed over the presidency of the society to Mr. B.F. Dada, who also handed over, after six years, to Mr. N.O. Fadayomi in 1988. Interestingly, these first three presidents were also the first to be given Honorary Fellowship awards, in 1993 by FISON, under the presidency of Dr. S.O. Talabi. Things was going slow and steady in FISON, with a mixed bag of successes and challenges, since that time.

I joined FISON in 1997 and have remained an active members since then. Even while I was at Bio-Organics, because I was the nutritionist in the house, I was the one representing the company at FISON meetings. From the very beginning, the Fisheries Society of Nigeria was established to encourage the business of fishery, to promote fish farmers, and, very importantly, to reduce the importation of frozen fish into Nigeria. By the time I joined FISON, there were no Nigerian companies involved in the production of fish feed, so, all the fish feed used in the country was imported from Belgium. However, some Nigerian companies began to attempt some local production, but the vitamin requirements for fish were not available in the country, which was why these companies were using vitamins meant for poultry feed to make fish feed.

When I left Bio-Organics in 2004, I initially decided to focus on two specific areas: I decided that I would focus on layers and aquaculture. Since I was an expert in nutrition, I then developed a premix for fish known as Hi-Mix® Aqua. This was done in conjunction with Professor Bamidele Oluwarotimi Omitoyin of the University of Ibadan, who helped me in testing the efficacy of the product at the University of Ibadan fish farm. When the product turned out well, I immediately introduced it to the

Nigerian market. By that time, some companies had started producing fish feed locally. But they were few: I remember that Top Feeds, Grand Cereals, CHI Ajanla Farms, Durante, and even Sabina Pad Farms were involved in this attempt. I was actually the one that encouraged Sabina to get into fish feed production.

Fortunately for me, Professor Omitoyin was a consultant to several fish feed producers; so, he was well-positioned to introduce my Hi-Mix® Aqua product to them, which they embraced and began to use in the production of their feed. The product was so successful that, in 2007, I got an award of excellence for it. As expected, this award was given by the Fisheries Society of Nigeria. Interestingly, my product was the first fish feed premix to get a NAFDAC registration number and that product became a standard against which others were judged by NAFDAC before being certified.

It was this award of excellence (given for the furtherance of fish feed development in Nigeria) that catapulted me into the limelight of the Fisheries Society of Nigeria. Hi-Nutrients was less than three years old by the time, and people in the industry thought it was simply amazing that such a young company could get that type of award so early in its history. Many people noticed this achievement, and it encouraged me to participate more in the activities of FISON.

Within this period also, Mrs. Foluke Ariola became the first female President of FISON, while I was nominated for Vice President Aquaculture. There was no doubt in my mind that my award, and the quick impact I had made through my product, were some of the factors directly responsible for being nominated for Vice President. I became the first entrepreneur to hold the position. Before my time, that post had consistently been held by members that were not players in the industry.

The Fisheries Society of Nigeria is actually made up of several blocks. We have entrepreneurs like myself, the artisans, and we also have the trawlers (those who use heavy equipment to fish in the high seas), the processors, the feed millers, and finally; the professionals, most of whom you will find in the universities as lecturers. As for fishery in Nigeria, there are other fisheries associations that promote the economic interests of their members. The good thing is that these associations are under FISON. They are, namely, Nigerian Trawlers Owners Association (NITOA); the Nigerian Association of Fish Farmers and Aquaculturists (NAFFA); the Nigerian Association of Ornamental Fish Exporters; and the Nigerian Union of Fishermen and Seafood Dealers.

The importance of FISON to the Nigerian economy cannot be overemphasised. Being the most important stakeholder in fisheries in Nigeria, it is FISON, not any other institution, that can play a role in tapping into the vast potential of the fish industry and earn Nigeria unbelievable amounts of money. Just to give a peek into what I mean, in 2016 alone, Nigeria recorded a deficit of 2.2 million metric tonnes of fish. This meant that that staggering amount of fish had to be imported from other countries just to meet local demand of fish. Imagine what would happen (in terms of employment generation, GDP growth, foreign exchange earnings, and wealth creation), if this humongous quantity of fish had been produced here in Nigeria. In terms of cash, the 2017 figure for fish importation into Nigeria was a staggering $190 million. This is equivalent to over ₦60 billion. Even Lagos State – Nigeria's richest state – will salivate over the prospects of earning such an amount. This is why I will continue to play my role as a member of the Fisheries Society of Nigeria (FISON) because, if there is any hope that this undesirable situation of massive importation will ever be corrected, the activities of FISON must play a pivotal role.

I feel fortunate to add that, apart from FISON, I am also a member of the Animal Science Association of Nigeria

(ASAN), which is the parent body of the National Institute of Animal Science (NIAS). In fact, I am proud of my credentials as a registered animal scientist. As an active member of both bodies, I have been officially informed that, I will be made a Fellow of the National Institute of Animal Science come September 2019.

Interestingly, I currently hold the post of Deputy Chairman of Feed Millers Association of Nigeria and the National Secretary of Feed Additives Manufacturers of Nigeria (FESMAN) under the presidency of Dr. Dele Oyediji. Furthermore, I was recently made a Fellow of the Institute of Agric Business Management of Nigeria, which has its headquarters in Ibadan but has an operating base in Lekki, Lagos State.

Over time, I have come to see the benefits of collaborating with professional colleagues in trying to move things forward in our sub-sector. I am also convinced that, without collaborating with like-minded Nigerians by participating in associations such as FISON, ASAN, NIAS, FESMAN, and others, the government will be unable to bring about the desired change that would position Nigeria to optimally utilise her potentials.

CHAPTER 20

MY BOTSWANA EXPERIENCE AND LESSONS FOR NIGERIA IN AGRICULTURAL DEVELOPMENT

Agriculture can be even more than the "new oil." One day, the oil would run out, but Sub-Saharan Africa will always have its fertile land, its rivers, its youthful workforce, and its huge domestic market. Investing now can turn that potential into prosperity.
Olusegun Obasanjo, GCFR

When Dr. Akinwunmi Adesina was Minister of Agriculture, he launched a very functional scheme called the Growth Enhancement Scheme, otherwise known as GES. It was one of the best government schemes I have ever witnessed at close quarters, with potential for so much good and subsequent positive chain reaction in the economy and the country at large.

The scheme was an attempt to establish cattle ranches in some of the states in Nigeria, especially in the north, in a manner that would move the practice of cattle rearing as close to modernisation as possible, and practicable in the Nigerian context. Through that scheme, I was opportune to produce and supply cattle feed to fourteen states of the federation including Kogi, Ondo, Kwara, Osun, Ekiti, Lagos, Oyo, Anambra, Imo, Akwa Ibom, Plateau, Gombe, and Niger, apart from the Federal Capital Territory. I cannot explain why this scheme was abandoned, but it was a very laudable idea, with potentials for preventing and eliminating the recurring farmers/herdsmen clashes that have become the norm in

Nigeria. The scheme also had the potential to drastically raise the standard of living of cattle herders, create employment for many Nigerians, and give the government an opportunity to do something meaningful for genuine cattle farmers.

The concept behind the scheme was simple: the cattle farmers targeted for support will pay 50% of the cost of setting up the ranch, while the federal government of Nigeria will pay the balance of 50%. For effectiveness, several ranches will be set up in a very large area with a common source of water supply, feed for their cattle, veterinary services, veterinary drugs, additives, and other requirements. Salt block (which is the mineral lick for cattle) would also be supplied to this area, which would be paid for by the government. The concept was much like that of poultry estates in Lagos State already mentioned ealier.

While it lasted, the GES promised a boom in the Nigerian agricultural sector. As a businessman, I became curious about the southern African nation of Botswana, which had a functional meat industry and was engaged in beef export. I decided to pay a visit to Botswana so that I could understudy their system to see if I could learn something that would be useful to me and my country. The fact that we had international super store chains operating in Nigeria selling imported packaged meat to us was also something I considered unacceptable. It was my intention to reduce such dependence by trying to see how Nigerian beef could replace imported beef in our stores.

I spent two weeks in Botswana and got to realise that the secret of the success of their meat industry was the implementation of a concept similar to what Dr. Akinwunmi Adesina had in his Growth Enhance Scheme initiative. But Botswana's system was a bit more robust. What I discovered in Botswana during my stay there was that they took cattle rearing as a very serious national business. For example, they relocated all cattle farmers to a specific region about four hours drive from the capital city, Gaborone. It was in this region that cattle were reared. In the region known as Lobatse, lands are allocated to specific farmers for use. Every form of support was then provided to the cattle farmers to ensure that they are able to care for their animals and make good business. There were small-scale industries that run the business of processing meat. These business owners patronised the farmers to buy live cows. There were also companies, involved in abattoir services for the meat packaging companies. Even the transportation of the animals was not haphazard, but based on rules and regulations to avoid health hazards and rascality in the practice. Everything was organised for optimum efficiency and productivity.

To encourage cattle farmers to support the initiative, there was a law that made it compulsory for anyone who wanted to practice cattle rearing to relocate to Lobatse. To avoid conflict, farmers are usually not allocated lands in the Lobatse area but in some other region of the country. The only cultivation you see in Lobatse is the planting of special grasses on some fields, which ultimately serve as food for the cattle. There was also a law in Botswana that prohibited the roaming of cattle anywhere other than the allocated area of Lobatse. Again, there was a law that stated that, any cattle that strayed from another country into Botswana becomes the property of Botswana. I could not but think about some excuses offered to explain the farmers/herders clashes in Nigeria. Sometimes, we get to hear that the herders that cause havoc in our farmlands are from countries like Niger Republic, Cameroun, or other neighbouring African countries. If this is true, none of these herders would dare to take their cattle close to Botswana's borders because, as soon as their cattle gets into Botswana land, they forfeit everything to the government.

Back in Nigeria, we punish our cattle herders who trek thousands of miles and face the risk of hunger, deprivation, and exposure to harm. We also put them at loggerheads with farmers thereby sustaining perpetual cycle of violence that is both unnecessary, expensive, retrogressive, appalling, and a testament to our lack of seriousness as a nation. It is true that, with over 19 million cattle, Nigeria's animal population is quite large. In fact, it is the largest in Africa. This ought to present the opportunity and incentive for developing a competitive beef export market, rather than serve as an excuse for inability due to assumed complexity. Failure to harness our potential in cattle has denied us peace and progress, and is even affecting the cohesion of the country. This has also denied us the utilisation of a huge revenue base.

Unfortunately, what is true of the cattle industry is also true of Nigeria as a whole. Nigeria is like a tragic movie. We started so well with so much promises, but, through mismanagement and imbibing of wrong attitudes, we have in no time lost our glory and are now struggling with countries who used to look up to us as the Giant of Africa. Some young Nigerians can hardly believe that there was such a time when Ghanaians flocked to our shores because they wanted a better life. There are several countries between Ghana and Nigeria; yet, the Ghanaians, knowing that Nigeria was far better and worth the stress of the journey, came in their thousands to find jobs, to attend school, and to live in a country that was more like a paradise, especially when compared to theirs. Today, the very opposite is the case.

I believe that the problem with Nigeria is not just with the government, but also with the people. I do not know where Nigerians learnt the terrible habit of trying to grab as much as they can whenever they have a small opportunity. When, for example, we want to talk about the issue of corruption, we must start from the level of the individual. Until the individual changes his or her orientation, the issue cannot be dealt with. If Nigeria must be built, it will be the result of several individuals who have decided to begin to do things the right way. Then when the number increases to what is known as a critical mass, things will swing the other way.

Lee Kuan Yew of Singapore could not have achieved what is normally attributed to him without the support and cooperation of the people of Singapore. His greatest task as a leader was to urge and convince them to see the need to go in the direction that he, their leader, had decided that they needed to go. But, if, for instance, the people of Singapore had failed to connect with the vision of Lee Kuan Yew, the story of that country would have been very different from what obtains today. No wonder the man took the issue of communication seriously. He knew that, with the buy-in of the citizens, there was no force that would prevent success – even the force of the threat of external aggression.

We need to have a heart of love for Nigeria and understand that there is nobody that would come from another country to develop it. Like John Kennedy rightfully said, "we should stop thinking of how we can get to a position and use that position to easily enrich ourselves"; rather, we should spend our time thinking of what we can do to make Nigeria better.

A musician can write songs to encourage people to love the country by highlighting its natural endowments, the resilience, and the history of the people. A teacher on his part can determine that, as far as the student depended on him, every student must receive quality education because one of his students may become the leader whose decision would affect millions of others. So, any bad foundation in the education of such student could have serious consequences. Residents can come together, through community development, to maintain public infrastructures in their locality. This act alone would make their street more beautiful, raise the value of their property, protect their vehicles and improve their longevity, and give them a better feeling when they are driving back home after a hard day's work.

We must change our attitude, and I do agree that leadership can instigate this change, but there is nothing wrong with this type of leadership coming from outside the official portfolio of leadership in the political sphere. Citizens can ignite a wave of change that would sweep the whole country, and we have seen wonderful Nigerians doing that. Just a few years ago, Doctor Ameyo Adadevoh became the epicentre of the global fight against the deadly Ebola virus in 2014, when she literally gave up her life to prevent an epidemic of the disease that would have consumed millions of Nigerians.

In fact, a movie titled 93 Days was produced in 2016 to honour the life of this woman and, while not praying for another threat to our national health, I believe that many doctors have been inspired to know that, like soldiers, they are at the frontier of the nation's health and must be ready to give their lives if need be to save the majority. On 27 October 2018, the internet search engine, Google, honoured the memory of this Nigerian doctor by placing her face on their official Google Doodle platform for the whole world to see and remember.

The story of Adadevoh is a very good and recent example of how one single individual can change the thinking of a nation. Not everybody needs to die, but we must understand the role we can play as individuals. Fortunately for us, there are many inspiring stories out there, and Nigerians themselves seem to be taking up the challenge of moving the country in the right direction, after years of waiting for the government to fix things and getting disappointed.

If we have self-denial, we would obey rules as simple and sensible as that of traffic lights. A person does not need any amount of education to stop a vehicle when the light shows red, wait when it shows yellow, and move only when it shows green. But Nigerians with sound education and even international experience routinely beat traffic lights. As for those with international travel, they would not dare to do these things abroad. I am often amazed how we willingly queue for services and other things while in foreign countries, but as soon as we feel the Lagos breeze at the Murtala Mohammed International Airport, it seems the demons we had kept back before travelling return with more violence, and we immediately begin to misbehave.

Another thing that creates problems for us in Nigeria is the issue of preferential treatment for the so-called "big men." I am happy that CNN and BBC normally show British Members of Parliament and even the British Prime Minister carrying their bags and walking alone into 10 Downing Street, which is the official residence of the Prime Minister. In Nigeria, the practice of selected judgement and preferential treatment are the norm. I believe that God created all of us equal and there is no need – except in emergencies – to bend the rules for anybody. There is nothing wrong with obeying rules all the time and it is my calm belief that the practice of disobeying rules, rather than prove power, is just a manifestation of indiscipline, pride, and selfishness. We must learn to serve before wanting to become leaders. People do not want to serve, but they want to become leaders.

Those in government must understand that they are not there to serve themselves but to serve the people. Leadership at whatever level is supposed to be a sacrifice, but many Nigerians see it differently. Political power to many is an avenue to enrich themselves and oppress the poor. No wonder, they are ready to do anything to either get to power, or hold on to it. I am happy that what happened in 2015 may become the beginning of a very good tradition that has the potential to sanitise the practice of politics in this country and cool down the high tension associated with general elections. I would remind Nigerians, that what happened in 2015 had already happened in Ekiti State, when incumbent Governor John Kayode Fayemi voluntarily conceded defeat to his main challenger, Ayodele Fayose. That was probably the first time such a thing had ever happened in Nigeria at the state level.

One former governor, who probably had plans to do the right thing was reported to have publicly cried out and said that the corruption of public officials was actually instigated by the people. This is not a good excuse, but, still, the man had a point. We, as so-called ordinary Nigerians, have become guilty by involving ourselves with the crimes of our public officers.

Why should you approach a person that has just been appointed minister, expecting that he will deep his hands into his pocket and give you a million naira, especially since you know that, apart from you, 100 others at least are going to pay him similar visit before the end of that month.

Nigerians need to get serious and stop deceiving themselves. Unless we change, this situation will not get better. Leaders should not be pressured for any sort of assistance beyond what they can comfortably do with their salaries and allowances. On their part, leaders should have the courage to use the resources under their supervision to build infrastructure for the public. There are blessings attached to doing what you are paid and empowered to do.

I wonder the type of orientation that would permit an elected official to divert money meant for the people for private use, knowing full well that that money is to be used to build a school, or a bridge connecting two remote villages, or to fix roads, or allocated to universities to conduct research that would improve our industries and provide jobs.

People need to consider the eventual consequences of their actions. One does not need excess wealth to be happy. Our leaders should focus on serving the people. Public funds should be channelled to social work, education, and the creation of an enabling environment in order to support industries and also to attract foreign investment.

My recommendation is also that people with no proven source of income should be disqualified from participating in politics. This will be good for our leadership recruitment.

I remember how people were very happy when they heard that I was aspiring for a political position. Many of them said I could be trusted because I was not a hungry man. I could take care of myself and my family, and that I did not achieve this ability through politics but through my God-given business acumen, through perseverance, hard work, and faith in God. I could be trusted because I am not likely to kill my opponent when I know that I am seeking a position that would require some sacrifice on my part; when I know that the position I am seeking is not necessary for my family members to feed or for me to educate my children.

Had it been that my account was in the red and I had no house, and my economic outlook was bleak, I would see the political contest as a do-or-die affair and do everything legal and illegal to get there. Furthermore, if by any mistake I get elected and become a leader, I am more likely to use the funds that come under my power to fill up my bank account and quickly try to build a house, buy cars, and improve my economic status. This is the thinking of most politicians and the reason for recommending that only those with proven sources of income be allowed to vie for public office.

No wonder I like Nelson Mandela: he was one of my key role models in politics and life. We also have Nigerians worthy of emulation in the likes of Chief Obafemi Awolowo, Alhaji Tafawa Balewa, and the Great Zik, Dr. Nnamdi Azikiwe, Chief Adekunle Ajasin, Dr. N.F. Aina, Col. Adekunle Fajuyi and even Herbert Macaulay. I have read the stories of these founding fathers, including the stories of characters like Anthony Enahoro and Bode Thomas, among others. These were men who had served Nigeria selflessly and it is for this reason that they are still remembered today. It was the inspiration gained from the legacies of these true patriots that caused me to start thinking about how I could play my own part in making my country a better place. That was partly why I decided to engage in active philanthropy.

The issue of tax payment provides a good paradigm to demonstrate the expected role of leaders and citizens. If the government is serious and responsive to the needs of the citizens, it is very likely that the citizens would in turn voluntarily pay their tax as and when due. It is simply disheartening when citizens pay their taxes promptly but are denied amenities that they cannot provide for themselves, such as good roads, electricity, and especially, security of their lives and property.

Politicians should remember that posterity will judge them. Nigerians should also remember that they have no other country to truly call their own, but Nigeria. This task of rebuilding Nigeria should be collective, but it has to start at the individual level.

As a player in the agricultural sector, I know that the key to Nigeria's prosperity and progress is in the development of agriculture. Without agriculture, industries cannot grow because it is agriculture that would provide the raw materials. For example, through cattle, hide and skin can be secured to develop the tannery industry; through cocoa, the beverage industry can be supplied for the production of several breakfast beverages. So, agriculture is the key and I believe that Nigerian can regain her dominance on the global stage and achieve self-sufficiency through it. The failure to improve on our agricultural potential is too expensive to sustain. Every year, we use a huge percentage of our scarce foreign exchange to import massive amounts of rice, fish, maize, and soya, when we could easily produce these things ourselves and even have enough to export. Nigeria is blessed with many water bodies holding fish, and also has the capacity for domestic fish production, apart from arable land covering tens of thousands of hectares. The current situation is both inexcusable and an embarrassment.

If farmers are given the support they need, they will achieve amazing miracles for themselves and for the country. In all my travel around the world, what I have noticed is that, farmers do not live in cities: they stay on their farms. Perhaps this is because they have access to very functional health services, water supply, electricity supply, security, good road, and other amenities. I remember a farmer I met in the United Kingdom. This man told me that he had not been to London in the last seven years, even though London was just two hours drive from his farm. When I asked him why he had not gone to London for that many years, he told me that he had no reason to go to London because everything he needed was available right in his farm, or very close by. So, going to London was quite unnecessary. According to him, his job was to produce crops from his farm and the job of the others down the value chain was to come to his farm and take the produce away, leaving him to consistently focus and achieve optimally.

As Nigerians, we must never forget our global indictment: we donated oil palm seedlings to Malaysia in the 1980s because they did not have it. Yet, these wise people mastered what was natural to our land and beat us in our own game to the extent that they are now the largest producers of palm oil in the world. If this does not cause us to rise in anger and do something differently, nothing else would, and that would be unfortunate. I believe that Nigeria will rise again.

Although we are the largest producer of cassava in the world, I believe that we have woefully failed to optimally utilise our position by producing ethanol from our cassava, animal feed, chips, and several other things. Each of this activity will require hands and directly provide jobs for many who are now unemployed. I do not see any other sector with the promise of thousands of jobs other than agriculture, and that is why I believe that Nigeria does not need to think twice about the issue. If we want to end the cycle of poverty for millions of Nigerians, the first step is to take agriculture seriously. Those of us already in the sector are willing and ready to play our roles and deploy our knowledge for the good of our country and our people.

As for the issue of farmers and herders clashes, I believe that the way forward is for the government to take the bull by the horn. There should be a law that pronounces that cattle rearing is a private business. Individual farmer should have his own cattle ranch. But, because it is not easy to establish a functional ranch, the government should come in and help significantly by providing incentives to the farmers. The government can follow the model of the Growth Enhancement Scheme of Dr. Akinwunmi Adesina and even raise their support for willing farmers to 60%. This thing may not be easy to pull off, but it is possible; and what we stand to gain as a country should provide the impetus for us to make the attempt. If Botswana could do it, if South Africa could do it, if Zimbabwe could do it, there is no reason for the Giant of Africa to be whining about not being able to do it.

Yes we can do it and we must do it.

Personal Pictures

At the inauguration of Dr. John Kayode Fayemi as Governor, Ekiti State, 2018

At Los Angeles, California, USA, 2014

At Iye-Ekiti, Ilejemeje local government during BAM foundation scholarship awards 2017

At an Award of Moba Elites, 2017

At Hi-Nutrients by Neovia Lagos office, 2018

At work as South-West Poultry Association of Nigeria Chairman, Lagos, 2018

At Hi-Nutrients by Neovia International Poultry Exhibition Abeokuta, Ogun State, 2018

At work in Lobatse, Gaborone, Botswana, 2016

At Ado-Ekiti, Ekiti State, 2018

Ontario, Canada 2017

At Erin Ijesa water fall, Osun State, 2017

As "fellow" Fisheries Society of Nigeria, 2018

At International Poultry show, Atlanta Georgia, PPE 2017, USA

At Markurdi, Benue State to visit customers, 2016

At Washington D.C. USA, 2017

At work in Ilorin, Kwara State 2017

With Senator Babafemi Ojudu, SA to President on Political Matters, 2017

Political Activities

Exchanging pleasantries with Jide Awe, former APC Chairman in Ekiti State, 2017

Moving to a meeting venue with loyalists in Otun-Ekiti, 2017

With some of BAM youths wing, 2017

Exchanging pleasantries with Mrs. Ibiloye and some party women leaders, 2017

Flag-off of campaign activities, 2017 for aspiration to become a Federal lawmaker at House of Representative

In a political town hall meeting, 2017

Bode with Honourable Ogunmola from Ijero-Ekiti, 2018

With Chief Mayegun, Former Ekiti State Commissioner for Local Government and Chieftancy Affairs, 2018

Prince Bode with Popular VIPs

Receiving an award at University of Benin presented by former Governor of Edo State, Chief Odigie Oyegun, 2017

With former Ekiti State Governor, Niyi Adebayo (Centre) and Senator Adeyeye (left) 2018 at Ado-Ekiti

Exchanging pleasantries with Chief Oyegun, former APC Chairman and Dr. Eniola Ajayi, 2018 at Ado-Ekiti

With the incubent Governor of Ekiti State, Dr. John Kayode Fayemi (JKF), 2018

With Otunba Niyi Adebayo, 2018

With Senator Olubunmi Adetumbi at Ado-Ekiti, 2018

With Chief Olusegun Obasanjo, former Nigeria President (Centre) and Alhaji T.J. Mohammed, 2017

With Mr. Francis Widmer, Economic Counsellor, Embassy of France, Nigeria, 2018

Prince Bode Adetoyi on a courtesy visit to Aare Ona Kakanfo of Yorubaland, Aare Dr. Gani Adams on his installation

From Right: Prince Olabode Adetoyi, Lagos Chairman, Poultry Association of Nigeria leads on a courtesy visit to General Olusegun Obasanjo

With Senator (Chief) Rashidi Adewolu Ladoja, former Executive Governor of Oyo State, immediate past Chairman, Hi-Nutrients International Limited

With Biodun Oyebanji, SSG to Ekiti State Government

With Pastor Mike and Pastor Mrs. Gloria Bamiloye

With International business colleagues in an interactive session at EDC, Lagos Business School

(L-R) Prince Adetoyi, Dr. Olusegun Ayodele Osinkolu with former Governor, Ekiti State, Ayodele Fayose at General Adeyinka Adebayo's Burial, 2017

With MISTAV Team Instabul Turkey, 2014

Prince Bode Adetoyi with Segun Oni, former governor of Ekiti State (centre)

International Travel Pictures

At A and M University College Station, Texas, USA, 2016

At world Aquaculture conference, Bassa, South Korea, 2015

At Cape Point, Cape of New Hope, South Africa, 2014

At Farmers Market, Atlanta USA, 2017

Hollywood, Los Angeles, USA, 2014

London, May 2017

Agota Horvath, Commercial Counsellor, Embassy of Hungary with Prince Bode Adetoyi in her office

At Atlanta, Georgia, USA, 2018

At beef-cattle farms training at Botswana, 2016

At Eiffel Tower, Paris, France, 2017

At Neovia Headquarters, We'nov Building, St. Nolf Vannes, France, 2018

At Tel Aviv, Israel, 2015

At United Nations Headquarter, New York, USA, 2017

At the Wailing Wall, Old King Solomon Temple, Jerusalem Israel (JP), 2015

At Ontario Canada, 2017

International Colleagues and Business Partners

Bayella H. Thiam, Director of African Business Development, Neovia Group, 2018

At an International Exhibition

With a friend at an International Exhibition, 2018

With friends at an International Exhibition, 2018

With Chief Joop Berkhout, Chairman, Safari Books Limited, 2017

2018

With Neovia CFO EMEA, Marin De-Lavenne, 2018

With Theodore, a colleague from Neovia South-Africa wisium office at an International Poultry Exhibition, 2018

With Patrick Waty, Neovia Head of Aquaculture, Lagos, 2018

Hubert De Roquefeulli, CEO Neovia, 2018

Mr. Kurt Seifarth, Regional Agricultural Counsellor of the American Embassy on visit to Hi-Nutrients, Lagos, 2015

With Chief Olatunde Badmus, Chairman Tuns Farms

With Dayo Obasanjo Director Obasanjo Farms Limited

With Dr. Olatunde Agbato, President, Animal Care Konsult Service Limited

With Leye Alayande MD. Hybrid Feeds

APPENDIXES

APPENDIX I

Awards

1. Fisheries Society of Nigeria Corporate Award of Excellence, November 2007.
2. Western Agric. Farmer Premix Company of the Year Award, June 2009.
3. Diamond Award for Professional Excellence, November 2009.
4. University of Ibadan Animal Science Student Association of Nigeria Merit Award, August 2010.
5. Distinguished Service Award as 3rd Vice President Fisheries Society of Nigeria, 2010.
6. Outstanding Recognition Award, Poultry Association of Nigeria, 2012.
7. Nigerian 50 Award for being among Top 50 Fastest Growing Company in Nigeria by All World Network, USA and The Tony Elumelu Foundation, March 2013.
8. Corporate Award of Excellence for Quality Products, Poultry Association of Nigeria (Ogun State Chapter), 2013.
9. Farming Advice Digest (FAD) 132 Farming Hero Award, 2013.
10. Award of Excellence, Nigerian Association of Agricultural Students, University of Ilorin, 2013.
11. Appreciation Award, Fountain of Greatness School, 2013
12. Productivity Merit Award by Fisheries Society of Nigeria, 2013.
13. Best Livestock Feed Vitamin Premixes Manufacturing Company of the Year Award by Institute for Govt. Research and Leadership Technology, Abuja, 2013.

14. Poultry Association of Nigeria (Ekiti State Chapter) Merit Award, April 2014.
15. African Quality Achievement Award for Best Quality Livestock Brand Company of the Year 2014.
16. High Professional Competence and Unquantifiable Support of the Food and Livestock Industries In Nigeria Award by The Nigerian Society for Animal Production (NSAP), 2014.
17. Nigerian Veterinary Medical Association Supporter Award, 2014.
18. Distinguished Merit Award by Association of Deans of Agriculture in Nigerian Universities (ADAN), June 2014.
19. Prominent Personality Award by Nigeria Association of Agricultural Students University of Ilorin, Aug. 2014.
20. Gold Support Award for Consistent Sponsorship of Animal Science Programme by Nigerian Institute of Animal Science (NIAS) and ASAN, September 2014.
21. Award of High Professional Competence by Nigerian Society for Animal Production, (NSAP), 2014.
22. Fellowship Award by The Institute of Brand Management of Nigeria, March 2015.
23. Fellowship Award Fisheries Society of Nigeria, 2015.
24. Outstanding Personality Award of Animal Science Association of Nigeria (Oyo State Chapter), 2015.
25. Award of Excellence Pillar in the House of God by St. Peters' Anglican Church Choir Diocese of Ekiti Oke, November 2015.
26. Honorary Award as Grand Patron Federation of Otun Moba Students' Union, FOMSU, 2016.
27. Fellowship Award as Fellow Fisheries Society of Nigeria, FISON, July 2016.
28. Distinguished Award by St. Anglican Church, Otun-Ekiti, June 2016.
29. Award of Excellence by Ekiti Youths' Conflation (EYC), August 2017.

30. Trail Blazer Award by Association of Deans of Agriculture in Nigeria, July 2017.
31. Moba Personality Award, 2017.
32. Award as Fellow Institute of Agribusiness Management of Nigeria, November 2018.
33. Entrepreneur Awards of Excellence by the Apostolic Church, 2018.
34. Meritorious Award of Recognition and Appreciation by Poultry Association of Nigeria, PAN, Lagos State Chapter, September 2018.
35. Award of Excellence in Recognition of Your Immense Contribution to Agriculture and Role Model to Youths and Young Farmers by the National Association of Agricultural Students, Obafemi Awolowo University, Ife Agric, 2018.
36. Best Personality in Humanitarian Services by National Youth Council of Nigeria, NYCN, Abuja, 2018.

APPENDIX 2

MY FAVOURITE QUOTES

" Richness goes with prosperity but wealthiness goes with posterity."

"The richest place in the world is graveyard, that is where the ideas that are conceived are buried. Share your ideas while alive."

"The content are more useful than the container."

"Opportunities will always meet preparation."

"When you put off opportunities repeatedly, you are bound to be poor."

"When you jump up, the law of gravity will bring you down, wait for your time."

"When you climb, you maintain, sustain and relax."

"If you are not born with silver spoon, get up and work harder to buy shinning silver spoon for yourself."

"After climbing a great hill. One only finds that there are many more hills to climb." - **Nelson Mandela**

In the Eyes of the People

As suggested by the title, this section contains remarks by some mentors, leaders, friends, professional colleagues, business partners, spiritual leaders, family members, and even political leaders. It is largely unedited, except for the slight restructuring sometimes required to transit from spoken English to written English. Every person's remark is stated after their individual particulars. The list does not follow any particular sequence and is not based on a ranking order.

Mrs Oluwabukola Florence Adetoyi
(Wife)

When I met my husband, it was divine because I never expected it. I heard nothing but good and godly things about him till I married him. He is so bold, intelligent, humble, respectful and God-fearing. He is a good husband and a wonderful father. I remember all the prayers and challenges we went through when he was trying to set-up his company: the disappointments, rejection from banks, and how everything turned around. I always pray that only the will of God will be done in his life and I am happy that he is fulfilling his purpose on earth.

Happy birthday to my darling husband. I wish you many more years ahead, good health, happiness and God's blessings always. Happy birthday once again to my friend, my confidant, and my soulmate.

I love you.

Finally, you will fulfil your destiny in Christ; you will wax stronger; you will see your children's children, and the Lord will give you the grace to serve Him for the rest of your life, in Jesus' name – Amen.

Adeola Adetoyi - D1
(Daughter)

If I was to describe my father in one word, it's going to be inexplicable. Words cannot adequately express how amazing his personality is but one thing I am sure of is that he is a very adventurous man who loves to travel the world and experience new things and he is very determined about any goal he sets for himself. One difficult challenge I have had with my dad was when I first came to Canada. My dad and I always had little misunderstandings and this made me feel like he did not understand me. But, at the end of the day, most of these misunderstandings were actually for my good. Now that I live thousands of miles away from home (Nigeria) I miss a lot of things: my family, friends, the food, and just Nigeria itself. Though it's challenging to be unable to see the people I would have loved to be seeing every day, it's still a fantastic opportunity for me to study in Canada and all thanks go to my Dad and my Mum.

I would love my dad to focus on his business and continue his philanthropy because he is so good at these.

Adetoyi David Jesufemi Adewale Toluwani - D2
(Son)

My father is a gentleman, but he does not take nonsense. He is a great man with many dreams; and dreams for his children too. He always wants the best for his children and for his family. He always takes care of our needs and ensures that we have the best of everything. I like the fact that he prays for us all the time, even though I know my mom does that more often. But one thing I don't like is that my dad travels a lot. And because his outings are always business-related, he cannot take us with him. My wish for my dad is that his dreams would come true. I am very proud of my dad and I will try to achieve more than he has achieved in my own life.

Prince Daniel Adetoyi - D3
(Son)

Daddy, happy birthday. I wish you the best on your 50th birthday. Have a long life and prosperity. I wish you good luck. May you see your children's children, live a long live, and may your efforts over us not be in vain. I love you: you are my darling daddy on your 50th birthday.

Otunba Niyi Adebayo
(Former Executive Governor of Ekiti State)

PRINCE OLABODE ADETOYI AT 50

It was not an accident that I met a young articulate Otun-Ekiti-born Prince, Bode Adetoyi. I remember vividly when he came to my office at Victoria Island on the 21st June, 2017 in the company of one of my political sons, Ayodeji Shiki. He introduced himself summarising what he was doing and how he would like to join politics of Ekiti in order to contribute his quota to serve his people. Seeing the enthusiasm of this young man, I wondered why he wanted to leave his booming business to join politics. Since he had made up his mind and I found him worthy, I had no option than to adopt him as one of my political sons and brother. I did not waste time in handing him over to Biodun Oyebanji to put him through the rudiments of politics and I am very sure he was coasting towards victory in his ambition to be an Honourable Member of the Federal House of Representatives in 2019.

However, the good news of the merger and acquisition of his company Hi-Nutrients with NEOVIA of France in June 2018 put a temporary hold on his ambition to serve his people. Without doubt, Bode has brought honour to himself, to Otun-Ekiti, to Ekiti State itself, and even to Nigeria as he blazed the trail to be the first indigenous agricultural company in the livestock industry to have achieved such a feat. I am also impressed with his philanthropic attitude. Prince Bode is unassuming, focused, dependable, and a fast learner in the game of politics. We will wait soonest to see him play an active political role in Ekiti and Nigeria as a whole. I am proud of him as a true born of Ekiti.

Wishing him a happy birthday at the golden age of 50.

Senator (Chief) Rashidi Adewolu Ladoja
(Former Executive Governor of Oyo State and Former Chairman of Hi-Nutrients International Ltd.)

Bode Adetoyi was introduced to me by Dr. Pension Smith, a friend of mine who is a farmer and has a production company dealing in agricultural products, as someone who is a specialist in the formulation of animal feeds and could help me with the cows and pigs in my farm in Oyo. Bode did the task brilliantly, and that marked the beginning of our relationship.

Few years later, he invited me to buy shares in his company – Hi Nutrients International Limited – and I served as the Chairman of the organisation. My son, Muyideen Ladoja, and I were Directors in the company till May, 2018.

The recent merger and acquisition of Hi-Nutrients International Limited with the Neovia group in France is a good development not just for the company in terms of increase in turn over, access to qualitative research and vast geographical presence, but also for the country and the feed subsector of the agricultural industry.

I know Bode to be an honest, hard-working and energetic individual. He is also multifaceted, engaging in various activities and excelling in them; notable among his engagements is his involvement with the Poultry Association of Nigeria (PAN). His weakness is that he is an incurable optimist and very trusting. However, his strength outweighs his weaknesses and I am sure that he will succeed in life.

Dr. Ayo Oduntan
(Group Managing Director Amo Byng Nigeria Limited; Former President, Poultry Association of Nigeria, 2012 to 2017)

I have been doing business with Bode all this while but I can remember our relationship developing when he started his business and was trying to convince us to buy his premix. I found in him at that time a very determined and very committed gentleman who was very keen on making his mark in the premix business. He was also very committed to his subject; you would not see him talking about anything other than premixes. He was very focused on becoming the number one in premix production in Nigeria. I always find that quality very attractive because I like people who know what they want and are ready to pay the price to get there. So, I saw that quality in him from the very beginning.

Bode has built a world-class company with world-class products. Interestingly, he achieved this in spite of the immense challenges he faced on the way. I am actually aware of some of these challenges, being a businessman myself. I know that growing a business in Nigeria is very tough: it is only people who have never set-up and run businesses that would think otherwise.

Bode started very humbly – with no money. For him to have been able to grow his business over the years to the level it is now is really commendable. I know that he faced quite a few financial challenges along the way. In fact, he was competing in a market that was filled with very sophisticated international competitors. Yet, through sheer tenacity and commitment, he was able to raise the profile of his company to match each and every one of those multinational companies. For those who know what it takes to achieve this type of feat, it is simply amazing.

So, in spite of these challenges, we can see that he has blazed a trail by being the first business in his category to attract foreign investment by way of a successful merger and acquisition, and that is really commendable. I cannot think of one Nigerian-owned and managed company, apart from Bode's company, that has been able to attract that kind of international attention.

The guy does not give up. He keeps at a goal until he achieves it. He is very mobile. He makes sure he cultivates his customers, befriends everything about them, he stays on his subject, and literally wears you down until you have no option but to succumb. You just must patronise Bode. The good thing is that his product matches up in terms of quality and in terms of pricing and there is no reason to decline his offer.

Hi-Nutrients International Limited has made us proud as the most successful indigenous premix manufacturer in Nigeria.

I turned 50 on the 7th July, 2018 and understand that Bode will be joining the club on the 2nd February, 2019. I would like to wish him many happy returns. Bode has been a great member of this industry and a great contributor also. But he has not only contributed to the poultry industry, he has played a role in fishery also and to agriculture and animal science as a whole.

I want to wish this very great man the very best, both now and in the future.

Mr. Ezekiel Ibrahim
(President, Poultry Association of Nigeria, 2017 till date)

Bode has been supporting the Poultry Association of Nigeria. There is something known as financial membership; but he has gone beyond that to support the association in many ways. For example, we are having a meeting now and he came here at his own cost. These are some of the ways he has been showing commitment and going the extra mile. The Poultry Association of Nigeria consists of four streams of players. We have the input suppliers and the feed millers; we have those into hatchery operations, and then we have the farmers. Hi-Nutrients International Limited is an input manufacturer and supplier and has been a major player in the industry.

The last time I checked, people in Belgium live up to 95 years. In fact, they are trying to cut down the intake of antibiotics in the population so as to concentrate on natural remedies, with the hope of increasing the longevity of citizens from 95 to 100 years. I wish Bode long life. May God give him good health and good children and give his wife long life also. I pray that his business empire will continue to expand.

May Bode's children learn from their father and realise that it is more blessed to give than to receive.

But you cannot give what you do not have;
And you cannot have if you do not work hard.

Mr. Onallo Akpa
(Director General,
Poultry Association of Nigeria,
2003 till date)

I have known Bode for many years. In fact, I met him in the early days of his company, Hi-Nutrients International Limited. He is one of those among us who has grown to become a big "masquerade." I celebrate his success. One notable thing about him is that he consults a lot. And he has consulted me on a number of issues. But better than that, he takes my advice.

Hi-Nutrients International Limited has greatly contributed to local content in the agricultural sector. When Bode was contacted by the French company for the merger and acquisition talks, he consulted me and I told him to go for it. I am happy that deal scaled through, becoming the first of its kind in the livestock industry.

Bode is not only a big boy but a big player.

With the new leap of his business and age, I wish him the good health and wisdom to manage the emerging complexities in the multinational business world.

JID Dada
(Former Managing Director Grand Cereals Nigeria Limited; Former Board Member, UAC Nigeria; Current Board Member, Grand Cereals)

Bode is a brilliant man. He is an enigma. I was fascinated with Bode from the early days of our interaction. I was Managing Director of Grand Cereals when I first met him. I said to myself: here is a young man; very articulate, very versatile. Bode knows his onions, as far as his business is concerned. He had that drive and was highly indefatigable. He was always pushing and pushing. So, I decided that we would give this young man a try because he was the sort of person we were looking for. We were looking for people who were credible, passionate, and could deliver. We knew there were a lot of cowboys in the business and wanted to relate only with genuine players. We had no interest in charlatans: we were interested in people who knew what they were doing, and that was the UAC tradition.

In Bode, we saw a person whose values aligned with ours and we felt we could do business with him. But we started by testing his products first. We gave him this opportunity in 2008 with a trial order. Naturally, there were some people who doubted his ability to deliver, but, as MD, I had seen something in the young man and had already decided that he was worth the risk, and giving him that trial order was certainly a risk. But he delivered, and we kept working with him before we hit him hard with a business deal that is still ongoing.

There are things about Bode that no one can take away from him. First is his passion, energy, drive and his focus.

As per the recent merger of Hi-Nutrients and Neovia, I would admit that I was impressed; but, really I was not surprised. Bode has become a goldfish, and the saying is that a goldfish has no hiding place. It was only a matter of time before such a thing happened, and I am glad that it has happened. I pray that all the objectives for which that partnership was formed will be achieved, in Jesus' name.

Part of Nigeria's challenges is that we have businessmen and women who are devoid of ethics. But Bode has ethics and he is consistent in upholding them.

As for Bode's 50th birthday, I am excited. Bode's life is proof that the Bible is true. The Bible says that a diligent man shall dine with kings and shall not dine with mean men. Bode's life has become a reason to believe that the Bible is a valid divine manual for excellent living. When I see the scripture being proven in the lives of people, I want to read more of the scriptures. In Deuteronomy 8:18, the Bible says that it is God that gives a man the power to make wealth. The power that Bode has to create wealth was given to him by God and it has been able to transform Hi-Nutrients into what we are witnessing today.

Bode is an employer; he goes to places; he is willing to share. I know of some of his philanthropic gestures. He is making effort to encourage young people. He is a mentor to several people. My joy for Bode at 50 is that the scripture has been proven in his life. He has become a point of contact, and may he continue to be a point of contact.

Secondly, the import of Bode at 50 for me is the idea that Nigeria needs role models. Today, the psychology of the average Nigerian youth is that one needs a godfather or a godmother somewhere in order to be successful. Some others believe that, except one travelled abroad to Europe or the United States, nothing good can come out of their lives. But Bode is a home-grown man who has hit the target and become a testament to the fact that something good can come out of Nigeria. Many people claim that there are no opportunities in Nigeria but Bode has proven that, wherever there are challenges, there are also opportunities. The two always go together and are optimistically referred to as challenging opportunities.

Bode shoots from both hips and goes full throttle in everything he does. People should learn from the life of this young man.

Finally, I believe that Bode is a case study: he is a living example. No need to go to Harvard or any of those big schools. I invite the Lagos Business School and top entrepreneurs in this country to make a case study out of Bode's story.

I wish Bode well and I wish his family well.

Otunba (Dr.) Adebayo Odunowo
(President, Biacom Agro Nigeria Limited)

I have known Bode since the 90s when he joined Bio-Organics Nutrients Systems Limited as a Sales Representative; I was then a Sales Manager at Rhone Poulenc Nigeria Limited. We collaborated together in furthering our company's interests in the marketplace and growth in the Nigeria Livestock Industry. Over the years, our relationship has been more of brother to brother relationship.

In general, Olabode Adetoyi is a very respectable and happy individual: one who is not only cheerful in himself but who gives much cheerfulness to others. He has a beautiful smile, a sense of humour, and a gentle demeanour. Bode is bright, logical, and systematic in his thinking and is always willing to share his ideas and information with others and you can see this in the way and manner he manages his company and people around him. I found him to be a splendid person of great intellect and a big heart.

Prince Olabode Adetoyi is a living proof of how fine a person can be. He is a loving husband to his wife (whom I first met during the commissioning of his factory years back), a devoted father to his children, and a good boss to his employees. He is also a good friend to many of his professional colleagues.

Prince Olabode Adetoyi's life is a life that exemplifies brilliance, a life that inspires emulation, and a life that burns so that others' paths could be lit.

In summing up the character of the life of the first 50 years of Prince Olabode Adetoyi's life (I pray that he lives for another

50 years so that we can have a centenary celebration), I would state that Bode is sincere, Bode is honest, Bode is loyal and Bode is dependable.

Albert Einstein once said that, "The value of a man should be seen in what he gives and not in what he is able to receive." In one word, Bode is a man who gives. He gave much to his work, and as such was able to grow his company from nothing in 2004 to a leading giant in the subsector he is operating today. Furthermore, he has done what his senior professional colleagues and I are afraid of doing, and that is taking Hi-Nutrients International Limited into the future by selling his majority stake in the company to a French Firm named Neovia. If he is not a giver, how could he have accomplished this feat?

Bode, as the founder and CEO of Hi-Nutrients International Limited, is a strategic thinker, a visionary who is brilliant, innovative and creative. He is passionately interested in poultry matters and also deeply concerned with improving livestock productivity in Nigeria; as a result, he generously gave his knowledge, his expertise and his skills to the poultry industry via his activities in the Poultry Association of Nigeria.

Bode is a trailblazer and an innovator: he is very keen to innovate, and this is what accounts for the many products Hi-Nutrients International Limited has introduced into the market.

Bode, you have made it through many challenges and come out stronger. As you celebrate your birthday, we celebrate years of great friendship and insight. You have been of essential and unforgettable impact in my life and organisation. I wish you all the best in life. Reach forward and grab the future and walk into it with confidence. You are a champion and a winner and this is to wish you a marvellous happy birthday.

Welcome to the 50s club!!!

Congratulations and happy birthday!

His Royal Majesty,
Oba Tijani Adetunji Akinloye
Sateru (II); Ojomu of Ajiran Land
(Founder, Akin Sateru Farms Nigeria Limited)

I knew Bode since his days at Bio-Organics. He was a salesman by that time. He is a very enthusiastic person. When he set-up his own company, I would say we decided to help him because he helped himself. He is a marketer. Even up till today, he is still involved in marketing. He is the chief marketer of his company. He is such a tenacious fellow: even if we say we want to leave him, he will not let us go because he keeps in touch seriously.

One other thing I have noticed about him is that he is not after exorbitant profit. Apparently, he believes in little margins spread over time.

I pray for the mercy of God to be on him. He has shown good business acumen and, by the grace of God, he will continue to prosper. I also wish him long life.

Chief Joop Berkhout, OON
(The Okun Borode of Ile-Ife, and Chairman,
Safari Books Limited, Ibadan)

My first encounter with Prince Bode Adetoyi was through a mutual friend, Patrick Obidoyin, who had just returned from the UK. The meeting was a brief one but it left me in utter amazement at what Bode had achieved in life at such an early age. Listening to him tell the story of his humble background and how he was able to go through the hardships of life to become a self-made man endeared him to me.

His life experiences are perfect demonstrations of my philosophies about life that irrespective of background, anyone can rise in life if the person is determined, and that society owes us nothing; but we owe the society.

During another visit Bode paid to my house, he intimated me of his desire to go into politics. I told him in clear terms that he was better off out of politics than being in it, as he could be of more influence and touch more lives as a private sector/business man than as a politician which is temporary. That piece of advice proved valuable as he eventually stayed away from politics to focus on his business. Today, not only is he better for that wise decision, but the Nigerian agricultural sector and business world in general are still reaping the benefits of his decision. In his business, he has achieved a rare feat as the first Nigerian to have started a livestock company which attracted foreign investors. That is a great achievement!

Bode is a unique and self-made man, without a godfather. He is a testament that Nigeria is a country full of great people. He is a thinker and a keen writer, always with a jotter and a pen to put down ideas as they come. If we have more of his kind in this country, Nigeria will be a better place and a great country.

I celebrate him and hope to see him in greater heights in future.

Tony O. Elumelu
(Founder, Tony Elumelu Foundation and Chairman,
Heirs Holdings)

Entrepreneurs (like Bode) are living proof that Africapitalism is changing Africa before our eyes. They are not only boosting Nigeria's economy and producing value-added capital, but are also giving back to the community by driving socially beneficial long-term development, such as creating employment.

Dr. Uzoma Kenny Acholonu
(Founder, Bio-Organics; Chairman, Nutri-Sciences
Nigeria Limited)

Bode, I am proud of you today. You are a big boy. I am happy I trained you. The kind of performance you showed (and that of your team) when you were with me was excellent delivery. Remember, if you started a company, managed it to an extent, and yet you are unable to sell it or attract foreign investment, then it means what you had was not a company. As for you, Bode, your success in attracting foreign investors to buy into your company shows that you had ran the company well and taken it to a global standard. You have done well for yourself. Remember the 3Ds in management: Discuss, Decide, and Deliver. Bode, as far as I am concerned, you have delivered.

Mr. Dick Obasoyo
(Former Production Manager,
Bendel Feed and Flour Mills,
Ewu Edo State
Now a Lecturer at the
Department of Animal Science
Ambrose Alli University, Ekpoma, Edo State)

Olabode Adetoyi – "The purposeful man"

According to J.C. Penney, "Give me a stock clerk with a goal and I will give you a man who will make history. Give me a man without a goal and I will give you a stock clerk".

Bode and I met while he was still working at Bio-Organics Nigeria Limited and when he came to Bendel Feed & Flour Mill Ltd, Ewu in 1999 to pursue his master's business. The expertise and strategy he exhibited was unparalleled; the commitment and dedication he showed was remarkable. He was patient, strong, and self-disciplined.

In gaining our confidence, we saw in him that:

- He values people;
- Accessible to everyone in the factory and a good listener;
- A good risk taker;
- Sensitive to customer's needs and desires;

- Problem solver and a balanced man of faith, family, and career.

In no distant time, he gained over 70% of our market share. When he eventually took the risk of starting Hi-Nutrients International Limited, he got our support and our market share too. His premixes were not only better in terms of performance, the quality and storage ability were excellent. We were also bold to introduce other Toll millers, farmers and other feed miller to the products. The growth over these few years have been phenomenal.

Personally, I am not surprised that his company has grown to become international. This success story is a function of the fact that Bode knows what he was doing and believed in it.

Our frequent trips to Atlanta Georgia, USA have yielded results. Congratulations!!!

His Royal Highness,
Oba James Adedapo Oladele Popoola,
Oore of Mobaland, Otun-Ekiti

He is a prince and wonderful son of the soil. He is resourceful, empathetic, and always ready to lend a helping hand. I wish Bode a happy birthday and pray sincerely that his days will be long, healthy, and prosperous.

Biodun Toki
(Managing Director,
Tom Associates Training)

Grounded, organised, exacting, socially deft, wonderfully outgoing and mentally capable, Bode has always been seen as dependable, practical, and able to get the job done – whatever the job may be.

Dr. Tunde Sigbeku JP; PhD; RAS
(Assistant Director/Head, Animal Feed and Premix Division, Veterinary Medicine and Allied Products, Directorate National Agency for Food and Drug Administration and Control (NAFDAC))

Bode and I met at the University of Ibadan in 1997 when we registered for the MSc course in Animal Science. Fortunately, we both resided at Obafemi Awolowo Hall on the campus. It was convenient for us to go to class together and also to the research farm. I actually met him through Rotimi Oyedele, who was my schoolmate while I was studying for my first degree.

Bode is open-hearted and very friendly and firm. He will always call you when leaving the hall for class, remind you of homework, and share meals with you – especially bread and akara. After graduation in November 1998, we all parted ways and there was no GSM phone then. I eventually joined NAFDAC and, one afternoon, Bode walked into my office to process an official permit that would enable him import raw materials for his new company – Hi-Nutrients International Limited. That was how we reunited after our University days. Ever since then, he has remained a wonderful colleague and friend. We often meet annually at IFRM in Atlanta, USA, and other professional meetings also. Bode is a very wonderful person to work with. He is very industrious and, as a regulator, I frequently advise him on regulatory issues and also get useful feedback from him on what is obtainable and practicable in the industry.

I will simply say that Bode is a brother from another mother. He is caring and wonderful. Very brilliant and God-fearing.

As he turns 50, I wish him the very best in life. I wish him long life and prosperity in good health and wealth. We usually celebrate his birthday at Atlanta and the last one I attended was during the IFRM, and he was there with his wife.

Wishing you well my brother. My humble regards also go to Bode's wife (Mrs. Adetoyi), his wonderful children, and the entire Adetoyi family. May the good Lord be with them all.

Jennifer Anazodo
(Bode's First Banker and Former BM, First Bank of Nigeria Plc)

I met Bode during my banking career as the Head of Retail Banking at the Agidingbi branch of First Bank, Lagos. After then, I became like a personal banker to him. He was very much enthusiastic about growing the figures in Hi-Nutrients International Limited, and he wanted to take advantage of the CBN Agric loan that was at a one-digit interest rate. After some trials (because there was no acceptable collateral in place), we finally scaled through with the first loan of ₦90m. Thereafter, we did quite a lot of loans, Invoice Discounting, Import Finance, LPO finance, Asset Acquisition and Agric loan. Bode practically moved his account to any branch I was transferred to.

As for his person, I would say he is a very humble, unassuming, but enthusiastic man. He puts in a lot of energy into what he believes in. He always strives to be the best and remains focused in his business. I also see him as generous, a team builder, and an exemplary leader. His staffs were always at ease with him and he carries them along in every transaction he had with the bank.

I have seen him grow from a small sole proprietor to a corporate business now sort after by most banks. He is a man of integrity.

After my exit from the banking sector, he has been a very supportive business partner. During the launch of my company, 'The Fifth Liner', he could not make it but ensured he sent a representative to the event, with apologies. That is Bode for you. He also registered as a financial member though he has never made it to any of our events.

I wish him the very best as he enters the golden age and as he moves to take over the international world in premixes and the agriculture business. I look forward to seeing him pick up important government appointments and represent Nigeria in agricultural matters.

When I see him pose with important dignitaries on his social media handles, I see a determined, fearless, and focused mind. His life shows me that, with determination and the fear of God, the sky is just a launching pad.

Pastor Bunmi Idowu
(General Manager, Obasanjo Farms, Ibogun)

I have known Bode for not less than twenty years. Since that time, I have seen that he is very focused, industrious, enterprising, and very good in customer relations. So, it is not surprising that, when he "retired" from his former place of employment, he decided to go and start his own business. As a fellow Animal Scientist, I must state that I love his commitment to professionalism. I had the privilege of attending the launch of his factory in 2007. I remember that I noticed the layout of the factory at the time and, even that showed that this was a person that was committed to doing things right; doing things professionally. And he has not rested on his oars. He has since left that first facility to a bigger and more modern one. If I have my record straight, I think his premix is the first to be registered by NAFDAC. Now, that is somebody who is committed to professionalism and excellence. He likes to ensure that he operates with best practices. And these qualities he has is properly reflected in the recent merger of his company with a foreign multinational company. We all know that, before such a foreign company will decide to merge with an indigenous one (and one that was started by a single person and a young person at that) they would have foreseen very good potential, strong fundamentals, and they must also have seen that Bode was somebody they could trust. As a rule, Europeans do not joke when it comes to trust in business.

So I believe that, by the grace of God, Bode has been able to put all of that together, and I am not surprised by the progress he has made over the years. All I can wish him is to first welcome him to the golden age.

His Royal Majesty Ayodele Kupoluyi
Oba of Temidire Town

We met in the Faith Chapel parish of the Redeemed Christian Church of God, Ojodu Berger, in the late 90s. He later joined the workers group. It was his conviviality that endeared him towards me, even before I eventually discovered that he was an Ekiti man. The bonding grew from there.

Prince is a man of many parts: a child of God, an entrepreneur, a philanthropist, and a 'politician'. Bode loves his parents to a fault and would do anything to honour them. We were in Otun-Ekiti when he lost his dad. He takes good care of his aged mum now. As a business man, he understood the dynamics of his field quite early and saw an opportunity in the sector. He therefore started Hi-Nutrients at an early age and made a success of it. Today, the company has gone global through foreign investment. As a philanthropist, he gives scholarships to his people and empowers them for self-sufficiency. My community was a beneficiary of this largesse in 2016 when he gave 25 students scholarship awards. No wonder, he won many awards which eventually made his zone to beg him to represent them in government. That's a story he will tell himself. It is also worth saying that he invested so much in building his parish when he was posted out of Faith Chapel. Shortly after he started Hi-Nutrients, he said he would give me his advertising business when it was time and, for over a decade, nothing happened. Suddenly, he called me recently and told me that a foreign partner is buying into his company and that he would want me to handle the advertising. For me, that is integrity. He kept to his words.

In spite of his achievements, Prince has remained a very humble person, God-fearing, loving, and caring. He is an astute business tycoon and he is very diligent in his business. I am not surprised that he has transformed the livestock sector from a docile sector to a very active one. His industry is very visible in the media due to the efforts and contributions of persons like him. As an employer of labour, he has put smiles on the faces of many homes and families. His products also compete favourably with imported ones, thus helping to reduce the influx of foreign products and also to preserve foreign exchange. He is helping to build a virile economy that is sustainable.

I wish him the very best of life at 50. I wish him more wisdom to excel, strength from the Most High, good health, and sound mind in years ahead in His service. I pray that he remains kingdom-focused and draw many to Jesus Christ along the way. May God help him to attain his political ambition in future for the betterment of Ekiti in particular and Nigeria in general. He has the potential to make a difference in governance from his experience in the private sector.

Finally, I urge him to spend more time with his family as he gets older.

Tade Matthew
(Fish Farmer)

As a young graduate then, he was an animal scientist and I was into aquaculture, and we had course to interact in the farm I was managing at the time. Bode is a very versatile and brilliant chap. When I discovered that, I felt that it was better for the two of us to work together and see how we could make progress in the field of aquaculture and agriculture in general. As a professional in aquaculture, I have been exposed to modern ways of rearing fish and I knew that, with Bode by my side in the area of nutrition, I would not have any problems. So, that was how we became friends.

I remember that I helped to set-up a fish farm for his in-law in Warri. I was in Warri for almost two years because I had to establish and manage the farm and train Bode's in-law in the practice. This recommendation from Bode was not a one-off thing. Any time he saw an aquaculture project, he will call on me and I will handle the project to the best of my ability without hesitation. And that is how we have been operating. He has been a good friend: very upright and very brilliant.

I wish him well; I wish him long life. I pray that his company will grow from strength to strength and that, at the end of the day, we would laugh together and remain good friends. I wish him all the best of everything in life. My own birthday is 15th February and I hope to attend his own on the 2nd of February.

Chief Chinedu Ahamneze
(Professional Colleague and Businessman)

I have come to see Bode as a man who is very resilient with objectives that are laudable and a good business man. I wish him more success, long life and prosperity.

Dr. Dele Oyediji
(Pioneer Registrar and Chief Executive of the Nigerian Institute of Animal Science, Abuja)

You are a very humble fellow who has built a reputation on dedication and honesty. Today, you are known as the biggest animal additive input supplier in Nigeria because of your aspiration to excel with good quality products and hard work. You have earned our respect. I wish you long life, happiness and continuous prosperity.

Mrs. Mope Omotosho
(Past President, Animal Science Association of Nigeria and Council Member, Nigerian Institute of Animal Science)

You are a hard-working person and you have grown in leaps and bounds. You have brought international exposure to the industry in Nigeria through the merger. I wish you a happy birthday. This is the beginning of better things in your life in all facets.

Professor Israel Folorunsho Adu
(President, Nigerian Institute of Animal Science)

You are an inspiration to the upcoming generation and we are proud of you. I wish you all the best and many more years.

Professor E. A. Iyayi
(Registrar, Nigerian Institute of Animal Science)

I have witnessed your meritorious rise in the industry and I am very proud of you. Thank God for your life. I wish you well and pray that God will strengthen you.

Professor Job Olutimehin Atteh
(University of Ilorin)

You have been a star: determined, highly focused, and ready to learn. You have made giant strides and we are proud of you. I wish you the best.

Professor Placid Njoku
(Pioneer President, Nigerian Institute of Animal Science)

As one of the great names from the industry, you have shown that you can achieve anything you set to achieve. I wish you great success as you grow your business to greater heights, and in all your endeavours.

Professor Enoch Olayiwola Oyawole
(Professor of Animal Science, Landmark University)

You are a worthy role model to the youths as you make waves in the industry. You will fulfil your purpose and I pray you continue to be a role model as people look up to you. I wish you the best of luck.

Nnenna Ugwu
(Alumni Director EDC)

A dedicated, unassuming, and humble man. A person I would like to identify with.

Dr. Peter Bamkole
(Founder and Director, EDC, Pan Atlantic University)

When I started to notice you, you were always humble and consistent with a never-give-up attitude. 50 is a year of jubilee. You have done well and I wish you all the best.

Olawale Anifowoshe
(Enterprise Development Centre (EDC); Pan Atlantic University, Lagos)

His genuine interest in supporting other start-ups in the agriculture value chain for investment opportunities is commendable. He is an exceptional person and we celebrate his achievements. I wish Bode a happy 50th birthday and many more years to continue to impact people and the nation.

Chief Emmanuel Folorusho Ogunnaike
(Chairman, FOLHOPE Limited)

From his days as an employee, I have known him to be trustworthy, faithful, and hard-working. I wish him long life in good health and the grace to reap the fruits of his labour.

Felix Olusegun Gbolagade
(Felima Aquaculture, Ijebu Ode)

Bode is a friend and a brother. I have known him for the past 15 to 18 years when we started this aquaculture thing basically in the western part of Nigeria. I have always been wishing him well. He considers me a mentor. In those days, whatever he wants to do, he will travel down all the way from Lagos to Ijebu Ode and tell me what he had in mind and then seek for my advice. I have always seen him as a hard-working man. I am always proud of him. The sky is his limit. The Lord is propelling him. He has joined forces with Europeans now and his products are higher than any other ones in the country. People are saying the products are expensive but my question is this: what is the result of the cheap products on your fish and other livestock?

I wish him long life; I wish him God's guidance. I pray that, by God's infinite mercy, we would mark his 60th birthday; 70th, 80th, and even his 100th. After he turns 100, he can decide to ask God if he should stay more.

Mrs. Toluwalashe Fashowape
(Former Deputy Chairman,
Poultry Association of Nigeria, Lagos State Chapter)

He is a friend, colleague and brother. A straightforward, hard-working business man; he is always aiming for the top and very respectful. I know his products and I use them mostly in my feed mill and on my animals – especially for my pigs. I don't compromise on Hi-Nutrients products. I have been using them over the years and the results have been excellent.

As he turns 50, I am so happy for him. He is welcome to the club. I am so happy for him. He is not even looking 50 anyway. I wish him all the best in all his endeavours: family, business, and every other aspect of life. I also wish him God's guidance in everything he does.

Mr. Godwin Egbebe
(Chairman, Poultry Association of Nigeria, Lagos Chapter)

I have known Mr. Olabode for at least 16 years and we have been patronising his products all this while and will keep patronising them. This is because we have seen that he knows what he is doing. His excellence in the industry is just as if he was born with the ability to manufacture premixes. I can say that categorically anywhere.

Bode is a go-getter; a dogged man. I took the baton from him as Chairman of the Poultry Association of Nigeria, Lagos State Chapter so I can say I know him well. Whatever he wants to achieve, he does everything and tries to achieve it. He has contributed a lot to the industry, especially in terms of information and financial support. He gives to the association to make sure that things are working. Also, when there is information, he tries to get it across.

I am proud of him and we are hoping that he will go into politics because we know that, once he is there, farmers will have more voice at the national level. I have been to many places and I see him supporting people through various humanitarian initiatives. I want him to keep up with this effort. And, whatever he is doing, he should continually look on to God because God is the ultimate.

Professor Emeritus Oyebiodun Grace Longe
(Nutritional Biochemistry, University of Ibadan)

As a Master's student, Bode demonstrated initiative, reliability, and responsibility in his project and coursework. He is very focused and humble even while serving a need in the industry. God has kept him till this golden age and will take him to greater heights, beyond his expectations. I wish him well.

Papa James F. Oyinloye
(Paternal Uncle)

As God would have it, I was one of those who brought Bode up. I was a teacher then. I noticed quite early that he was intelligent and very ready to learn. When he was younger, I used to call him Bode Thomas, in honour of the real Bode Thomas – the popular Action Group politician and former Minister of Finance. He was so rich that he was one of the financiers of the Action Group in those days. There was an occasion when Bode Thomas is reported to have said openly that he was born with a silver spoon in his mouth. Bode Thomas was such an interesting fellow and I saw that Bode Adetoyi was also going to have an interesting life; so that was why I used to call him Bode Thomas.

I remember that, one day, I called Bode aside and asked him if he knew why I often called him Bode Thomas. When he said he did not know, I told him that I did that because Bode Thomas was very rich and was even a millionaire as a young man. And I told him that I wanted him to work hard so that he also would become a young millionaire in the future. In those days, most people went to the university to study geography or history, with the hope of becoming teachers. But I advised Bode to go to the university and study a professional course so that he will become a professional. Bode took to my advice and, today, thank God, he is one of the forces to be reckoned with. He is now a young millionaire (if not billionaire) as I anticipated he would be.

Bode has helped so many people; he is a philanthropist and I wish him the best. I am very happy for him.

Olabode Odunsi
(Bourdillon Feeds, Ijebu Ode)

When I went into the livestock industry in 2007, Bode was one of the first people that I met. He was supplying us with his Hi-Nutrients premixes.

Very remarkably, I can say that, except for Bode and his excellent products, I probably would have left the industry by now. There was a time we had a problem and our fishes were turning yellow because of a certain meal we were giving them. I told Bode about the issue, which was so serious that it threatened to force me out of the business. Bode told me to simply increase the quantity of the Hi-Nutrients premixes he was supplying me and to reduce the quantity of the special feed we were giving the fishes, and, like magic, the problem vanished. This problem happened shortly after I established my fishery, and it would have damaged the business. No wonder, up till today, I use Hi-Nutrients products and also supply my customers the same products.

Bode is now more than a business partner to me. He is now a brother. For the past ten years that I have known him, my house has become his house. Anytime he comes to Ijebu Ode, he must come to my place. When my mother was alive, he would give her some cash, play with my children, and make everybody feel good.

Bode is an agile man. He can control a whole state: in fact, he can control two states in Nigeria at once. With the level of his intelligence, he can be the governor of a state. Bode did not get his money from politics, and yet he is spending his money in philanthropy. I don't think his recent attempt to go into politics is because of money. It is to help people.

I wish him good health.

Ikemefuna Frank
(Rainbow Feeds, Sapele, Delta State)

My relationship with Bode has been a long one. When Bode was with Bio-Organics, I was the General Manager of Top Feeds. He was a salesman then and was supplying us some products. That was when the friendship started. But that friendship took a new turn when he left Bio-Organics and I also left Top Feeds. We started our respective companies almost at the same time. When I started, I think the very first vitamin premix I bought was from him. We have been together all these years. It has not been smooth sailing, but we are still together. He has been a friend. There have been times I have visited Lagos and he would lodge me and pay my hotel bills. I have even slept in his house before, and this goes to show just how close we are.

I am happy that he is making progress, and I know that he is also happy with the progress we are making, even though we lack government support and are not moving as fast as we could. It is unfortunate that our politicians do not know how easily agriculture can provide countless employment for our youths.

I know how small Bode started, and I know where he is today. I remember he used to tell me that he was interested in having partners who will invest in the business. I am glad that his goal has been achieved with the recent merger. That is the kind of thing we want. I am happy with him and for him.

Bode, you are now joining the elders, and I pray that God will keep you until you get to three score and ten years – and even beyond. Your business will also grow far better than what it is today. I want you to be happy.

Adewunmi Ayo Ajibade
(PRO, Prime Club of Otun-Ekiti)

I consider Bode an asset to our community. But I do not only consider him an asset: I see him as an answer to the prayer of many generations for God to raise a person who is intellectually sound, who is morally upright, who is financially capable, and who has vision and the social standing to mix with all sorts of people and lift up the status of our community. If you see the kind of thing that Bode is doing, you will easily deduce that, one of these days, Otun-Ekiti will also have a Dangote.

What has allowed Bode to help many people is his mind-set. His own kind of mind-set is that, anybody from Otun-Ekiti is his brother and his sister. You do not need to be related to him by blood to benefit from his philanthropy. This is a young man that has moral values: the kind of values you don't find in many people around. Intellectually, he cannot be found wanting because he is well educated. So, because of his moral values and high intellect, he is able to do a lot of things that other businessmen cannot do; he is able to relate with people from different parts of the world.

Bode has all the qualities we need in leaders and I was very delighted when he said he wanted to join politics. I told him that he had all it takes to aspire for any position in Ekiti State. I know that he has had to backpedal because of his international business merger, but, I am convinced that, in the near future, he will be one of the symbols of our democratic progress as a people. We need a higher institution in Otun, and one of the people who can get it for us is Bode Adetoyi. So, I believe the time has come when we may need to force people like Bode to run for political office.

I wish him all the best. I love him, and I want him to concentrate on his business for now. I am very proud of Bode, anytime any day.

Dr. Leye Alayande
(MD/CEO Hybrid Feeds Ltd, Kaduna)

Bode and I were employed at about the same time in 1999 at Bio-Organics Nutrient Systems Ltd. Bode covered Ibadan region whilst I worked in Kaduna. What immediately struck me about Bode was his knowledge of the product and the industry even at the early stage of our working together. He was always willing and ready to take up technical issues that may arise on the field in a bid to resolve them. These qualities stood him out and enabled us to foster and develop a great working and personal relationship. Bode is a go-getter who remains undaunted, even in the face of challenges. His diligence at work is infectious; no wonder, he has been able to inculcate this trait in the lives of his friends, colleagues, and workers.

Bode is a foremost livestock practitioner that started from humble beginnings, but has become a household name in the industry. This is reflected in his latest merger, which will enable him to achieve even more in the industry. The sky is not the limit for him; rather, it is the starting point. As a testament to this, we are one of his numerous customers and he has lived up to our expectations.

May he be blessed abundantly today, tomorrow, and in days to come.

Mrs. Abiodun Oluwaseyi - Bode's Former Staff
(Registered Animal Scientist & Senior Livestock Development Officer, Department of Animal Husbandry Services, Federal Ministry of Agriculture and Rural Development, Abuja)

The first time I met Mr. Ezekiel Olabode Adetoyi was when I came for a job interview in his company. My first impression of him on the day of the interview was that he was an accommodating person and quite passionate about his profession. He was happy to interview a female Animal Scientist and he eventually gave me the job. While working with him, our relationship was cordial; he is a good boss, a brother, a mentor, and a spectacular person who has made our connection stronger over the years. Sometimes we disagree to agree and I feel blessed to have worked under him.

As a person, Mr. Adetoyi is very smart, a go-getter, a giver, a person of integrity, determined in professionalism, and a good marketer. He appreciates hard-working people and he is a God fearing person. He loves his family so much and does not joke with the welfare and education of his children. He also loves his mother passionately. Bode loves God and gives liberally towards kingdom expansion.

I remember when I was given a Presidential award. He was the first person to break the good news to the other staff. He was so happy to have me working in his organisation and he appreciated me with a good sum of money, which shows that he loves the progress of his workers.

I wish him good health, long life, much success, not just today, but always and all through his life.

Mr. Abiodun Elutilo
(Senior Driver at Hi-Nutrients International Limited)

I have been working with Hi Nutrients for about 14 years now. When I got to Hi-Nutrients, something told me that the company will grow beyond imagination because my boss, Mr. Bode, has always been a versatile and resilient man. I used to drive my boss to several locations in Nigeria and I have enjoyed working with him.

Like every other company, Hi-Nutrients has had its own challenges, but our MD, Mr. Bode was ever ready to face all challenges and, to God be the glory, he always finds a way out.

My boss is resilient and always optimistic. He teaches us to always tell the truth at all time and that has been our principle till date. He leads by example. There has never been a day I ever thought of quitting my job at Hi-Nutrients.

Definitely, there is no gain without pain but I am happy working with Hi-Nutrients and am happy working with Mr. Bode Adetoyi.

Gabriel Popoola Adetoyi
(Eldest Brother and First Born of the Family)

He is a star in our family: he will continue to soar wherever he goes. In whatever he does, God will always be with him.

Mrs. Alice Akanke Odia
(Elder Sister)

I pray that, as God has blessed him and has been protecting him, may He continue to do so. I normally pray for him because he travels a lot. It is by the grace of God that he enjoys safety because, some people move just a few kilometres and become involved in fatal accidents, but God has been helping Bode and granting him journey mercy. We give God the glory for his life and we really thank God for his achievements. We also thank God for the entire family because God has been helping us.

May God continue to bless and promote Bode in all his endeavours. May God continue to guide and protect him. God will help him to achieve all his goals, in the mighty name of Jesus. As he is successful, may God enable all his children to be successful also. May God also bless his staffs and raise them up. May his staff be able to train their children to be responsible citizens of our country.

Bode will never lack a helper in his business and no calamity shall befall his factory, in the mighty name of Jesus. God will make his staffs faithful and diligent in their work; he will never mistakenly employ anyone who will trouble his business or bring disunity to the workforce, in the name of Jesus.

As he celebrates his birthday, I pray that he will celebrate many more birthdays in the future, in Jesus' name. May God also give our mother many more years so she will enjoy the fruit of her labour, in the mighty name of Jesus.

No evil shall befall Bode; no evil man or woman will cross his path. Any time he is going out, God will go with him; any time he is coming in, God will come with him. God will continue to be his umbrella and continue to protect him. He will continue to succeed.

Prince Adetoyi Joseph Adebamiji
(Elder Brother)

Bode was lazy; he hated farming when he was younger: but he was brilliant in school. As his elder brother, I used to count it all joy when I managed to take the 8th or 9th position in primary school. But Bode was so brilliant that, the day he took the 2nd position in primary school, he cried so much and nearly became depressed.

Whenever it was time for farm work, he used to pretend to be sick just to avoid going to the farm. I am baffled that, today, he is a great farmer. It gladdens my heart that he is a career farmer. He is even farming beyond my imagination and I thank God for this irony.

Bode is my immediate younger brother and I boast of him everywhere I go. I am very proud of him. I give God the glory for his life. And I pray that he will live up to 100 and even 120. He will not die prematurely. He has done well. He has played a vital role in uniting our family. He has also done well in our community. Every year, he gives scholarship to many students of tertiary institutions from Mobaland. This scholarship is restricted to the children of parents who are not well to do so as to make it meaningful. He has even gone beyond our local government and even our federal constituency to extend the benefit to other areas within Ekiti State.

Mr. Adekunle Frank Alarapon
(Branch Manager, Wema Bank; Dopemu Branch)

He is one man for whom I can go the extra mile because I believe in his prudence. I believe in his passion. I believe in his vision, and I believe in his knowledge and integrity. We have done business together that we now have a mutual friendship and I am very proud of his achievements.

Mr. Henry Odiachi
(Head of Accounts, Hi-Nutrients International Limited)

One remarkable thing about Mr. Bode, my MD, that is very inspiring to me is that he is somebody that does not give up. I like that quality when I see that it is part of a person's principles. He is a very good sales man also. He can bulldoze the market and takeover whatever he wants to takeover: he is very good at that. He practises guerilla marketing.

On the other hand, he is a very articulate person; a good leader, persistent and consistent in achieving a set goal. Turning 50 is a lofty achievement, coupled with building an international company. I say big congratulations. He deserves the accolades for being visionary and achieving milestones.

Dr. (Pastor) Babatunde Owolabi
California, USA

Bode and I went to the same primary school. Apart from that, his mum and mine were good friend, and, by virtue of this, we became friends automatically and I took him as my younger brother. Our relationship has been cordial and one of mutual respect. He is fond of calling me *egbon*, meaning elder brother. Aside being his family and company doctor for more than 20years, we are bound together spiritually as we are both ordained ministers of God in the Redeemed Christian Church of God (RCCG).

A whole book would not be enough for me to describe Bode, but I would simply state that he is a hard-working, dedicated, honest, determined, fearless, trustworthy, purposeful, go-getting, and astute businessman. He is also God-fearing, humble, and well connected. I remember that he came to me and told me when he wanted to resign his job and start his own business. By that time, I had already started my own private medical practice. It was a risk worth taking and thanks be to God today that is enjoying the blessing.

Bode, as you clock 50, I wish you more years of great achievements, perfect health, divine wisdom, and revelation, God's protection and provision.

OWO AYE KO NI BA E

Greater heights in Jesus' name.

Welcome to the 50's club.

Please, Bode, as you start the second half of your life, do not forget God. Make Him your anchor and support; serve Him more than ever before.

The sky is just the beginning;

Keep soaring my brother;

Happy birthday to you!

Congratulations!

Taiwo Lemoshe
(Former RCF President, University of Ibadan)

Mr. Olabode and I met on the campus of University of Ibadan while he was doing his postgraduate course and while I was an undergraduate. We met at the Redeemed Christian Fellowship and were both members of the executive committee of that fellowship and served under the great leadership of Pastor Tunji Olasunkanmi.

To me, Mr. Olabode is a dogged go-getter. It is amazing how he has built his company from the scratch to what it is today. It takes foresight and doggedness to make such happen in our kind of country and economy; yet, he did it by the grace of God.

I pray that the next decades of his life will be ten times better than the past ones.

Pastor Asaolu S. Taiwo
Iro-Ekiti

Olabode and I have known each other since from childhood and we grew up together in the same village. His late father and my late father were both wool farmers in Ekiti State. My late mother also had a good relationship with his mum. I know that, for a while, we did not see each other but we met again after his programme at the university. I eventually became his fashion designer, that being my profession. This business relationship began right from when he was still with Bio-Organics. I also hold prayer sessions with him many times, pleading with God to establish him. To the glory of God, all of the prophecies that came during these prayers sessions came to pass at their appointed times.

My sincere wish for him is that he will celebrate many years on earth if Christ tarries. He should keep trusting God and continue being humble. Also, he should always remember that the more he raises many, the more God will enlarge his coast.

Atolani Olanrewaju James
(University Coursemate and Brother-in-Law)

A very bold and interesting man, even from our days as students. With the way he impacts the lives of people wherever he goes and leaves footprints, I had no doubt that my sister was in good hands. He is someone I would recommend at any time.

Mr. Olaitan Alatise
(Master's Degree Programme Classmate; University of Ibadan; First Degree Classmate; University of Ilorin; now Deputy Director of Agriculture, Moba Local Government, Ekiti State)

One thing is that Bode is a go-getter, and he has a unique strategy for difficult challenges. If Bode wants to get something in the next two years, he would start making some moves today; but people around him may not know what he is up to. Bode is highly industrious and very focused. This is not something he just picked up. Even right from our undergraduate days, that was how he was. Bode has excelled in everything he has done in life. I am not surprised by his present status because I know him and what he is capable of.

If Bode has a target, he will make sure he achieves that target, no matter what. If the person that has what he needs is a small boy, Bode is ready to prostrate before that boy, if that is what it would take to get what he wants. He is very humble

I am aware of his brand of philanthropy, which is unprecedented in Mobaland and other local governments in Ekiti North, and was happy when he was given an award on Otun Day some years back. He supports education with his resources because he knows the value of education, and I have been seeing some pictures of him on social media delivering lectures in different places.

There is nowhere you will put Bode that he will not perform. I know the impact he made on the company he used to work for. He made a difference in that company and it is no wonder that, with his own company now, he is making a difference in the industry and even in Nigeria as a whole. Bode's success both as an employee and a CEO of his own company is in line with a Yoruba proverb which basically avers that the way you treat another man's business is the way you will treat your own. So, his success and commitment as an employee in another's man's company was bound to result in success and commitment in his own company. There is nothing strange about that.

I wish him long life, peace, more blessings, more achievements, and, to crown it all, I want him to age with grace.

Mr. Dele Atolani
(In-Law)

We thank God for his life. We thank God for how he started, where he is now, and where he is headed. We bless the name of God for his life. He has been very good to us. Any time we seek for assistance from him, he does no shy away.

My advice to him is to be patient in life and to be serving God. He should also be slow in taking decisions – especially major decisions. I also would encourage him in his philanthropy.

I wish him long life and pray that he would be more devoted to God.

Mrs. Dele Atolani

Prince Olabode is a very generous, kind, respectful, and friendly man. He does not look down on people and I just have a natural admiration for his person since I got to know him after he married my sister-in-law.

As he turns 50, I wish him many happy returns in good health and wealth. His expectation shall never be cut short in life. Multiple blessings will radiate in him with the new age he has attained. He shall always be honoured, in Jesus' mighty name – Amen.

Aderemi Onipede
(Member, Covenant Givers' Group, RCCG Faith City)

Worshipping with you in church for 17 years, I have come to know you as a man of vision and a true lover of God. I remember how we used to pray together to become business owners. I am not surprised that, today, you own a thriving business. I wish you a happy birthday and more of what God has in store for you because God is fulfilling His words in your life. I pray that it will be well with you and that you will grow from strength to strength all the days of your life. As you have gone international, there will be no cause for losses in Jesus' name. I wish you the very best.

Austin Dominique
(Member, Covenant Givers' Group, RCCG Faith City)

You are a God-fearing, kind, and approachable man who likes to help people indiscriminately. It is evident that God gave you the revelation, the gift, and talents, and you have used them well. I wish you the best of luck in life. You will continue to go higher; God will continue to use you well as you hold on to Him. I wish you growth and pray that you will continue to be in peace in Jesus' mighty name.

Kayode Oluwashona
(Member, Covenant Givers' Group, RCCG Faith City)

Bode is a very unassuming man. He is true to himself, and he does nothing for selfish reasons. He is someone I would stick out my neck for. Resolute, down to earth, determined, focused, and hard-working. All your hard work is yielding fruits and you are making huge progress. Your good deeds precede you and I wish you more strength, long life, more achievements, and accomplishments. I wish you a very happy birthday.

Pastor Muyiwa Adeyemo
(Member, Covenant Givers' Group, RCCG Faith City)

You are a go-getter. Once you set your heart on something, you always go after it and get it. This the beginning: you will go higher and increase on every side. I believe God for you that you will attain greater heights. The Lord will keep you and preserve you and your family. You will see many years in Jesus' name. It is well with you. God bless you and happy birthday.

Pastor Femi Adekunle
(Pastor, RCCG, Hope Assembly Parish, Fagba)

You have been my very good friend for close to 23 years. I already knew you would go far because you are very hard-working, versatile in your work, very diligent, and you have made impact on people's lives. I know that at 50, life just begins, so I wish you the best in your career, your business, your family and I welcome you to the club of 50.

Pastor Michael Harrison Kpolu
(RCCG, Faith City Parish)

Bode, you are a friend, a brother and you are focused on the vision God has given you. I trust you to keep believing in God and trusting Him to take you to the height that He has purposed for you.

Pastor Gilbert Aimufua RCCG - Abuja
(The Pastor that invited Bode to join RCCG in 1995)

Our assignment as children of God is to reach out to as many souls as we come across. Bode happened to be a child that we came across and he is a loving son. As a loving son, we developed interest in him; that is, myself and my wife. And we tried to extend the love which Christ had already showed us to him. When we look at the life of Christ, we can see that He cared for both the physical and the spiritual needs of people, and He is still doing that today through

His people on earth. Fortunately, Bode responded to this and was attracted thereby to the Redeemed Christian Church of God.

I thank God for keeping Bode all this while. I am not just referring to his being a member of the Redeemed Christian Church of God, I am thanking God because Bode is still in the Christian faith. It is one thing to be in the church and quite another to be in the faith. My excitement is that Bode has remained in the faith, and not just in the church. As a pastor, my daily prayer is for God to preserve in Him, all those we have been privileged to minister to. There is no man good enough or strong enough to preserve himself in the Christian faith; so that is why I constantly make this prayer and why I thank God for keeping Bode in the faith.

Bode has gone through many challenges and we have tried to encourage him. But, one day, some years after he started working, he told us that he had set up his own company. And I thank God today and have greater joy that, the company which started like a child's play has gained an international image. It is a thing of joy to me to see him growing higher and higher on daily basis, and not having any reason to say he is in any sort of lack.

My prayer is that God will keep him in the journey which he has started in Christ Jesus. I pray that God will uphold him and strengthen him in wisdom and knowledge and understanding such that, when the trumpet would sound, he will be ready. My prayer is that God would keep him, even in this level he has attained. I pray that the Spirit of God will constantly humble him in all situations; that he will not allow pride to enter into his life. I know him; but my knowledge of him cannot be compared to God's knowledge of him. So, I pray that God, Who knows him more than I do, would sustain him and keep him focused on the things of God, and not just on earthly things. May God help him to focus on heavenly things such that, when the trumpet would sound, none of us would be left behind.

Mrs. Gilbert Aimufua

I see Bode as a very determined and focused young man who is not ready to give up in the face of any challenge in life. Even when he wanted to go for his Master's degree, it was as if that would not be possible. But he took the bull by the horn and did whatever he could do and was able to achieve his dream. So, I find in him somebody that has a focus and works towards it. When I got to know how he started and the things he had been able to achieve, I knew that he was somebody that would surely go far in life. He is very articulate and also has a lot of business acumen. He is a true entrepreneur. He started with nothing, and look at where he is now. The place Bode is now is the place normally occupied by people who inherited successful companies from their parents, or who used inherited wealth to easily set up companies. But, in his case, he started from nothing.

Each time I see him, I get excited in my spirit and I believe that nobody should give any excuse and say that the government is not helping or that an uncle or friend is not willing to help. From the life of Bode, it is clear that, if one is determined and then decide to push ahead, you will surely make it. But, above all, the God factor was the secret of his success.

I wish Bode long life and I pray that he will fulfil his days. His destiny would not be truncated and God will take him to higher heights and he will impact nations. Where others have failed, he will prevail and God will take him to the next level.

Olakunle Ojo

Prince Bode and I attended the same church in the Berger area of Lagos beginning from over 15 years ago and we became friends from then. I have known him as a resourceful and respectful person. He rose through pain and doggedness to be who he is today. He does not have an end to his quest for knowledge. He is also willing to share his knowledge with others and the less privileged. As the

Bible says, a man's gift will make a way for him. Through the grace of God and his unquenchable search of knowledge, he has been able to dine with "Kings and Priests". He has travelled widely all over the world and has become an enigma on his own. He is a typical example of a self-made man, unlike the numerous "big men" we see around who amass wealth by looting the common pot of the nation/state.

I recall selling Bode his first car and recall how he constantly shared his plans with me during the formative years of his company. I see him as a person that genuinely desires and genuinely seeks wise counsel.

I wish him the best there is in life in good health and prosperity. I pray that God's perfect will shall be done in his life and that he will live long to eat the fruits of his labour in health and happiness. I pray God will elevate him to more prestigious and honourable heights in our nation.

God is the author and finisher of our faith. In all you do, Bode, remember to give God the glory because wisdom, knowledge, understanding, and goodwill come from Him alone. God bless you and happy golden birthday once again my dear brother.

Elder Mecha Udo
(RCCG Graceland Parish)

Being an active member of the men's fellowship, your willingness to be deeply involved was remarkable and we are proud of you. Let the will of God continue to reign in your life; let it manifest to its fullness because what we see now is the tip of the iceberg. What you are standing on today is just a stepping stone to your glory. The Lord will take you to places and you will conquer territories in Jesus' name.

Pastor Gabriel Oni
(RCCG Graceland Parish)

From the first time I met you, you have been a very wonderful man, doing the work of God, selfless and being a philanthropist too. It is a golden jubilee and the Lord will grant you the blessings attached to this golden age. God will still take you to greater heights and I wish you long life in good health.

Pastor Tope Abbey
(RCCG Graceland Parish)

I first met you during the Networking Sunday programme. I found in you a very resourceful man filled with ideas, energy, and vision. I believe your best is yet to come because I see you becoming a global player.

Adekoya Olatunde Owosibo
(Principal Lecturer, Federal College of Animal Health)

You are a go-getter; a very rugged man and knowledgeable too. You have made a very big impact in the agricultural industry because of the quality of your products and the merger. May God give you long life, prosperity, and continue to expand your coast.

Kameed Olubukola Azeez, PhD
(Soil Fertility and Plant Nutrition, Farm Manager)

You are a wonderful person and you have what it takes to succeed. This is just the beginning; the sky is the starting point for you. I wish you success in all your endeavours.

Mr. Raymond Obiajulu Isiadinso
(MD/CEO Mid-Century Agro-Allied Ventures Limited)

A passionate, result-oriented, result-driven man. Your dedication to work motivated and drew me to work with you. You are an asset to the industry and you have been brought to the spotlight with your strategic alliance and achievements so far. I wish you good health, strength, wisdom and limitless opportunities.

Ojo Oluwaseyi Temitope
(Business man)

It has always been a pleasure doing business with you. I wish you the best, long life and prosperity.

Olugbenga Adeniran Ogunwole
(Zonal Coordinator, ASAN South-West)

You have been an industry veteran and you have achieved great feats. I wish you excellent and perfect health.

Professor M. A. Bamikole
(National President, Faculty of Agriculture Dean of Nigerian Universities)

You are a rare gem and I am privileged to have taught you. I pray that God grants you long life, good health, and many abundant blessings.

Pastor Ajibola Odukoya
(Nutritionist)

I am proud of you and I will recommend your products to anyone any day because of their high quality. I wish you long life, good health, and more success in your future endeavours and career.

Raji Adebayo
(Livestock Nutritionist)

Bode is a very knowledgeable man in the industry.

Taiwo Adeoye
(National President, Animal Science Association of Nigeria, ASAN)

You are a distinguished animal scientist, an industrialist, and a promising industry leader, who has achieved a great feat in the industry. I wish you the very best and in this new phase of your life, God will grant you good health and wisdom to enjoy the fruits of your labour.

Timothy Makeri
(Former Procurement Manager, Grand Cereals Limited, Jos)

You are a vibrant, dynamic, and energetic man. I congratulate you for attaining the golden age, for your achievements, and your impact in the livestock industry.

Mrs. Winnie Ifeoma Lai Solarin
(Deputy Director, Federal Ministry of Agriculture and Rural Development)

You have achieved a giant feat by bringing international attention to the industry in Nigeria. God will bless you and your generation shall reap the benefits. This new year you have attained will be golden for you and everyone around you.

Chief Simeon Owhofa
(Second Vice President, Nigerian Institute of Animal Science)

I wish you growth, wisdom, and prosperity in all your endeavours as you attain this new age.

Dr. Ademola Raji
(Pioneer Director, Federal Department of Animal Husbandry and Awardee of Nigerian Institute of Animal Science 2018)

I know that you are a doer, who always brings out the positive of anything. I congratulate you and welcome you to the club of the fifties.

Professor Festus Ayodeji Sunday Dairo
(Animal Nutrition and Feed Management Resource)

You have been one of the pillars of the industry with your contributions to the institute and the economy. You have done well and I pray that you will become more relevant as you pursue your career.

Professor Adeseyinwa Akinyele
(Pioneer, Animal Science Association of Nigeria)

A man who is teachable and dogged: such combination has made you a person I would like to associate with, all the time. I wish you success as you clock 50.

Afolabi Abiodun
(President, Enterprise Development Centre (EDC) Alumni Association)

You are a man filled with so much distinct ideas, and who would never compromise on values. The values you have added to the market has distinguished you. I wish you more prosperous years.

Chief Dr. Bayo Olufunwa
(Businessman; Former Chairman, Poultry Association of Nigeria, Lagos State Chapter)

Your combination of genuine hunger for more knowledge, hard work, strong business acumen and humility has shot you up to where you are and I couldn't be any prouder than I am about your achievements. I wish you continuity and more success.

Dr. Gbenga Oluyemi
(Former National General Secretary, Nigerian Veterinary Medical Association)

I have known him as a very God fearing, intelligent, and hard-working nutritionist who knows his onions. I wish him long life so his light will continue to shine.

Dr. Babatunde Olofinbiyi

He is a man worthy of emulation and I am proud to call him my friend.

Lanre Bello
(Former Chairman, Poultry Association of Nigeria, Lagos State Chapter)

Bode has always been a promising man; very respectful and diligent in his job. He has made tremendous contributions to the country and has achieved a lot. I wish him the best of luck.

Professor Bamidele Oluwarotimi Omitoyin
(Dean of Faculty of Renewable Natural Resources, University of Ibadan)

I came to know him as a resilient and very focused man while he was an employee and it drew me closer to him. He is always willing to learn and that is why he is achieving milestones. I am happy with him. I wish him many more successes and the fulfilment of his destiny.

Professor Bolarinde Joseph Obebe

Having a father who was successful as a farmer, the apple did not fall far from the tree. I remember telling his father that Bode was not a usual farmer. Bode is an excellent man, dedicated and hard-working with humility. He is someone to be proud of.

Pastor Sunday Adebowale RCCG

There are so many things to say about Bode. He is a child of God, he loves God and has served Him consistently. He does not discriminate among people. I wish him a glorious birthday. In good health, he will enjoy the rest of his days.

Bode, you will have breakthrough in all areas of your life and I wish you the very best.

Pastor Toromade Francis
(Director of Marketing, Rome Business School)

Very amiable, enterprising, and humble. His customer-centricity and marketing skills are so exceptional, they endeared him to me. Bode is a force to be reckoned with in business. I wish him longevity and perfect health and pray that his path will continue to shine.

Rev. Abayomi Oyinloye
(Director of Home Missions in Nigeria, Foursquare Gospel Church)

He is a very enthusiastic man with an inquisitive mind and I knew he was going to be a great person. I wish him all the best in this new phase of his life.

Venerable Samson Olubunmi Omitade
(Vicar, St. Peter's Anglican Church Otun-Ekiti)

Bode is an easy-going man, a philanthropist, and a very good mentor of the youths. He has given back to society and made very strong impact in the Otun-Ekiti community. Let the will of God continue to reign in his life and let the purpose for which God has created him be fulfilled. I wish him expansion and more successes.

Blessing Isioma Alawode
(Chairperson, Poultry Association of Nigeria, Ogun State Chapter)

The only way I can describe Bode is that he is a go-getter. His genuine love for the industry and adding real value is evident in his products, services and support. I pray that God will allow more of his dreams to become reality.

Dr. Joseph Deji Folutile
(Veterinary Surgeon, Publisher, *Farming Advice Digest***)**

I saw Bode as a dynamic young man some years back: I respect him a lot. He has been able to drive business with his good strategy and dynamism. He is a man of integrity; very accessible and very humble. He always impacts the minds of people who come across him. As he turns 50, I want him to know that he is appreciated. I also want to encourage him to grow bigger.

Mrs. Olabisi Ayo-Hamilton
(Deputy Chairman, Poultry Association of Nigeria, Lagos Chapter)

Bode Adetoyi is an intelligent and a dynamic man. I would say he is all over the place. He knows his onions. In the industry, he is very wide. I knew him since his days in Bio-Organics and he has been very active. Hi-Nutrients International Limited has been pleasant; Bode Adetoyi has been pleasant. I still buy his products for my shop.

Bode has worked very hard for the sustainability of the Poultry Association of Nigeria. He has been recognised as one of the big guys in the industry that has sustained poultry in Lagos State. He has received awards in this regard. And he is not only good in poultry but in the livestock industry in general, especially in aquaculture (fish) and cattle.

I wish him all the best he wishes himself: long life and better things to come. I know he has a great vision and I pray that God will make his vision a reality.

Mr. Olukayode Oladipo
(West Africa Representative, Impextraco Belgium)

Mr. Olabode was one of my first key customers when I started Impextraco Belgium for Nigeria. We had a very good business deal to kick-start our relationship at that level. That deal with him was one of the stabilising factors for the business and I appreciate him for that. Incidentally, we actually discussed and sealed that first deal in Atlanta. He still remains a very good customer of mine and a very worthy elder brother. He is an outgoing man and he always wants to do his best for people around him.

For him, the sky is the limit. He should just keep pushing, and I know the best will always come.

Mr. Wole Adediji
(CEO JIKS Global Ventures)

I have known Bode for a while now: he is very industrious and he is an aggressive marketer. He has made progress and I believe that there will be more to come because I know he will do well.

Jide Asaolu
(Electrical Supervisor
Nigerian Bottling Company Limited
Ikeja, Lagos)

I grew up with Bode and consider him a family member. Despite the fact that we were not from the same father and mother, Bode took me as a blood brother. We were childhood friends from the earliest stages of our growth. He remains my dearly loved brother; he is NOT just a friend. Most especially during our days at Otun Comprehensive High School, Otun-Ekiti and even beyond, we related like twin brothers.

Olabode Adetoyi has proven himself to be a man of success. Also, he is a man of the people. He is an active farmer, a giver, a hard-working man, and a man of high intellect. Bode's unique love and special interest in me is immeasurable. I wish him long life in sound health and happiness. May he continue to be a positive voice and a source of blessing to others. I wish him all the best. I pray that the grace of God will not depart from him.

Bode, please do not relent in doing good.

You are blessed.

Mr. Seyi Alade
(Accountant at Hi-Nutrients International Limited)

The story of Hi-Nutrients is a typical story of "from grass to grace". In years past, we have had several challenges, the most important being the problem of funding. But now, things have changed with the merger with a foreign company.

My Managing Director, Mr. Bode Adetoyi, is a boss and a mentor. He is very hard-working and very diligent in his work: he can go an extra mile to achieve the goals of the organisation. As far as I can see, he is a true entrepreneur. He has been of great help and an instrument in helping us as staff members to grow and master what we do. I have never been tired of working with Hi-Nutrients and Mr. Bode in particular. He is a professional to the core.

Dr. Abayomi Waheed
(Surgeon, Childhood Friend and Secondary School Mate)

Bode was one of the brightest lads in Otun-Ekiti Comprehensive High School, while I was one of the top boys at Moba Grammar School in the same town in the early '80s. This was the era of chalks and blackboards, Cortina leather sandals and white tennis canvas wears. I had heard through a mutual friend, the cerebral Tunde Olofinbiyi (now a consultant gynaecologist) about a brilliant chap who could recite offhand the elements in the Periodic Table; who knew ALL, yes, ALL the laws and principles in O Level Physics by Nelkon like Newton's Laws, Faraday's Laws, and Archimedes'; who had read from cover to cover the *O Level Economics* textbook by O. A. Lawal; and who had other intimidating credentials. This was in 1985 and we were all in Form Four. But you must affix, in block letters, SCIENCE CLASS, which was in itself another CV.

I quickly told the Moba Grammar School Team about this young Einstein, but I was surprised that they all knew about him. This gingered us to read harder because we had to academically settle the rhetoric of "who be the Oga" between the two schools. We all looked forward to the day we would meet formally and officially for the records. Back in the days, we tested strength through quiz competitions, debates, sports, and omoluabi wits.

Bode has always been an impeccable dresser. He had come to see Tunde, and was in an Addidas athleisure with his white tennis canvas shoes while I was in white-on-brown shorts MGS uniform atop Cortina sandals when we accidentally met. An improvised blackboard was staring at us. Tunde was going to be the impromptu quiz master. We just sampled randomly. I was slightly better than him in biology, literature, and English, but he was a guru in physics, maths, economics, and agricultural science, while we tied in the others. Little wonder he's richer than me today. We prayed we would meet officially but that never happened because the two schools were always "seeded" in competitions except sports, and we were not good athletes. Thence commenced a bosom friendship that has lived for almost four decades – and still counting. My relationship with

Bode has been an epitome of true friendship devoid of the rancour of creed, tribe, or politics.

As a person, Bode is honest, kind, brilliant, altruistic, and is a man with a very good business acumen.

By way of going down memory lane, I remember while we were preparing for the O Level exams in 1986; I was virtually sleeping on his bed at Aafin just to be taught some little more of maths, which was my weakest subject. Bode the brilliant chap would come to our house at Ile Balogun to call me whenever there was a maths tutorial either in his school, or at his house. Anytime we showed up for tutorials, his very kind mother was always on hand to feed all of us with bread, or corn meal, or garri, or whatever she could lay her hands on.

As he turns 50, I wish my good friend a long healthy life full of God's blessings, His grace and protection, His favours and mercies. Nothing less than the very best.

You this Ekiti man, my name is Waheed, and not WAIDI

Orji Ugoeze Lois
(Student)

I am so proud and happy to meet such a wonderful and great courageous man like you. You keep me motivated everytime I view your status. I wish one day I will work so hard to be like you.

You are my mentor and I celebrate you sir.

Mr. Adebisi Adeyinka Ibukun - Mentee
(CEO, Fortrans Express Logistics, Lagos)

Nothing else for me to say than the fact that you are a typical example of results of GRACE. People see you in public places and think it all begin today; they do not know when you burned yourself out in the night and in the day to carve a niche for yourself. I notice something each time I'm in your office: YOU ALWAYS WANT TO BREAK NEW GROUNDS'. I'm more than inspired seeing you achieve great heights; I'm infected and sold out to the course of what I see in my head everyday. If you can make it, yes I can: if you can go all the way to get yourself a fantastic education in prestigious universities of the world without the support of anybody, I have made up my mind to do the same.

I'm inspired by your commitment, dedication and never say die approach you give to life; I am inspired by your unrelenting disposition toward success.

One day, I will be bold to say I'm glad to have you around as an example of great possibility even when the cloud is thick beyond necessary and the future looks so bleak.

I doff my hat sir!

Dr. Bisi Olasehinde
(Senior Lecturer
Federal Polytechnic Ado-Ekiti,
Ekiti State)

BODE ADETOYI I KNOW

I have known Bode Adetoyi since when he was in secondary school at Otun-Ekiti and my first contact with him was when he and Ganiyu Saloro came to me and asked me for assistance in teaching them physics and chemistry. I obliged to do so and our usual meeting point was Bode's house.

What I noticed in him then was his yearning and desire for knowledge and this attribute in him is what has been sustaining him in life. No wonder, when I read through the profile of Bode Adetoyi, I was not taken aback. His desire for knowledge took him to University of Ilorin, University of Ibadan, Harvard Business School Boston, USA, Lagos State University, and Lagos Business School, now Pan Atlantic University.

Bode's life after he had acquired the desired knowledge has been that of service to humanity. As an employer of labour, he has made an impact in the lives of many employees who are gainfully employed in his companies. As a scholar, he has made an impact in the lives of many students who have benefitted from his scholarship scheme over the years. As a farmer, he has contributed significantly to the Gross Domestic Product (GDP) of the nation through various productions that are going on in his local and foreign companies.

Obviously, Bode is qualified to be called a scholar, an inventor, an investor, a mentor, an employer and a philanthropist.

His tenacity of purpose in life has made him productive in all spheres of human endeavours.

Olufemi J. Obebe
(CEO Dukeall Tech,
Selby United Kingdom)

Prince Bode Adetoyi's life and achievements is a testament to his unwavering faith in God, his outstanding vision, and commitment to success. He embodies an ideal leader and all that is good in business management, customer care, and contributions to the community. This book will challenge and empower future generations.

Engr. Patrick Obidoyin
(Manchester, United Kingdom)

Prince Olabode Adetoyi is an exceptional Nigerian. He never ceases to amaze me. He is very passionate about everything he does; farming, business, et cetera.

He has successfully overcome key challenges and major constraints in Nigeria. His mind-set and sheer dedication should be emulated by all Nigerians. This book will serve as a source of great motivation to all Nigerian youths who have lost hope in Nigeria.

Babayemi Ganiyu Adewale
(Childhood Friend and Secondary School Mate)

Bode, a man who sees opportunities in difficulties

Bode is a friend of almost four decades. We have been doing things together since our Form 1 days in secondary school at the Otun Comprehensive High School, Otun-Ekiti, Ekiti State. Some of our other friends then are Olofinbiyi Babatunde, Asaolu Ezekiel, Aborisade Adebayo, etc. Through our progressive spirit and excellent relationship, our parents became very good friends too because they all saw something in common in us: that is, we were all ambitious and concerned about the future.

Bode has always been a very brilliant, charismatic, intelligent, and brave person, with a rugged determination to succeed in life. He has a trait in him that prevents him from believing that there is something unachievable. He is also a man who does not joke with opportunities and he never procrastinates any action that requires his attention. He always wants to learn new ideas. If you come with any innovative idea, he will come down to your level to gain from you. This trait in him was what initiated the idea of teaching ourselves when our teachers were not around to take us on any subject and even during our free period or after school hours when other students would have left the school. This initiative really helped us in all our subsequent examinations such as WAEC and JAMB. He went to the University of Ilorin to pursue Agricultural Science with specialisation in Animal Science while Bayo, Tunde, and myself, went to the Obafemi Awolowo University. Tunde later joined him at Ilorin to pursue Medicine. Initially, we were all keen on pursuing a career in medicine, but Bode is someone who believed he could equally build his career in any profession he eventually found himself. Hence, I'm not surprised that he is making waves in his chosen path today and, to the glory of God, he has proven himself to the whole world.

I pray that the Almighty God will continue to guide you and order your steps. I wish you happy celebration of your golden age.

Congratulations!!! The Almighty God will bless your new age and you will celebrate many more years in sound health and prosperity.

Forward ever, backward never.

'Bosun Dudubo
(Former Banker at UBA)

This book amplifies the unique quality that saw Prince Bode Adetoyi from growing up as a young student from Otun-Ekiti to the entrepreneurial world, nurturing Hi-Nutrients International Limited from infancy in a small flat at Ogba Lagos to becoming a global brand in Nigeria's challenging and unstable business environment. It also captures his spirit of giving by establishing a platform on which he grants 150 indigent Ekiti students scholarship every year, and his servant-leadership style by delving into politics to serve the good people of Ekiti State.

The Entrepreneur... a good template for the youth and must read for every entrepreneur.

Lawyer Lekan Adetoyi - United Kingdom
(Elder Brother)

Bode and I grew up and spent our entire early life living within the confines of our community at Otun-Ekiti. We were fortunate to have parents who inculcated the spirit of hard work in us. Our father was a peasant farmer; however, I will call him a farmer among farmers.

Bode is an intelligent and hard-working individual; he spent most of his time with me in Lagos. Whilst other children were gallivanting about, Bode was "burning the midnight candle". He had no time for social activities except to attend church with me on Sundays.

Bode is not just a farmer, he is a motivational speaker, teacher, pastor, philanthropist, and, above all, a father and a husband to his lovely wife and children. He awards university scholarship to many students every year and has been doing so since 2014.

I quote from one of his speeches as a motivational speaker during one of his numerous interviews on Channels television. He said, "If you are not born with a silver spoon in your mouth, work hard and make one for yourself". This message encapsulates the beginning of what we are witnessing today. Bode was not born with any spoon in his mouth, let alone a silver one. He worked hard to get to where he is today.

I hereby state on record that the first contract executed by Hi-Nutrients International Limited was delivered with an Okada (motorbike) because he could not afford to charter a taxi. What we are witnessing today is a product of hard work, diligence, and perseverance, but, above all, the blessings of God.

I wish our father was still around to witness what is happening today; he would have been the happiest man on earth, knowing that one of his sons had come this far. However, we thank God Almighty because our mother who is 92 years old is still here with us.

I wish you a happy birthday my lovely brother and we are happy to have your type in ADETOYI'S family.

Elijah Ayokunle Falade - Mentee
(CEO, First Amazing Global Concept Company)

An anonymous quote once said "The mark of a true visionary is his ability to imagine the future and act on it, yielding great results in the process and then using this success for the benefit of others." Prince Ezekiel Olabode Adetoyi is not just a leader but a leader with a clear and distinct vision of goal getting and raising a breed of followers with a difference. He has no doubt stood out in all ways, thereby making himself more than just a force but an household name for all to behold.

BAM, like we call him, is a man that gives you a challenge to responsibility, motivates you, and supports you to the last. He is indeed a man for all and a true model to follow. A man full of sincerity of purpose, vision, and purpose-driven; a generational thinker and a rare breed.

I can't but appreciate his fatherly role, his mentorship, and guidance at all times. He has had a positive influence on me and changed my thinking towards the world.

Sir, there is no doubt that you have that key to people's heart through your kind and generous acts.

Keep soaring;
Keep winning;
Keep flying;
Keep making us proud; as you blaze the trail we follow.
My Role Model At 50.

Emmanuel Bamidele Okusanya
(Friend and Church Minister, USA)

Prince Olabode Adetoyi is a friend and we've been relating for almost a decade now. His inner tenacity and enthusiasm for success and excellence in life's endeavours is unparalleled. I have personally studied him over the years and can state that his high level of leadership and entrepreneurial acumen is very remarkable and something I really admire. I have seen him practically taking a business (Hi-Nutrients International Limited) from the very scratch at the local level to an unimaginable height in the international market, which has given him global recognition. Bode is also an ardent lover and giver to God's work.

I celebrate you as a rear gem on this occasion of your 50th birthday and the presentation of this classic book which is truly a reflection of your leadership strength. You are truly an exceptional leader, and an entrepreneur per excellence who has redefined agribusiness.

CONGRATULATIONS!

Olumide Akinola
(CEO Ecocities Innovations Limited)

I was privileged to meet Pastor Bode Adetoyi on a trip to Israel to attend Agritech 2015. From the moment we had our first encounter, I just knew he was not the 'usual' person. I never knew he was such an achiever until I visited his office and saw the walls replete with awards, certificates, and all manner of endorsements from both local and international entities.

In my opinion, Pastor Bode is committed to a life of excellence and scholarship, considering the number of international conferences, seminars, workshops, and trainings he has attended (and still attends) around the world. He has an insatiable appetite for knowledge!

In the coming years and by the grace of God, I really look forward to knowing him better.

More power to your elbow sir!

Oyinloye Oluwasegun - Leo D'Prince
(Federation of Moba Students' Union (FOMSU) President Emeritus)

Golden Age of a Goal Getter

It is said that a good captain is one who knows the way, goes the way, and shows the way. My captain, Prince Bode Adetoyi is a blessing to the younger generation, particularly youths and students. His philanthropic role to this duo is second to none. Every year, he gives bursary awards to students from Moba Local Government Area of Ekiti State and even beyond.

He was inaugurated as the Grand Patron of the Federation of Otun Moba Students' Union, FOMSU, by the leadership of the Union during my tenure as the National President in 2016.

Prince Bode has touched the lives of our dear youths and students greatly and has never relented till date: this is why we, as youths, always throw our weight behind him at all times.

On behalf of the entire students of Otun, Moba, Ekiti State and beyond that have benefited from your Educational Support Programme as individuals, and also on behalf of FOMSU, I say: HAPPY BIRTHDAY TO YOU SIR ON YOUR GOLDEN JUBILEE CELEBRATION AND BOOK LAUNCH!

Felix Ayoyinka
(Banker and Fellow University of Ilorin Alumni)

Mr. Bode Adetoyi is more than a friend. He is a brother whose love for his neighbour did not just start today. Both of us were neither age mates, classmates, nor secondary schoolmates, in our growing years in Otun, yet he helped me settle down as soon as I entered the University of Ilorin. In 1993, Bode allowed me and one other guy to join him in his one-bedded space without one single day of animosity.

I pray that God will continue to bless you and grant you many happy returns in the land of the living in Jesus' name.

Ibrahim Sanuth
(Relationship Manager (Agric) First Bank Lagos & Ogun)

Prince Bode has kept a good business relationship in an environment like Nigeria with unstable business policies, constantly challenged by deficit of leadership and lack of national interest in the hearts of our economy.

Prince is a great business man/partner of high entrepreneurship acumen, integrity, and armed with a great spirit that supports the win-win ideology.

Prince is passionate and open minded.

I wish him a happy birthday and more fruitful years on earth.

Gbadebo and Bunmi Ajiboye - USA
(Childhood Friend and Classmate in Primary School)

Bode Adetoyi and I grew up together at Aafin Street, Otun-Ekiti. His father's house and my father's house were next to each other. We were both born into families with poor background and we had nothing but a lot of hope that things would be better in the future if we did well in our studies. One special thing about both of us was that we were both born same day and same month – February 2nd! However, our parents never celebrated birthday due to their educational background. Growing up with Bode Adetoyi was a very big task and it was very challenging considering his intelligence and brilliance in academics.

During our elementary school at St. Peter's Anglican School Otun-Ekiti, attempting to compete with Bode academically usually resulted in heavy defeat. Eventually, we went to Comprehensive High School, Otun-Ekiti and graduated in 1986. We played together, ate together and went to farm every Saturday. I remember that his father's farm was at Iro-Ekiti. I did go to their farm periodically to eat and farm with him. Due to our fathers' influence in the church, we had to go to church every Sunday to robe as choristers. No excuse for not going to church or making your parent proud as a chorister.

When we got to Comprehensive High School, his curiosity, passion for science, and his ambition to be a medical doctor made him to join the science class while I was in accounting together with Olawale Olajide and others. He was in the company of other "scientists" as they liked to call themselves in those days, with the likes of Olofinbiyi Tunde, Raji Ganiyu, and Bayo Aborishade, just to mention a few. We did call him "Doctor Adetoyi" at the time. When we all finished secondary school and moved on to the next stage of our lives, I got to know that Bode had studied Animal Science instead of Medicine. I was shocked but, as is now obvious, God knew what He was doing. Now, Bode is known as one of the reputable Animal Nutritionists, not just in Nigeria, but in other parts of the world. Bode Adetoyi is also a philanthropist, a politician, and a generous man!

Now Bode, I have a question for you? Do you regret not being a doctor? I am ready to answer the question for you; absolutely not!

Bode is a good Christian and a devoted man of God. May God continue to be with you and your family. Bode's wife (Bukola Adetoyi nee Atolani) is like my sister because her father and my father were best of friends when her father was alive. Who knew that I would also be in the medical field in the United States of America today, as against my passion for accounting initially? We thank God for all he has done in our lives, and for giving us this opportunity to reflect on our humble beginnings.

On behalf of my family, Bunmi and I wish you happy birthday.

Omooba Stephen Adedapo Adebisi

Growing up and knowing Prince Bode Adetoyi has been pleasant. Bode is an amiable person with a pleasant personality. He is a notable and highly connected politician and a worthy prince of Otun-Ekiti in Ekiti State.

As the MD/CEO of Hi-Nutrients International Limited, Bode is highly productive and is a philanthropist per excellence, a core entrepreneur, an ideal man of many virtues, a political leader of note, and a God-fearing man. His high level of productivity has earned him many awards both home and abroad. He is an alumnus of Lagos Business School, a visionary leader, a great achiever, and a great investor.

Among our peers, I call him "BABA AGBE" meaning a great farmer. His love for his profession and the agricultural sector of our country has no measure and, as a philanthropist, he has made it a call by ensuring that he supports students through scholarship yearly.

I sincerely and heartily congratulate you as you celebrate your Golden Jubilee. May God in His Grace continue to direct all your thoughts, guide all your decisions, uphold you in all your undertakings, perfect everything that concerns you and your family, and grant you the grace to be closer to Him and the grace to do more for humanity.

Congratulations and happy golden jubilee Ore mi.

Olagunju Ayodele Joseph
(Joejoy Academy Otu)

He is a nice man, he is a father, he is a leader.

Bode Adetoyi is a philanthropist. He is positively affecting many Nigerian students through his offer of scholarship awards.

He is a diligent man, a role model to many youths who would like to emulate him. He is indeed a business mogul and an inspirational speaker.

I wish to at this time join scores of people to celebrate Prince Bode Ezekiel Adetoyi on his 50th year birthday celebration.

Happy birthday celebration sir.

Long live Bode Adetoyi!

Long live Hi-Nutrients International Limited!

INDEX

A

Aaye town, 14–15
Abajadiewon, 12
Abayomi Oyinloye, 346
Abayomi Waheed, 350
Abiodun Elutilo, 327
Abiodun Oluwaseyi, 326
Abiodun Toki, 163, 311
Abolarin, Ade, 242–43, 246–48, 252
Acholonu Uzoma, 99–100, 107–8, 110–11, 113, 115–16, 130–31, 163, 197, 217
Adebayo Adedeji, 62
Adebisi Adeyinka Ibukun, 351
Adebola Adetoyi, 28
Adeboye, Enoch adejare, 206, 210, 244, 246, 248
Adedotun Agbojo, 216
Adegoke Olubummo, 256
Adekoya Olatunde Owosibo, 340
Adekunle Fajuyi, 288
Adekunle Frank Alarapon, 175, 329
Ademola Raji, 343
Adeola Adetoyi, 298
Adeoye Taiwo, 342
Aderemi Onipede, 334
Adeseyinwa Akinyele, 344
Adetoyi, John, 21, 23, 29, 34
Adetoyi David Jesufemi Adewale Toluwani, 195, 298
Adewunmi Ayo Ajibade, 251, 324
Adewura Farms, 216
Adifala, 17–18
African-American Business Forum, 117
Agricultural Students University of Ilorin, 294
Agriculture Business Management Programme, 59
Ahmadu Bello University, 110
Ajanla Farms, 276
Ajibogun, 9–10
Akinsateru Farms, 138, 216
Akinwunmi Adesina, 117, 279–80, 290
Akunyili, Dora, 106
Alatise, 64, 69, 83, 94–96, 189–90
Alawode Blessing Isioma, 347
Alhaji Aliko Dangote, 117
Alhaji Kosoko, 207
Alhaji Mohammed Ola, 93
Alhaji Ola, 93, 95
Alhaji Tafawa Balewa, 288
Anazodo Jennifer, 313
Aroyinkeye, 20
Asaolu Taiwo, 194, 332
Ashaka Cement Company, 85
Atlanta, 163, 312, 348
Atolani Olanrewaju James, 332
Atterbury, Ian, 267
Avian Flu, 223
Ayangbemile, 38–39
Ayodeji Shiki, 299
Ayodele Fayose, 286
Ayo Oduntan, 220, 228–29, 233, 235–36, 259, 301

B

Babatunde Owolabi California, 330
Bamkole, Peter, 3–4, 104, 121, 319
Bayagbona, 275
Berkhout Joop, 254, 308,
Biodun Toki, 311
Bio-Organics Nutrients Systems Limited, 98–101, 105, 107–15, 118–21, 124–25, 127–32, 138, 162–63, 169, 175, 182, 184, 188, 217, 306, 308–9, 310
Bloomberg, Michael, 266
Board of Directors of Hi-Nutrients International Limited, 140, 150–51
Bode Adetoyi Movement, 238, 254
Bode Thomas, 288, 322
Botswana, 260, 280–81, 290
Bourdillon Feeds, 323
Britain, 29–31, 35
Bukola Adetoyi, 246, 361
Bunmi Ajiboye, 360
Bunmi Fabiyi, 63
Bunmi Idowu, 314
Bush, George W., 266

C

Chapel, Faith, 207–9, 315
Chevron Petroleum Company, 182
Chief Adekunle Ajasin, 288
Chief Chinedu Ahamneze, 317
Chief Folorunsho Ogunnaike, 137, 217, 230
Chief Johnson Arumeni, 114
Chief Ladipo, 215
Chief Ladipo Daniel, 215
Chief Obadofin, 13

Chief Obafemi Awolowo, 250, 288
Chief Obanla Osasona, 25, 26
Chief Saade Ogunleye, 52, 54
Chief Simeon Owhofa, 343
Chief Tunde Badmus, 217
Comfort Jinadu, 209
Comprehensive High School, 41–42, 44, 52, 63, 360

D
Dada, Joe, 178
Dawodu Kolawale, 18
Dayo Adetoyi, 27, 83
Dele Atolani, 334
Dele Oyediji, 131, 278, 317
Demir Farm, 80
Doctor Ameyo Adadevoh, 284
Drucker, Peter, 1

E
ECOBANK, 136
ECOWAS, 62
EDC (Enterprise Development Centre), 104, 132, 160, 319, 344
Ekiti-Parapo war, 17, 32
Ekundayo Adeyinka Adeyemi, 256
Elder Mecha Udo, 339
Elder Olaniran, 85
Elegido, Juan, 121
Elijah Ayokunle Falade, 356
Elumelu, Tony, 4, 118, 309
Emmanuel Bamidele Okusanya, 357
Enahoro, Anthony, 288
Enoch Olayiwola Oyawole, 319
Europe, 1, 35, 192–93, 224, 259, 305

F
FAD (Farming Advice Digest), 293, 347
Farms, Ola, 93–95, 97–98, 104
Fayemi Kayode John, 252, 254, 286
Federal Institute of Industrial Research, Oshodi (FIIRO), 94
Federal Ministry of Agriculture, 161
Federal Ministry of Agriculture and Rural Development, 326
Federal Polytechnic Ado-Ekiti, 352
Federal University of Technology, 170
Felix Olusegun Gbolagade, 320

Fellow Fisheries Society, 294
Femi Balogun, 68
Femi Falana, 176–77
Femi Faniyi, 136, 139, 227–30
Femi Kupolati, 68–69
Festus Ayodeji Sunday Dairo, 343
FIIRO (Federal Institute of Industrial Research, Oshodi), 94
Fisheries Society of Nigeria Corporate Award of Excellence, 293
FISON (Fisheries Society of Nigeria), 261, 273–78, 293–94
Flour Mills, 138, 201–2, 310
Folarin Afelumo, 215, 226
FOLHOPE Farms, 137, 320
FOMSU (Federation of Otun-Moba Students Union), 243, 294, 358–59
Fountain of Greatness School, 293
Foursquare Gospel Church, 129, 215, 346
France, 1, 35, 104, 169, 179, 200, 259–60, 300
French Agricultural Cooperative Group, 1

G
Gabriel Popoola Adetoyi, 23, 203, 327
Gilbert Michael, 153–54, 264–65
Glorious Parish, 86–87, 204
Grand Cereals, 110, 140, 145, 149, 152, 156–57, 179, 276, 304
Grooming Enterprise Leaders Programme, 59

H
Harvard Business School, 161, 266–67, 352
Hi-Mix, 2, 275–76
Hi-Nutrients, merger of, 104, 170, 174, 176, 238, 304
Hi-Nutrients' Hi-Mix, 165
Hi-Nutrients International Limited, 1–2, 145–46, 149–52, 154, 160–61, 172, 175, 194–95, 200–201, 245, 300, 302–3, 307, 311–13, 356–57
Hi-Nutrients premixes, 323
Hope Assembly Parish, 336
Hybrid Feeds, 110

I
Ibidun Taiwo, 68
Ibidunmoye, 12, 21
Idio, 109
Ifeyinwa, 109, 129
Ignatius Sancho, 31
Ikemefuna Frank, 324
Isiadinso Raymond Obiajulu, 260, 341
Iyayi E.A., 318

J
Jayeoba 87
Jide Taiwo, 130, 194, 208-209
Jones Melvin, 257

K
Kalejaiye, 184, 205
Kameed Olubukola, Azeez 340
Kate Robinson, 267
Kempex, 286
Kennedy John, 283
Kpolu Grace, 208
Kuala Lumpur 269, 270
Kunle Ojo, 208, 38
Kupolati Femi, 68-69
Kupoluyi Ayo, 244, 315
Kurz Sebastian, 35

L
Ladipo Daniel, 215
Ladoja, Rashidi Adewolu, 147, 160, 168, 244-6, 300
Lagos Business School, 3, 4, 59, 104, 116, 118-120, 123, 129-150, 208, 306, 352, 361
Lai Solarin Winnie Ifeoma
Lamido Sanusi, 117
Lawal O.A., 350
Lawson Olusola, 87
Lemose
- Kehinde 205
- Taiwo 205

Lobatse, 281

M
Macaulay Herbert 288
Macron Emmanuel, 35
Makeri Timothy, 342

Mandela Nelson, 103, 288, 296
Martin Luther King, Jnr 143
Matthew Tade 316
McNamara, Robert S., 267
Mecca, 63
Medunoye Olubisi, 91
Mensah Adeola 194, 207, 209
Mensah Tetteh 207, 208
Midgley Clare, 30
Mitchell Farm, 215
Murtala Mohammed 62, 285
Mussolini, Emperor 263
Muyiwa Adeyemo 208

N
NAFDAC 106-9, 161, 276, 312, 314
NAFFA 277
Neovia 1, 2, 79, 104, 158, 160, 163-169, 170-1, 173-79, 200, 205, 238, 300, 307
Newton Isaac 120-1, 350
NIAS, 132, 278, 294
NITOA 277
Njoku Placid, 318
Norgem Nigeria Limited, 157, 158, 165
Novus, 157-9, 160, 165
NSAP 294-5
Nwachukwu Ben, 110, 129
Nworga, Mrs. 157
NYCN 295

O
Obadofin, Chief, 13
Obanla, 25
Obasanjo Farm 87, 109, 137, 173, 314
Obasanjo Olusegun, 56, 57, 62, 65-6, 87, 92, 106, 119, 137, 215, 217-8, 252, 254, 256, 279,
Obasoyo Dick, 138, 220, 310,
Obebe Joseph Bolarinde, 51-8, 61-5, 66-8, 83, 84, 92, 101, 119, 345
Obegirimo Oore, 16, 19, 21
Obidoyin Patrick, 308
Obuh, 204
Odia Alice 28, 71, 84, 157
Odiachi Henry 175, 330
Odukoya Ajibola, Pastor 342
Odundun Asodedero Oore, 20
Odunowo Adebayo, Otunba 306

Index 367

Odunsi Olabode, 323
Oduntan, 220, 228, 233, 235-7, 259, 301
Ogbechie Israel, Pastor 208
Ogbogodo Mr. 138, 202
Ogbomoso, 147
Ogbonisan, 52
Ogijo, 91
Ogunleye Saade, Chief 52, 54
Ogunnaike Folorunsho, 137
Ogunode Femi, 208
Ogunwole Adeniran Olugbenga, 341
Ojemai Farms, 114
Ojo Johnson, 69
Ojo Olakunle, 338
Okinbaloye Oore, 16
Okonjo-Iweala, 117
Okusanya Emmanuel, Bamidele 357
Olabisi Ayo-Hamilton, 347
Oladimeji, 21
Oladipo Olukayode, 348
Olagunju Ayodele Joseph, 362
Olajide Olawale, 360
Olalekan Adetoyi, 28
Olaniran Elder, 29, 85
Olaniyi Adetoyi, 27
Olapade Mrs. 136
Olarenwaju Bello, 60
Olasehinde Bisi, 352
Olasunkanmi Tunji, 205, 331
Olateru Engr. 233
Olaudah Equiano 31
Olawale Olajide, 360
Olayiwola Oyawole Enoch, 319
Olelebioke of Imoje, 13
Olofinbiyi Babatunde, 43, 38, 345, 350
Olubalekun, 13
Olubinyin Ewedumoye, 19
Olubisi Farm, 91-5, 104
Olubukola Kameed Azeez, 340
Olubummo Adegoke, Professor, 256
Olufawo Olushoga, Alhaji, 216, 225
Olufunwa Bayo 93-4, 97, 104, 215, 344
Olugbenga Adenira Ogunwole, 341
Olukayode Oladipo, 348
Olutimehin Job Atteh, Professor 318
Oluwabukola Florence, 181, 297
Oluwarotimi Omitoyin, 385
Oluwasegun Oyinloye 358

Oluwaseyi Abiodun, 326
Oluwashona Kayode, 335
Oluyemi Gbenga Dr. 169-171, 260, 344
Omitade Olubunmi Samson, 346, 32
Omooba Stephen Adedapo Adebisi, 361
Omotosho Mope, 317
Onallo Akpa 232, 303
Oni Gabriel, 340
Oni Segun, 252, 254
Onigbode Wale, 177, 208
Onipede Aderemi, 334
Oritsharemi P.M., 131
Orji Ugoeze Lois, 351
OSCAS 51-2, 64, 73, 79
Oshomo Adekunle, 215
Osioma Blessing Alawode, 80
Osoba Awoyinka, 25
Owa Obokun, 10
Owafonran Oore, 12
Owhofa Simeone, Chief 343
Owolabi Nike, 208, 330
Owosibo Olatunde Adekoya, 340
Oyatoki Layi, 156-7, 177-9
Oyawole Enoch Olayiwola, 319
Oyebamiji Abiodun, 253-9, 299
Oyebiodun Grace Longe, 322
Oyedele Rotimi 205, 315
Oyediji Dele, 131-2, 278, 317
Oyinloye James f., 254, 322
Oyinloye, Oba, 25-29
Oyinloye Yomi, 100, 129-30, 346

P

Pascal, Captain, 31
Pfizer, 107
Plato, 240
Popoola Gabriel, 27, 203, 327
Popoola Oba James Adedapo Oladele 7, 20, 243, 311
Porter Michael, 161

Q

Quaker 31
Quraysh, 262

R
Raji Ganiyu, 48, 360
Rhone Poulex Nutrition Animale 169-71, 260, 306
Roche 108-9
Rome 224, 346
Rommey Mitt, 266

S
Saloro Ganiyu, 352
Samuel Adebayo Olufunwa, 215
Samuel Ajayi, Crowther, 31
Sani Abacha, General, 256, 106
Santa Rosa, 59, 264,
Sanusi Lamido Sanusi, 117
Sanuth Ibrahim, 359
Sao Paulo, 59
Sarah Abolarin, 28, 90, 91
Sateru, Oba Tijani Adetunji Akinloye, 308
Scortia Bank, 205
Selassie Haile, 263
Sheba Queen, 261, 262
Sigbeku Tunde, 312
Sofayo Toye, 173-5

T
TACSFON 203
Taiwo Funke, 208
Talabi, S.O., 275
Toluwanimi, 195

Trafalgar Square, 116

U
UAC, 140-1, 144-6, 147-157, 179, 208, 226, 304
Uche Okpalanmo, 109, 129
Utomi Patrick, 3, 118, 121, 123-5, 151

V
Vassa Gustavus, 31
Vivax Limited, 171, 260

W
Walter Hass Jnr., 267
Whitman Meg, 267
William Perry, 257
William Prince, 7
Wilson Badejo, 215
Wollstonecraft Mary, 30

Y
Yakassai Murktar, 179
Yakubu Gowon, General, 62
Yew Lee Kuan, 283

Z
Zik, 288
Zartec, 109, 222

www.ingramcontent.com/pod-product-compliance
Lightning Source LLC
Chambersburg PA
CBHW070805300426
44111CB00014B/2427